THE AUTHOR in one of his daily discussions with Goering, Hess, and
Ribbentrop during the Nuremberg trial

THE PSYCHOLOGY
OF DICTATORSHIP

*Based on an Examination of the Leaders of
Nazi Germany*

By

G. M. GILBERT, Ph.D.

ASSOCIATE PROFESSOR OF PSYCHOLOGY
MICHIGAN STATE COLLEGE
FORMERLY PRISON PSYCHOLOGIST AT THE NUREMBERG TRIAL
OF THE NAZI WAR CRIMINALS

GREENWOOD PRESS, PUBLISHERS
WESTPORT, CONNECTICUT

Library of Congress Cataloging in Publication Data

Gilbert, G   M   1911-
    The psychology of dictatorship.

    Reprint of the ed. published by Ronald Press,
New York.
    Bibliography: p.
    Includes index.
    1. Dictators. 2. National socialism.
3. Germany--Biography. I. Title.
[HM141.G55 1979]   301.15'5   79-15335
ISBN 0-313-21975-3

Published in 1950 by The Ronald Press Company, New York

Reprinted with the permission of John Wiley & Sons, Inc.

Reprinted in 1979 by Greenwood Press, Inc.
51 Riverside Avenue, Westport, CT 06880

Printed in the United States of America

10 9 8 7 6 5 4 3 2 1

To My Sons

ROBERT, JOHN, AND CHARLES

PREFACE

This study of leading personalities in the Nazi dictatorship is an attempt to achieve some insight into the relationship between psychodynamics and social conflict in the modern world. A unique opportunity to obtain first-hand data concerning this interplay of personalities and social processes, as it existed during the rise and fall of an aggressive ideological dictatorship, was provided by the international war crimes trial of 1945-46. As prison psychologist at Nuremberg during the period of the trial, the writer had free access to the major German leaders who had survived the war. The study was conducted under conditions well suited for continuous close observation for a full year, from the time of indictment to the time of execution of sentence. Rapport was enhanced by the fact that the writer was the only prison officer to whom all of the prisoners could talk at will and in their own language.

The method of study evolved was a combination of individual clinical examination and daily intimate observation of behavior in the group, the writer informally assuming the role of "participant observer" in this well-structured social situation. Although nothing approaching "depth analysis" was possible under these circumstances, the members of the group did speak rather freely about each other, themselves, and their Führer, and reacted rather revealingly to the stimuli provided by their trial. It was thus possible to obtain a great deal of data on their character development and emotional conflicts, their interpersonal relationships, their motivating social values, and the nature of their group identifications, loyalties, and hostilities. These interviews and the reactions of the participants also supplied a substantial amount of information concerning Hitler and his career. Three years of subsequent study and research have helped to crystallize meanings and relationships which we could only dimly perceive at the time.

This report, combining the approaches of clinical and social psychology in a first-hand study of the leaders of a modern dictatorship, has been prepared primarily for students of psychology. Nevertheless it is hoped that its broader implications will not be lost upon students of other social sciences and informed readers generally.

I am most indebted to Professor Robert W. White of Harvard, Professor Otto Klineberg of Columbia, and Professor Hadley Cantril of Princeton for their critical reading of the manuscript and the numerous constructive suggestions made for the final revision and editing. Various questions that arose in the treatment of the Nazi characters in their cultural setting were clarified by Dr. Arpad Pauncz and Dr. Marianne Beran of the Lyons (New Jersey) Veterans Administration Hospital. Permission granted by various authors and publishers to quote the excerpts used in this book is likewise gratefully acknowledged.

G. M. Gilbert

Princeton, N. J.
June, 1950

CONTENTS

PART I

The Genesis of Dictatorship

CHAPTER   PAGE

1 THE EMERGENT PATTERN OF DICTATORSHIP—A PSY-
CHOCULTURAL VIEW 3
The Authoritarian Cultural Lag. Scope of the Present
Study.

2 ADOLF HITLER AND THE NAZI MOVEMENT . . . 16
Early Life History. Viennese Period. World War I.
First Political Activities. From *Mein Kampf* to Dic-
tatorship.

PART II

Selected Case Studies

3 THE REVOLUTIONISTS 81
Hermann Goering, Dictator Number Two. Rudolf Hess,
The Führer's Deputy. Hans Frank, Devil's Advocate.

4 THE DIPLOMATS 154
Ex-Chancellor von Papen. Foreign Minister von Ribbentrop.

5 THE MILITARISTS 205
Field Marshal Keitel, Chief of Staff.

6 THE STATE POLICE 237
SS-Colonel Hoess of Auschwitz.

PART III

Psychological Implications

CHAPTER   PAGE

7 CLINICAL AND PSYCHODYNAMIC ASPECTS . . . 265

Authoritarian Regressiveness. Cultural Pseudopathology. Defense Mechanisms in Value-Conflict. Psychopathic Personalities.

8 SOME SOCIAL RELATIONSHIPS 287

Persistence of Prejudices and Stereotypes. Leadership and Social Interaction. Leadership in History.

9 DICTATORSHIP AND ADAPTIVE SOCIAL BEHAVIOR . . 304

The Authoritarian Value-System. Dictatorship and the Mechanization of Aggression.

REFERENCES AND BIBLIOGRAPHY 319

NAME INDEX 323

SUBJECT INDEX 325

PART I
THE GENESIS OF DICTATORSHIP

Chapter 1

THE EMERGENT PATTERN OF DICTATORSHIP
—A PSYCHOCULTURAL VIEW

Since wars begin in the minds of men, it is in the minds of men
that the defenses of peace must be constructed.
—Constitution, UNESCO

From a psychological viewpoint, history may be regarded
as the developmental record of man's adaptive social behavior
in the struggle for survival and security. It is within that
framework that one may understand the development of social
institutions like government, progress in science and industry,
cooperative and competitive behavior in various cultures, and
even such historical crises as wars and revolutions.

In modern history, man's quest for collective security through
self-government has been characterized by an increasing revolt
against submission to the autocratic rule of royal dynasties.
These revolutionary reactions to royal despotism have taken
two significant and opposite directions in Western civilization:
representative democracy and ideological totalitarianism.
World War II has generally been regarded as a climax in the
continuing struggle between these two incompatible systems
in the government of men. In a larger sense, it was an acute
phase of the conflict between constructive and destructive
potentialities in man's social behavior—a conflict in which no
nation or system of government may be presumed to have a
monopoly on the good or the evil. Nevertheless, the extremes
to which a fanatic dictatorship can go in organized aggression
was demonstrated by Nazi Germany as perhaps never before
in human history.

The question may well be raised whether the psychological
examination of leading personalities in that dictatorship can
provide any significant insights into social conflicts of such

3

magnitude and deep historical roots. It would admittedly be unrealistic to overestimate the importance of the psychodynamics of leading personalities in producing these major social upheavals, as against the socioeconomic, political, and historical forces at work. Nevertheless, we must recognize that such forces do not exist as pure abstractions, but become manifest only through the behavior of human beings; that throughout history social movements of far-reaching consequences have been decisively influenced by leaders, and that the behavior of such leaders is necessarily motivated to some extent by psychological tensions rooted in their individual character development. We must furthermore recognize the fact that the personalities of political leaders, like all human beings, are largely the products of their cultural mores and social tensions, and that they become leaders only if they effectively express the aspirations (or frustrations) of significant segments of their contemporary society. The study of political leadership thus provides a fertile field for interrelating psychodynamics with the broader social processes involved in these historic conflicts.

Before proceeding to the examination of the leaders of Nazi Germany, therefore, we shall want to get our bearings on some of the psychocultural relationships involved in the historical emergence of modern dictatorships.

The Authoritarian Cultural Lag

The Western revolt against royal despotism first came to a head at the end of the eighteenth century. This social upheaval was marked by the outbreak of major republican revolutions in Europe and the New World, and the revolutionary dictatorships which followed in their wake. The link between dictatorship and democracy has been generally overlooked in the assumed incompatibility of these two systems of government. Yet that link does exist from a psychocultural viewpoint, and is of the utmost significance for our study.

The Napoleonic rule which followed within a decade after the French Revolution is generally conceded to be the prototype of modern dictatorships. It was the forerunner not only historically, but psychologically as well, for it demonstrated a principal function of dictatorship as a psychocultural emergent: *a reversion to authoritarian rule after a too drastic attempt to impose democracy on an authoritarian culture.* Napoleon's assumption of the role of dictator and then emperor, with the wholehearted support of significant segments of postrevolutionary French society, illustrates a fact that has been true of virtually every dictatorship since then: the inability of an authoritarian culture to absorb too much self-government too suddenly without reverting, at least temporarily, to some form of paternalistic-authoritarian rule. From the first French Republic to the German Weimar Republic, it has been proved again and again that, while the outward forms of democracy may be achieved overnight by revolution, the psychological changes necessary to sustain it cannot.

On the contrary, there is invariably a cultural lag (in which we emphasize the psychocultural aspect, rather than the technological) that leaves both the masses and the leaders of entrenched institutions psychologically predisposed to support any reversion to their accustomed way of life. This involves not merely the obvious material motivation of the "vested interests," which have been abundantly treated elsewhere,[1] but the socioeconomic and psychological insecurity of the common people that follows in the wake of any drastic social change. It is a psychological truism that man abhors the insecurity of lost meanings as much as nature abhors a vacuum. In the confusion of revolutionary social change, the security of familiar patterns of behavior and a reliable frame of reference for social meanings and values are not readily abandoned, unless the social change immediately provides its own adequate rewards and substitutes. Since social upheaval invariably accentuates psychological and socioeconomic insecurity, and the acculturation process in personality development is not readily reversed, there is apt to be a

---

[1] Cobban, for example, points out that the triumph of reason in the French revolution "was not quite so simple. Divine right monarchy fell, but . . . the allies and dependents of monarchy—the Church, the aristocracy, and even the wealthy bourgeoisie—were not willing to commit suicide without greater persuasion." (13)

persistence of the older patterns of behavior for at least a generation or two after the revolution.

Great statesmen have had insight into this cultural lag long before social psychology developed its sophisticated terminology. Thomas Jefferson, evaluating the prospects for the ultimate success of democracy in his generation of republican revolutions, wrote to Adams in 1823:

> The generation which commences a revolution rarely completes it. Habituated from infancy to passive submission of body and mind to their kings and priests, they are not qualified when called on to think for themselves; and in their inexperience, their ignorance and bigotry make them instruments often, in the hands of the Bonapartes and Iturbides, to defeat their own rights and purposes. This is the present situation in Europe and Spanish America. But it is not desperate. . . . As a younger and more instructed [generation] comes on, the sentiment becomes more intuitive . . . some subsequent one of the ever renewed attempts will ultimately succeed. (38)

Jefferson's insight and faith were vindicated by the ultimate triumph of democracy in France and in some of the other European and Latin-American countries. But it was not surprising that the France and Latin America of Jefferson's time should have reverted to authoritarian rule after going through revolutions to throw off the yoke of royal tyranny. The masses could not be educated overnight to understand democracy and to adopt it as a way of life, nor could truly democratic leadership suddenly spring from their midst after centuries of autocratic rule had firmly established an authoritarian frame of reference for their thinking and behavior.

It is our thesis that authoritarian leadership, like any other, reflects the nature of the culture in which it emerges. This is expressed, first of all, in the social values developed among the potential leaders of the given culture. Case histories of Napoleon and other dictators (whose biographies provide us with some clues) would necessarily reveal the authoritarian influences in their upbringing and the cultural channeling of their aggressions. The cultural lag is also expressed in the nature of the support available for any revolutionary or counterrevolutionary movement. Not even a power-driven dictator can seize and hold supreme power in the modern state by sheer personal dominance, as if it were a boy's gang or a seal's harem. His success depends principally on the support he is able to muster from other powerful and influential leaders and the institutions they represent. Historians have pointed out that even Napoleon could not have seized and maintained his power except for the support of other powerful militarists, certain politicians, financiers, etc. The emergence of a dictatorship requires an expression of the cultural lag in terms of the support of influential leaders whose purposes are thought to be served by reversion to autocratic rule.

It must not be assumed, however, that the dictator is merely the passive tool of cultural forces. On the contrary, we must recognize that social interaction implies a two-way process, in which cultural mores help to determine the nature of political leadership, and the latter in turn influences the development of the cultural pattern. It would be fruitless, in the absence of first-hand observations, to speculate on the psychodynamics of Napoleon's drive for power and the way in which it affected the course of European history. But there would presumably be ample room for the investigation of personality differences and individually motivated aggressions among dictators and their supporters. Certainly there has been as much variation in the personalities of dictators as there has been in the personalities of kings—from benevolent despots to destructive maniacs; and the history of their reigns has varied accordingly.

Yet it was precisely to eliminate that element of caprice from government that men were beginning to rebel against rule by the "divine right of kings." In the case of the successful republican revolutions, the purpose was achieved. But even where the rebellion resulted in dictatorship, the original purpose must not be lost sight of. Napoleon came to power, not merely as a reversion to the despotic-paternalistic emperor-figure, but as a strong symbol of peace and security, sanctioned by the will of the people. This may appear ironic, if not slightly incredible in retrospect, but there too Napoleon was the prototype of the modern dictator. For Napoleon, as historians point out, was supported by men of power and influence and was welcomed by the people, not so much to tyrannize them or to wage aggressive wars as to put an end to the chaos and insecurity of life in the postrevolutionary republic.[2]

The struggle for security, which is an underlying motive of all social behavior, was necessarily a predominant motive for all these revolutionary changes. With the expansion of the ethnic identification group from the primitive tribe to the modern state, the socially identified security of the individual has been correspondingly extended. The aggressive nationalism that has characterized many dictatorships must be regarded as an enlarged manifestation of that continuing quest for security through group solidarity. As we have already intimated, dictatorship provided an easy solution in cultures that had always conceived of personal and group security in an ethnocentric-authoritarian frame of reference. But there was a conflict of value judgments in this revolutionary period following the Enlightenment. On the one hand, men realized that there was greater security for the group and freedom for the individual if they asserted their right to self-government. On the other hand, the man on horseback was, and continued to be, the recognized symbol of law and order, strength and security for the nation. The heroic myth persisted even after men had rebelled against the mailed fist of royal despotism. To reconcile the apparently incompatible, Napoleon and his supporters had merely to resort to a device that dictators have repeatedly resorted to since—the "free plebiscite" with formal deference to constitutional government (13). Even a constitution presented no serious obstacle to dictatorship, since many of its provisions could be suspended in a "national emergency" where the security of the nation was threatened; and such emergencies, as Napoleon knew only too well, could always be provided by propaganda. Nevertheless, the people were enabled through these

---

[2] Vandal (62) cites abundant evidence from the writings of the times tending to prove that Napoleon was regarded as the guarantor of the peace and that he gave his wars the appearance of defensive strategy for the protection of French national security. We have abundant evidence that Hitler followed the same pattern.

devices to maintain the illusion of government by popular mandate, while merely substituting a new form of despotism for the accustomed one.

Dictatorship thus emerged in an era of democratic revolution as a retrogressive phenomenon in man's quest for security through self-government, representing a compromise between his revolt against old symbols of suppressive authority and his inability to structure his purposes without them.

What was true of the Napoleonic era applied to the revolutionary period following World War I. The war had brought to a head the growing revolt against the remaining symbols of suppressive authority in Continental Europe, while the cultural lag perpetuated the quest for new authority. But now this quest took a new form: the political ideology. It was not any longer the "man on horseback" but the man with the ideological panacea who now represented authority for security. Heroic mythology was beginning to give way to political demagoguery in the modern version of dictatorship.

This was essentially a modern development. The early barbarian war lords had been able to dominate their hordes and lead them to conquest or defeat without the benefit of fanciful ideologies. Ethnic cohesion and authoritarianism were too deeply imbedded in the cultures of early civilization to require justification. Even Napoleon required little more than lip-service to the idea of self-government to secure allegiance to his autocratic rule and conquest. But the gradual enlightenment of the people and their growing revolt against autocratic rule in modern times placed a high premium on plausible ideologies to justify aggressive leadership and totalitarianism. There was a greater spread of social awareness among the people and their potential leaders, brought about by more widespread education and intercommunication, by the widely communicated gospels of social and scientific thinkers, and by the now well-established examples of self-government in the Western democracies. All this served to intensify the revolt against political and economic privilege, but on a slightly more sophisticated plane and broader base of popular comprehension than had been possible in Napoleon's time.

The revolutionary movements that came into being at the turn of the century expressed and appealed to the need for security by offering a variety of politico-economic ideologies. Essentially, this was a perverted recognition of the growth of social science since the nineteenth century. Unfortunately, in view of the cultural lag, it was still a case of a little insight being a dangerous thing. The discovery of human evolution, translated into theories of ethnic struggles for survival by men like Spencer and Nietzsche, provided one pseudoscientific rationalization for the aggressive ideologies of modern dictators. The discovery of economic laws, translated into doctrines of implacable class warfare for the fruits of production by Marx and others, provided another. There was more than a grain of truth in these philosophies to begin with. It was their perversion into aggressive ideological dictatorship that was of crucial significance from the psychocultural viewpoint. For these ideologies represented formidable sources of confusion and digression in man's quest for security through self-government.

The clash of ideologies came to a head in the period of social disorganization at the end of World War I. War, defeat, and social chaos had created new demands for social and political reform. Ethnic tensions had been strained by war-born hostilities and postwar "settlements." The breakdown of old institutions and the economic chaos were creating increasing mass frustration. The meaning and justification of old values, authorities, and institutions were being questioned by many and stoutly defended by others. The literature and arts of dissent were flourishing as a symptom of social unrest. Revolutionary movements gathered momentum while political parties multiplied.

To the authoritarian mind the propaganda of idealists and demagogues alike took on an aura of ideological panaceas amid these social tensions. To many the socioeconomic ideology became a faith to fill the gap left by religion in the material realities of the modern world; to others religion became the focal point of the political ideology. The demand for representative government vied with the demand for strong leadership and ethnic solidarity; socialist revolution grappled with the demand for stable economy; nationalism with internationalism; democracy with dictatorship. In most European monarchies, the people were sure of only one thing: their desire to abolish the old ruling dynasties that had subjugated them and plunged them into war for centuries. As in the French Revolution, social unrest demanded the abolition of old authority, but just how to establish order and security without it was not so clear. That appeared to be an interplay of the cultural lag with numerous other factors, including the existing constellation of leadership and group interests in each country—the ideology they preached and the skill with which they pursued their goals, the nature of the underlying socioeconomic conditions that caused the social unrest, and the critical historical incidents that influenced the outcome of the conflict at each stage of its development.

In several countries the struggle started with attempts to establish representative government and liberal social reform as antidotes to suppression and politico-economic privilege. The war was scarcely over when the Communist revolutionists under Lenin overthrew the Czarist regime in Russia and established a socialist republic. Revolts shattered the remains of the Hohenzollern dynasty in Germany, and the Weimar Republic came into being under Allied auspices. A fascist movement under Mussolini with a pseudo-radical reform program established a constitutional "corporate state" in Italy. Some years later a liberal republic was established in Spain. But in every one of these countries (and several others that need not concern us here), it was dictatorship, rather than free representative government or truly liberal social reform that eventually emerged.

Of the numerous factors that may have contributed to this reversion to totalitarian government in these countries, the authoritarian cultural lag would appear to be at least one fundamental common denominator.[3] As in postrevolutionary France,

---

[3] To the proponents of economic determinism we would point out that (a) even where the politico-economic ideologies were diametrically opposed, as in the fascist and communist movements, the wielding of supreme power reverted to the established cultural pattern and (b) even though the Western democracies were rocked by the same economic catastrophes in the postwar depression, they achieved a measure of socioeconomic reform within the framework of established patterns of representative government.

more than a century earlier, the attempts to impose the forms of representative government were defeated in part by the inability of these cultures to absorb too much self-government too suddenly, especially in the social chaos and insecurity that followed the overthrow of the old institutions. The long tradition of submission to despotism which had prevailed for centuries in Germany, Russia, Spain, and Italy had left too strong a trace of authoritarian thinking and ego-involvement among the people and their potential leaders to be readily abandoned in favor of the democratic-socialistic millennium.

Certainly that was the case in Germany. After centuries of subservience to the Junker aristocracy, church authority, and the military caste, neither the common people nor the leading members of the various social identification groups were prepared for democracy. Political freedom and equality were but awkwardly imposed on a social structure that still bore the heritage of class privilege, race consciousness, militant nationalism, and a deeply ingrained psychology of dominance-submissiveness in hierarchies of power and authority. Even in electing a president of the newly created Weimar Republic, they inevitably turned to the very embodiment of ancient symbols of authority—the aged Junker Field Marshal von Hindenburg. The potentiality of democratic leadership was not lacking, and it might conceivably have prevailed, given time and a more favorable combination of leadership and circumstances. But the growing insecurity of the people in the postwar chaos was running against the democratic tide. The people were clamoring for strong leadership and an authoritative formula to put an end to the politico-economic chaos, in accordance with the well-worn pattern of authoritarian regressiveness. At this juncture, Adolf Hitler was already making his violent bid for power, offering an ideological panacea concocted of aggressive nationalism, social reform, and racial solidarity. Like Napoleon and other dictators, he soon won crucial support from other leaders when his interests appeared to coincide with theirs. With their support, a popular following, and a favorable series of crucial events, he was able to force his way into power on "a mandate from the people" and to consolidate that power into a formidable dictatorship.

Thus the emergence of successful dictatorship would seem to be determined in large part by the interaction of (*a*) *social unrest* carried over from the revolt against royal despotism; (*b*) an *authoritarian cultural lag,* with its persistent quest for security through strong leadership and political demagoguery; (*c*) a *favorable constellation of leadership* and the group interests they represent, providing the authoritative formula and its material implementation; (*d*) *crucial events,* sometimes of minor intrinsic significance, which favor the establishment and continuance of the dictator in power.

SCOPE OF THE PRESENT STUDY

We shall approach the study of dictatorship through an examination of the personalities in the constellation of leadership in Nazi Germany. This constellation of leadership breaks down into three principal identification groups or group-clusters that appear to be characteristic of such movements:

1. The *revolutionary nucleus* of fanatic rebels, idealists, and outright adventurers, under whose ideological banner the movement and the dictatorship come into being

    In this case the revolutionary group consisted of Adolf Hitler and his "Old Fighters," identified as a new in-group from the days of the Munich *Putsch.*

2. The *"political bandwagon"* of less fanatic, more or less opportunistic politicians and businessmen, "vested interests," etc., who support the revolutionary movement just before or after its success is assured

    In this case it consisted of an overlapping cluster of Junker-Diplomat-Industrialist identification groups, which we shall designate as "The Diplomats."

3. The *agencies of aggression,* including the traditional *militarists* and that special creation of the totalitarian state, the *state police*

    In this case they were the Prussian militarists and the SS-police network.

We shall have more to say about each one of these groups in turn, but first a word about our approach.

These groups of personalities, when examined in the light of social interaction, can provide the key perspective to the entire pattern of emergence of such a movement. The character development and behavior of leaders has more than clinical scope. It reflects not only the basic psychodynamics of their early emotional development through early family experiences, but their indoctrination in the social mores and cultural values, their identification with social groups and group interests, and the selective impact of social unrest on their personalities. This broader conception of psychodynamics is essentially *motivational development in interaction with society and culture,* so that the individual level of explanation cannot be fully understood without reference to the social and vice versa.

We are thus interested in tracing the early development of Hitler's emotional conflicts, not merely to judge the nature of his neurosis, but to understand how such conflicts, interacting with the values and frustrations of his contemporary society, affected the lives of millions of people. We are interested in Goering's early manifestations of aggression, not merely to judge whether he was an aggressive psychopath, but to see how such a personality found expression through an aggressive political movement and exploited the social tensions that precipitate war and genocide. We are also interested in seeing how fairly normal though ambitious men, like Franz von Papen and General Keitel, played their roles in a revolutionary dictatorship that actually violated their Junker sense of values.

By adopting this broad psychocultural frame of reference in the study of personality development, we can better understand the processes of social interaction that produced the Nazi movement and its accompanying social catastrophes. We may also achieve a better understanding of aggressive ideological dictatorship as a modern aberration of social behavior in the quest for security.

It is obvious that such an approach does not allow of any narrow doctrinaire bias such as might have a limited validity in approaching human behavior at one level for one specific purpose (e.g., psychoanalysis, behaviorism, economic determinism). We shall, on the other hand, freely make use of any concepts that appear valid for the interpretation of data at the relevant level of explanation. If any designation of this approach is required, it might best be designated as *dynamic eclecticism*. This does not mean the building up of a patchwork of arbitrary partial explanations, but a systematic framework of dynamic interrelationships, without doctrinaire bias. Our unifying concept is adaptive behavior in social interaction, seen against the larger framework of biosocial evolution. Only such a broad framework has appeared adequate for the study of political leadership.

In pursuing this line of investigation, we shall want to throw some light on a number of questions of academic and human interest: What kind of men were the Nazi leaders, and how did they get that way? How did a would-be dictator hold the loyalty of his entourage, appeal to the masses, and win the support of other leaders to achieve his power? How did he maintain that power and mobilize a whole nation to such extremes of aggression?—was there unity of purpose among the leaders?—did the people acquiesce? What was in the minds of men who planned aggressive war and collaborated in wholesale atrocities? What is the relationship between psychopathology and social pathology on that scale?—between personality and leadership? —between leadership and history? How do stereotypes, prejudices, group tensions and loyalties operate in such a political movement? Just how can one evaluate the authoritarian value-system? Where does it fit into the picture of adaptive social behavior? And finally, what is the significance of aggressive ideological dictatorship at the present stage of social evolution?

This is a broad and ambitious program, but nothing less will do justice to the magnitude of the problem of dictatorship. Even a little insight achieved from the examination of a few of the leaders of Nazi Germany would be of inestimable value.

Our first task is to trace the character development of the dictator himself, using his "case history" as a focal point for the development of the movement up to the consolidation of power. We can then round out the picture by direct examination of some of the other principal characters in the constellation of leadership in Nazi Germany, whom we studied in Nuremberg.

Chapter 2

ADOLF HITLER AND THE NAZI MOVEMENT

EARLY LIFE HISTORY [1]

The Austria of Hitler's youth had already begun to feel the undercurrents of social unrest that were to mark the turn of the century. Beneath the sentimental tranquillity of Emperor Franz Josef's reign, there was a rekindling of the long-smoldering rebellion against the Hapsburg dynasty that had dominated Central Europe almost since the days of the Holy Roman Empire. The effects of industrial revolution, migration, and urbanization were being translated into social conflict and new political ideologies. The gospels of socialism, Pan-Germanic nationalism, and racism were winning new adherents. All of these social influences were destined to have their impact on the development of Hitler's character, and he in turn was destined to leave his decisive mark on the development of these social tensions. To understand why this social interaction took the course that it did in Hitler's case, we must first understand the emotional tensions that were built up in his youth.

Family Background.—Hitler's father, born Alois Schickelgruber, was an illegitimate child who had borne the family name of his unmarried mother, Maria Schickelgruber, in accordance

---

[1] Since this study of Hitler was not based on direct examination, as was the case with other Nazi leaders, a word of explanation about our source materials may be in order. The principal sources were: (a) information and reactions obtained from the other Nazi leaders, especially those closest to him ever since the early days of the Munich *Putsch;* this included documentary material, such as a 1,000-page essay on Hitler and the Nazi movement written by his lawyer, Hans Frank, before he was hanged; (b) the usual documentary historical sources, supplemented by evidence presented at the Nuremberg trial; (c) recent reports by others who knew Hitler, particularly his closest companion in Vienna.

with the Austrian law governing illegitimate births. However, he had been "legitimized" (i.e., claimed as an actual son born out of wedlock) by the man his mother later married. He had acquired the name Hitler along with his belated and questionable legitimacy when he was thirty-nine years old. It is not certain whether the real father of Alois Schickelgruber-Hitler was the same as the foster father who later claimed him as a legitimate son. The foster father had, in fact, legitimized him so many years after his marriage to Maria Schickelgruber that it might well have been an afterthought to give legitimate status to an illegitimate stepson.

The question then arises as to the identity of Alois Schickelgruber-Hitler's real father (Adolf Hitler's paternal grandfather). This is a question of more than academic significance, since it raises a question about Adolf Hitler's own "pure Aryan" status. The confirmed facts [2] are that a Jewish family for whom Maria Schickelgruber worked had paid "alimony" for the support of Hitler's father until he was fourteen years old. Whether this was charity, parental responsibility, or blackmail money is uncertain. With this cloud of illegitimacy over his birth, Hitler's father had been brought up with a very negative family life, receiving little parental affection and no education to speak of. Small wonder that he, in turn, proved to be very unstable in his own marital relationships. His first marriage was to a woman fourteen years his senior. She obtained a separation because of his adultery, which produced an illegitimate child. Alois' second marriage was to his mistress after the death of the first wife, but she, too, left him after a year. After the death of the second wife, Alois Schickelgruber (now Hitler) married his twenty-five-year-old ward, Klara Pölzl, a second cousin twenty-three years his junior.

Adolf Hitler was the fourth of five children by this marriage. He was born on April 20, 1889, at Braunau-am-Inn, near the German border. The home environment was far from healthy mentally or physically. Three of the siblings died in childhood, and Adolf himself was rather sickly and emotionally high-strung

---

[2] Details set forth in the Frank MS. (18)

as a child. Partiality of affection developed quite early, the evidence being that Adolf loved his mother but hated his father. The latter had had a rather shifty career, achieving the low civil service status of border patrolman in the Austrian Customs Police. He retired at the age of fifty-six to speculate in land. His life having been marked by continual frustration in his attempts "to make something of himself" in spite of his inauspicious beginnings, Alois Schickelgruber-Hitler had become an embittered, ill-tempered alcoholic by the time Adolf was born. Understandably sensitive about his social status, Hitler's father carried his assertion of parental authority to a neurotic extreme. He was very strict in demanding the respect of his children, both legitimate and illegitimate, requiring that they address him with the formal *Sie,* while the mother was addressed with the familiar *du,* as was customary among family members. He went to extremes in enforcing an outward show of respect by harshness, even outdoing the traditional Germanic pattern of paternal authoritarianism. It was in this setting that Adolf grew up as a friendless, hostile child who would break out into temper tantrums at the slightest provocation. Hitler's half-brother, Alois Hitler, Jr., describes young Adolf's behavior in the family as follows: "He was imperious and quick to anger from childhood onward and would not listen to anyone. My stepmother [Adolf's mother] always took his part. He would get the craziest notions and get away with it. If he didn't have his way he got very angry. . . . He had no friends, took to no one and could be very heartless. He could fly into a rage over any triviality." [3]

Some of this furious hostility can undoubtedly be explained by the father-son relationship. In his childhood Adolf frequently had to go after his father to bring him home from the beer taverns, and he was frequently beaten for his disrespect. The beatings were apparently sufficiently frequent and severe to constitute a traumatic experience. Adolf repaid this hostility as best he could, nursing his wounded ego with spite, stubbornness, and hatred. On one occasion he read that the stoic Indians did

---

[3] Interview reported in *Wiener Wochenausgabe,* September 11, 1948.

not cry out when hurt but bore their pain in silence. He resolved never to cry again when beaten, and to spite his father
with a show of silent determination. The next time his father
beat him he did not utter a sound, much to the family's amazement, and he never cried again when beaten. Instead, he built
up and suppressed violent hostility toward his father, while
seeking to impress his young, indulgent mother with his bravery
and determination in the face of this "persecution."

Hans Frank, Hitler's lawyer and close confidant during the
rise to power, described for the writer the paternal relationship
as he got it from Hitler himself:

> His father suffered from an uncontrollable addiction to alcohol
> which often led to the most painful family experiences for the boy,
> Adolf Hitler. How often did this boy have to fetch his father late
> at night out of the tavern, after the latter had been guzzling
> alcohol for hours on end. Hitler himself related to me in 1930—
> when we were speaking about his family relationships (in con-
> nection with a blackmail threat), "Even as a 10 or 12-year-old kid
> I always had to go late at night to this stinking, smoky dive.
> Without being spared any of the details, I would have to go to the
> table and shake him as he looked at me with a blank stare. Then
> I would say, 'Father, you must come home! Come now, we've
> got to go!' And I often had to wait a quarter or half hour, beg-
> ging, cursing, until I could get him to budge. Then I would
> support him and finally get him home. That was the most terrible
> shame I have ever experienced. Oh, Frank, I know what a devil
> Alcohol is! Through my father it became my greatest enemy in
> my youth!" (18)

Armed with this information and a little clinical insight we
may go a step further in reconstructing the psychological tensions of Hitler's home environment. Scrutinizing *Mein Kampf*
for autobiographical clues, we come upon an interesting hypothetical description of "the thorny road of a laborer's child."
Although Hitler was never given a projective personality test,
we suggest that this description actually amounts to a projection
of his own psychodynamic conflicts. The details represent a
juxtaposition of known elements in his father's life, his own
early family life, and his later experiences in the slums of Vienna.
The father and son figures can easily be identified.

Take the following case, for example. In a stuffy 2-room cellar dwelling there lives a laborer's family of 7. Among the 5 children there is a boy of, let us say, 3 years. . . . The crowding in this narrow space is an unfavorable condition to begin with. . . . They don't just live together, but keep rubbing each other the wrong way. Quarrels and brawls are inevitable. . . . For the children it is bad enough . . . but when these battles are fought by the parents themselves, almost every day, with a degree of crudity which leaves nothing to the imagination, then the results of such upbringing sooner or later have a disastrous effect on the children. When these fights take the form of brutal abuse of the mother by the father, and go so far as drunken attacks on her, then anyone who is unfamiliar with such an environment can hardly imagine it. At the age of 6 the poor youngster senses things that would horrify even a grownup. Morally poisoned, physically undernourished, his little head full of lice, the little citizen now trudges to grammar school. A bare knowledge of reading and writing is all he manages to squeeze out. . . . At home, nothing remains unreviled, from the teacher to the Head of the State. Church, morality, government, society, everything is cursed in the most obscene manner and dragged through the filth of their dirty minds. When the boy leaves school at the age of 14, it is hard to decide which is worse: his incredible stupidity or his sheer impudence and immorality. . . . (33)

This is a remarkable passage, for Hitler's own repressed and suppressed conflicts apparently come to light with brilliant clarity. The fact that Hitler was semiconsciously projecting his own childhood conflicts into this picture of the "Viennese worker's family" can be verified in part by certain objective similarities: Hitler was one of five children of a poor family whose father was a drunkard and was known to have beaten him. Hitler also muddled his way through school as a sacrilegious little rebel until the age of fourteen, as we shall see presently. Here Adolf unwittingly betrays the fact (as we interpret it) that his father also went so far as drunken attacks on his mother. He further states that "anyone who is unfamiliar with such an environment cannot imagine it. At the age of 6 the poor youngster senses things that would horrify even a grownup." What Adolf "sensed" we can only surmise. It is safe to assume that the drunken father's behavior toward the mother in their crowded home was such as to stir up intense psychosexual conflicts in the child, who already hated his father for the beatings he administered and the disgust he engendered. Although we need not subscribe to the universality of the Oedipal conflict, the evidence certainly points to it in Adolf Hitler's case. The scene of pure Nordic womanhood being attacked by a drunken sot of a laborer (father-son figure) was potent enough imagery for the projection of psychosexual conflicts into political symbols. It was probably before he wrote *Mein Kampf* that Hitler first became aware of (and repressed) the possibility that his own drunken father was a half-Jew. His obsessive anxiety over the rape and pollution of Aryan womanhood, later in life, may well have originated in this repressed psychosexual conflict. We shall have to follow that clue later. In the meantime, further clues to his personality are provided by the early educational influences.

Educational Influences.—Adolf received his education in and around Linz up to the age of fourteen. At first he was a fair student, but his emotional conflicts affected his scholarship more and more adversely. His father wanted him to study so that Adolf could achieve a higher place in civil service than he himself had been able to achieve. He was also worried lest Adolf turn out to be a shiftless ne'er-do-well and jailbird like his half-brother, Alois, Jr. But for conscious as well as unconscious reasons, Adolf hated everything his father stood for. He obtained a secret satisfaction (as he later confessed) in thwarting the old man's desires, while his own fancy turned to other things. The more his father insisted on his becoming a *Beamter* (civil service official), the more determined Adolf says he was never to become any such thing.

His studies suffered, except for his interest in German history. This provided a rich milieu for the heroic fantasies born in frustration. As he himself related in *Mein Kampf,* at an early age he read an account of the Franco-Prussian War of 1870-71. "It did not take long before the great heroic battle became my greatest inner experience. From now on I longed more and more for anything that had any connection with war and militarism." In the Realschule (high school) in Linz, Hitler was most influenced by a history teacher by the name of Dr. Leopold Pötsch, whose portrayal of the history of the German people "sometimes even moved us to tears. . . . Indeed, he unintentionally made a young revolutionary out of me even then. How could any one study German history without becoming an enemy of the State whose ruling family had so miserably influenced the fate of the nation? . . . Didn't we youngsters already know that this Austrian State did not and could not have any love for us Germans?"

It takes very little interpretation to see how at an early age the study of history enabled Hitler to resolve some anxiety by identifying himself with the heroic and persecuted German people, while the contemporary authoritarian figures were persecuting this heroic specimen of German manhood who bore his pain in silence.

His heroic fantasies were soon channeled into a desire for artistic expression. At the age of twelve he witnessed his first performance of *Lohengrin*. "At one stroke I was captivated. My youthful enthusiasm for the master of Bayreuth now knew no bounds. . . . All this emphasized my deep inner resistance to the profession my father had chosen for me, especially after overcoming the early growing pains (which were particularly painful in my case). I became more and more convinced that I could never be happy as a civil servant. Since my artistic talents were recognized in high school, my determination was all the greater. Neither pleas nor threats could change that. I wanted to become a painter and no power in the world could make me a civil servant." (33)

Hitler continued to fancy himself the great classical artist in the romantic tradition of his culture. His mother indulged this whim, but his father began to despair of his ever amounting to anything. The divided affections were mutual. In *Mein Kampf* Hitler states that he honored his father but loved his mother. From some of his later associates we got a slightly different story. He not only hated his father, but felt that the father could never understand him because he was so ignorant and boorish. This cruelty and lack of understanding apparently drove him further and further into the world of romantic fantasy provided by his culture. His father died when Adolf was thirteen. We can only surmise the mixed feelings of relief and guilt on the part of a son who had hated his father so intensely, and had probably wished him dead more than once. In *Mein Kampf* he merely makes the enigmatic statement that his father "had entirely unwittingly sown the seed for a future which neither he nor I had yet understood"—another little clue to Hitler's semiconscious awareness of the psychodynamics of his own aggression.

At any rate, the father's death did give his career-fantasy freer rein. His mother now dutifully tried to encourage him to study for civil service as his father had wanted him to, but Adolf could now rebel with impunity. His schooling suffered more and more because of his unwillingness to apply himself to serious study. This was undoubtedly due largely to the emotional conflicts of his home environment, since we have reason to believe that he was not intellectually mediocre or subnormal.[4] However, the antiquated pedagogy of some of the old teachers around Linz probably also had its effect in discouraging many a student from serious study. This was particularly true in the case of young Adolf, who was already rebelling against all the forms, conventions, and aspirations of the *Kleinbürger,* and longing to be left alone with his romantic fantasies. His interest in studies was therefore selective, to say the least.

For one thing, the altogether too literal religious dogma and biblical precept handed down by his teacher in the compulsory course on religion did little to inspire this rebellious adolescent in an age of increasing skepticism and materialism. Along with his classmates, Hitler enjoyed baiting the old professor of religion with prankish questions of feigned pious interest: the

---

[4] This is not merely assumed on the a priori grounds that even a successful demagogue requires a higher-than-average I.Q. We have additional evidence, such as the militarists' testimony that Hitler was capable of prodigious feats of memory when it suited his purpose; the diplomats' testimony that he overcame his educational handicap to some extent by the prolific reading of history. That his *judgment* was clouded by emotional conflicts is, of course, another matter.

gory details of the martyrdom of saints who had been boiled in oil, gorged with water, flayed alive, drawn and quartered, burned at the stake; the flagellation and self-torture of penitents; the plagues and pestilences, the punishment of sins by hell-fire, etc. They delighted in embarrassing him with trick questions about the infallibility of the Pope, the daily routine of life in heaven and hell, the Jewish parentage and virgin birth of Jesus, all of which the old professor ardently described or defended. Hitler even went so far as to write and circulate copies of a smutty version of the Immaculate Conception and then became a momentary martyr among the anticlerical students and faculty when he was punished for it. The combination of too dogmatic religious instruction and a young mind already obsessed with the need for rebellion against authority only turned the Bible into a vehicle for protest and iconoclasm. The study of German history on the other hand, with its racial, militaristic, and nationalistic bias and its heroic legends, provided him with a vehicle for the projection of heroic fantasies as well as objects for his latent hostility. As for the study of the German language, Hitler claimed that the memorization of verb forms and grammatical formulas was enough to drive one to despair. The same applied, apparently, to any other language and to most of the subjects in the curriculum.

He received the grade of "unsatisfactory" in mathematics, stenography, German, and geometry. His mother began to despair of his ever amounting to anything. Hitler's own fantasies probably dispelled any such doubts, but the alternatives of studying for a career he despised or being dropped out of school as an outright failure presented a serious dilemma to one with such keen inferiority feelings. At about that time (age fourteen) as Hitler relates it, "an illness suddenly came to my rescue and decided my future in a few weeks." Because of a respiratory ailment the doctor advised his stopping school temporarily. This illness, following on the heels of his father's death, conveniently put an end to any serious study for a career in about the middle of secondary school. He was now free to dab at water color and drawing, to read about the heroes of German legend and military history as the spirit moved him, and to loaf about in friendless isolation. A considerable portion of his adolescence was apparently spent in this aimless and indigent existence. It was to be but a foretaste of his early adult life.

We may thus sum up the psychodynamics and social inter-action in Hitler's early emotional development: Beaten and repulsed by a somewhat degenerate old father, while dominating his indulgent young mother, Adolf Hitler grew up with a seeth-ing reservoir of suppressed hostility, unresolved psychosexual conflicts, and intense feelings of persecution and inferiority. The cultural influences were such as to provide some outlet through heroic fantasies and ethnic identification, while his aggression was displaced to the emperor-figure and a vague enemy out-group.

In early adolescence these were still largely unchannelized conflicts that could take any turn. The direction they finally took was partly predetermined not only by the emotionally toned symbols of his early life experience but by the further interaction of these personal conflicts with the socioeconomic conflicts of the society into which he grew. We shall attempt to trace the course of this development.

Viennese Period

Frustrated Artist.—When he was about seventeen, Hitler's mother died and "put an abrupt end to all these beautiful plans. . . . Need and hard reality now forced me to make a quick de-cision. My father's meagre means had been mostly used up by my mother's serious illness; the orphan's pension which was due me was not enough to live on, so I was forced to earn my own bread somehow. With a suitcase of clothing in my hand, an unshakable will in my heart, I rode off to Vienna. As my father had succeeded 50 years before, so I hoped to master my fate. I too wanted to 'amount to something'—but not a civil servant." (33)

Now completely on his own, Hitler went to Vienna to apply for admission to the Academy of Fine Arts. He had failed this admission test once before because the drawings he submitted showed no evidence of the talent he had supposedly demonstrated in school. Undaunted, he now tried again. This time he suffered an even more humiliating blow to his artistic aspirations. The professor to whom he went for admission to the competitive entrance examination had him produce another sample of his work and then decided, out of kindness, not even to subject his work to official judgment. Instead he advised Hitler to take up some trade. Thus humiliated and frustrated, Hitler could only retaliate by judging his judges.

His reactions at this time are described at first hand (though in retrospect) by his artist-companion of these years, Josef Greiner, as follows: "After this [rejection] Hitler was very downcast over his failure in painting and architectural drawing. He showed neither the desire nor inclination for any work and called the professors stupid, since the true artist requires no school grades. If he had wanted to go through with it, he thought his drawings would certainly have been qualified as good. It was a chief failing of Hitler's that he was always stubborn and self-righteous and always put the blame on the other party whenever he failed in anything. When he tried to take the test in the Art Academy the second time and failed, he naturally put the blame on the professors." In other words, where sublimation of his ascendancy needs failed, he resorted to the projection of his inferiority feelings.

Hitler drifted about, alternately loafing and doing menial odd jobs, even begging for a time. At first he had to sleep on the park benches of the Prater, later taking a bed at the Obdachlosen-Asyl, a temporary shelter for vagrants. Finally he settled at the Männerheim, a cheap rooming house for destitute men where a room could be had for a few cents a night. The few kronen he had brought from home soon dwindled to nothing. Another destitute panhandler had offered to try to sell his water-color cards for him at a commission, since Hitler indulged in some pretenses at being an artist. His principal technique was to make a grid over a picture postcard, then copy it on a larger sheet, square for square, and finally fill in the colors. This could then be sold as an "original water-color." As his sporadic daubing failed to bring in enough for a regular meal card or bath at the

Männerheim, he was forced to sell the little decent clothing he had, piece by piece. The result was a picture of shabby destitution which made even some of the beggars at the Männerheim look down on him. His behavior at this time is described as extremely shy, with ample evidence of sensitivity and feelings of inferiority for which his only compensatory outlet was hostility in argumentation. This endeared him still less to his neighbors at the Männerheim, who went so far as to request the manager to throw out this disagreeable, unkempt boarder. Only the help of the slightly more capable artist-companion-in-misery, Greiner, saved him from outright expulsion.

Equipped with some pieces of fresh clothing and a few kronen provided by Greiner, Hitler continued to try his hand at advertising art. It was apparently at this time that the magic of propaganda was first impressed on him. The drawings that he and his friend were asked to make for advertising displays started him thinking. Indeed, he seemed quite inspired by the success of a Viennese woman who advertised a lotion which could grow long, seductive tresses like those of the Lorelei on any woman who used it. She even had thankful, but fictitious, testimonials to prove it. "That's advertising for you!" Hitler observed excitedly. "Propaganda, propaganda!—just keep at it until the people actually believe that this junk can really help you. . . . Propaganda—just keep at it until it is actually believed and one no longer knows what is imagination and what is reality." Hitler was sure that with enough propaganda the people could even be led to believe that this wonderful salve would grow hair on a billiard ball. Propaganda thus opened up new vistas for sublimation of his ascendancy needs : through propaganda one could make the people believe whatever one wanted them to believe and thus show one's superiority. What better proof of one's own superiority than the contemptible gullibility of the masses? Here indeed was the beginning of a new philosophy of life. "All you need is propaganda; the dumb ones will never know the difference. Propaganda is the basis of every religion, whether that of heaven or of hair ointment. Belief strengthened by propaganda brings blessings to priest and

advertiser alike." (28) A form of religious indoctrination
that had provided nothing but gory dogma in school now de-
generated in his mind to the level of cheap propaganda.

But the political implications of propaganda were by no
means lost on the frustrated artist, even then. It was in the
Viennese metropolis that the country boy first learned the meaning of public opinion and the power of the press, and it made a
lasting impression on him. Writing with ill-concealed contempt
about public opinion some years later in *Mein Kampf,* Hitler
stated :

> . . . Even as a young man in Vienna I had the best opportunity
> to get acquainted with the masters and spiritual creators of this
> mass-education machine. At first I was astounded at how easily
> this worst power in the State was able to create a definite public
> opinion, even when it involved a complete falsification of the real
> inner wishes and views of the public. In a few days, a trivial
> matter could be made into an important affair of State, while
> at the same time vital problems were forgotten. . . .

The evil men who controlled this dangerous weapon, just
like everything else, he had discovered, were Jews—which
brings us to the early formation of Hitler's political attitudes.
Frustrated in his aspirations, and having derived nothing but
aggressive nationalism and a cynical iconoclasm from his previous education as a basis for social values, he continued to formulate his own attitudes from daily experience. These were
built up selectively from environmental influences that provided
abundant outlet for his neurotic needs : rebellion against religious and secular authority, contempt for the masses, feelings
of persecution and racial superiority, aggression directed against
readily available scapegoats, a cynical amorality which virtually
worshiped successful deceit and power drive. It was within this
framework of largely hostile social values that Hitler began to
formulate his political attitudes.

Political Indoctrination.—The political milieu in which
these attitudes were formed was one of ethnic conflict and revolutionary protest. The Hapsburg monarchy rested uneasily on
a foundation of tenuously resolved ethnic group interests and
prejudices, whose origins were obscured in the history of the

Holy Roman Empire and even more ancient history. Serbs, Croats, Hungarians, Czechs, Slavs; Jews, Catholics, and Protestants of all nationalities; capital, labor, and militarism—all had their heritage of prejudices, their special problems and interests, in the social conflict of nineteenth-century Austria. The conflict was only aggravated by the complex interrelationship of these group identifications, by increasing migration which confused the distinctions between in-groups and out-groups, by increasing industrialization and population growth in Europe, and by the ever more insistent demand for representative self-government. The social unrest that had begun to simmer at the turn of the century was slowly coming to a boil, and nowhere did it sputter more heatedly than around the slums of Vienna.

Thrown together with the struggling proletariat of many nations, all competing to eke out a bare existence, if not some security and status, Hitler became deeply impressed by the contemporary rabble-rousing political movements. One such movement was the Christian Socialist party of Karl Lueger, the violently anti-Semitic mayor of Vienna. Another group was the German Nationalist party of Anton Schönerer. Each vied with the other in providing scapegoats for the socioeconomic frustration of the masses as well as for the competitive needs of the various identification groups. The recent influx of Jewish refugees from the East provided the easiest target.

Many thousands of Jewish families who had fled from Polish and Russian pogroms had taken refuge in Vienna around the turn of the century. Their struggle for existence no doubt strained the already limited Austrian economy and excited opposition to class privilege—an age-old problem in refugee migration. The ancient prejudices against Jews on historic religious grounds had long since ceased to be an important factor in this animosity, except among the more unenlightened religious fanatics. But the socioeconomic conflicts and the forces of social lag had kept it alive, as with many such hostilities, to provide ready scapegoats for every kind of frustration. The process was merely repeating itself in the Vienna of Hitler's youth, though it did not become acute until after World War I.

As is usually the case, the psychosocial processes inherent in prejudice helped to perpetuate it as much as the motivation involved. For one thing, the social discrimination that had confined many Jews to Eastern ghettoes had created certain subcultural differences. This, in turn, provided easier identification for further discrimination and a barrier to easy assimilation in the Viennese population. It likewise aggravated the xenophobia of the more provincial inhabitants of this metropolis. The partly self-protective and partly forced segregation in the slums of Vienna only served further to perpetuate the prejudicial stereotype of "dirty foreign element." Even the defensive reactions of such minority groups provided the prejudiced with specious rationalizations. As out-groups suffering from old prejudices and discrimination, they were often more critical of political and economic privilege than the underprivileged members of the native group.[5] This made it easy for the conservative members of the society to identify them as "disturbers of the social order—why don't they go back to where they came from?" The native underprivileged, with similar rebellious tendencies, were a far larger group, but the selective association inherent in prejudice did not take account of that fact. On the contrary, these underprivileged were made to think that their struggle for existence was being made all the harder by the "foreign element"—again, a demonstrable reality, if one ignored the more basic aspects of economic competition. As some of these refugees began to work themselves out of their inferior status and assimilate with the native group, they further incurred the envy and hostility of all those whose status-needs were dependent on the prejudicial status quo of the "outsiders." The most dependent were naturally those who were the most insecure economically and psychologically. Thus Adolf Hitler, like millions of frustrated Austrians, found a needed outlet for his frustrations in the demagoguery of Mayor Lueger, who was

---

[5] This picture of prewar Vienna is extracted from Hitler's biased account in *Mein Kampf*, corrected by the more objective picture drawn for us by the later Nazi Chancellor of Austria, Seyss-Inquart, and several Viennese refugees.

making political capital out of the Jewish scapegoat. Unfortunately, as often happens in persecuted minority groups, this demagoguery was sometimes silently aided and abetted by assimilated Jews who also wished to get rid of the embarrassing "foreign element." Thus even the reaction formation of the scapegoat group itself helped to perpetuate the stereotype and the prejudice. On the other hand, the fact that men in all classes of Austrian society shared its conflicts and contributed to its culture, regardless of ethnic background, provided no corrective to the biased perceptions of those who needed or exploited scapegoat propaganda.

The German Nationalist party of Anton Schönerer likewise capitalized on inflaming the anti-Semitic sentiment, but offered bigger and better scapegoats than the incumbent mayor. Schönerer also attacked Roman Catholicism, the House of Hapsburg, and the Slavic element in the population, espousing a racial Pan-Germanic expansionism. An Anschluss with Germany was a major feature of his program, but the economic necessity was camouflaged by the racial ideology. The street corners and meeting halls of Vienna often resounded with cries of "Cut loose from Rome!" "Throw out the Jews!" "Anschluss with Germany!" "Down with the Hapsburgs!"

These political identifications and hostilities served Hitler's need for aggressive defenses against his own feelings of frustration and inferiority. Hitler had already absorbed some of these prejudices from his admired history teacher, Dr. Pötsch, in Linz, but he experienced the actual needs and the social facilitation of these attitudes during his indigent life in Vienna. For if his mediocrity and indolence prevented him from living up to his aspiration level, he could at least vent his aggressions on the ready-made scapegoats: (a) the "ruling classes" who were persecuting and exploiting the workers and (b) the "inferior foreign elements" who were making life more intolerable for them. The former had provided the universal battle-cry of revolutionaries throughout the ages, sometimes exaggerated, often justified. The latter gave the revolutionary sentiment a reactionary twist which distinguished it from twentieth-century leftist revolution.

As we have already seen, Hitler's identification with the poor working class was not without a loathing for the inferior status and stupidity of the masses. Obversely, his hostility to the "ruling class" was not without a concealed envy of the superior status to which he himself aspired. He had no doubt been predisposed to this ambivalence by familial and cultural influences, but now it was becoming socially conditioned into political attitudes.

Hitler's anti-Semitism was probably further inflamed by the frustration of his first love—the only authentic instance we have of sexual trauma in his Viennese period. Greiner reports that Hitler became wildly infatuated with a seventeen-year-old girl who had been engaged to pose for some underwear ads which Greiner had been commissioned to sketch. Hitler met her in the studio and was immediately smitten by her Nordic beauty. He tried to play the sophisticated fellow-artist, but the girl nevertheless refused to undress in his presence. Hitler wooed her with poetry, but was likewise rebuffed on that level. She even ridiculed his pretenses at both poesy and art. Still unable to withstand frustration, Hitler attacked her while she was undressing in the studio. She beat him off, and Hitler reacted like a mongrel wounded in heat. Thanks to Greiner's interference, he was prevented from doing more than inflict some bites and scratches on her body, and he sulked off to a cheap bordel. Greiner had to dissuade the girl from pressing charges against her assailant.

A short time later she became engaged to a promising young businessman, who happened to be of half-Jewish parentage, though baptized. Hitler was beside himself with anguish, but the fiancé's background provided a ready rationale for his aggression. "A Jew! A Jew!" he screamed to Greiner, who tried to point out the inaccuracy and irrelevancy of his denunciation. "They're all dirty pigs (*Saujuden*) and it makes no difference whether they've been baptized or not. No water or priestly hocus-pocus will ever convert a Jew into an Aryan!" (28) Hitler ranted on that he would throttle the swine who dared to be the lover of his Aryan beauty. He then wrote an insulting and threatening letter to the fiancé, in which he incidentally treated himself to the vicarious thrill of claiming that he was the girl's original lover and would not give her up to any *Saujude*. He even went so far as to create a scene when encountering the couple on the street, by screaming his threats and urging mob action against Jews who seduce "our German women." When he attempted to repeat the performance at the wedding, he was hustled out by a couple of plain-clothes policemen posted to handle the emergency with the least disturbance. Thus ended Hitler's first love affair. He swore off women, but continued to be obsessed with projected anxiety over the violation of Christian girls by Jews.

All in all, it was in this Viennese school of daily frustrations that Adolf Hitler, a man of the masses, learned to displace his psychosexual aggressions, to project his feelings of inferiority onto the most popular scapegoat of the time, and to structuralize his political attitudes on these defense mechanisms.

Still a failure after five years of shiftless poking around in the slums and political rallies of Vienna, Hitler left "the city which is for so many the epitome of careless gaiety, the joyous scene of happy people, but for me only the living memory of the most unhappy period of my life." It was, indeed, the period in which his feelings of inferiority were most painfully confirmed, and he left it with nothing but an accumulation of hatreds: against royalty, the Catholic church, Social Democrats and Communists, civil service, Parliament, Slavs, Jews and "foreigners" generally—everything except German militarism and nationalism.

WORLD WAR I

Munich Interlude.—From 1912 to the outbreak of war in 1914, Adolf Hitler lived in Munich, "A *German* city!! What a contrast to Vienna!" Still an unsuccessful dauber in water color and dabbler in odd jobs, he found here some solace in being accepted among the less cosmopolitan and less sophisticated Munich *Bürgers* as a German among Germans. Actually the common ground was in the religion, dialect, provincialism, current prejudices, and other cultural factors common to Bavarians and rural Austrians. The question of an Anschluss of Austria and Germany was also a live political issue in Catholic Bavaria. Hitler warmly supported this solution to his own ego-needs, but for reasons of racial rather than religious identification. Nevertheless, he had to content himself with listening to political debates in beer halls, chafing at the bit, while the others talked and he craved action. Neither the satisfaction nor the sublimation of his needs having succeeded, overt aggression became a crying necessity. If his old history teacher, Dr. Pötsch, had inculcated in him revolutionary ideas even as a youth, years of frustration in every direction had only served to fixate and intensify his revolutionary cravings. It was thus that the outbreak of war in 1914 came as a godsend to his pent-up aggression by his own confession: "To me that day seemed a resolution of all my tortured youthful sensations. I am not ashamed to say even today that I sank to my knees, overcome by passionate inspiration and thanked heaven with an overflowing heart for having granted me the good fortune to be living at this time." (33, chap. v.)

This revelation of ardent aggressive nationalism is valid enough as far as it goes; however, we must recognize further considerations, both material and psychological. In 1914, at the age of twenty-five, Adolf Hitler was still actually a vagabond who did not know where his next week's food and shelter were coming from. He was without background, without companions, without occupational or social status, without any acceptable group identification. Having dodged the Austrian draft, he was virtually a man without a country. The outbreak of war solved all his status-needs at one stroke. He was now a *German* with the privilege of volunteering for the German army to fight for the cause of *Kaiser und Vaterland* like the German heroes of old. Besides, he would always have a roof over his head, adequate clothing, and fairly regular meals. In fact, shortly before the outbreak of war Hitler had finally decided not to avoid the compulsory military service of Austria any longer, but he had been rejected anyway as unfit for military duty. We may therefore well believe that Germany's declaration of war came as a relief to all his tortured youthful sensations—of poverty and inferiority.

War Service.—Hitler immediately volunteered, for according to his own account he could hardly get to the front soon enough to prove his right to sing *Deutschland, Deutschland über Alles, über Alles in der Welt!* He did not remain at the front very long, however, for he was soon able to get assigned to regimental headquarters as a dispatch carrier. Some biographers who are familiar with conditions of trench warfare on the German fronts during World War I point out that any position at regimental headquarters was a good spot for a common soldier who wanted to keep as far behind the front-line trenches as possible. Furthermore, Hitler's emotional instability and unsociability did not lend itself to the camaraderie that made life in the front-line trenches more bearable and promoted the company *esprit de corps.* His company commander is reported to have stated, "I'll never make a non-com out of this hysteric." We may also infer from the fact that Hitler had been rejected in the draft just prior to the outbreak of hostilities that he was not an asset in combat, whether for physical or mental reasons or both. Since he was not equipped by training even for clerical work at company or regimental headquarters, the job of regimental dispatch carrier was apparently one of the few things that he could qualify for. To Hitler, being attached to regimental headquarters was not only a more comfortable assignment but provided a vicarious identification with authority. The orders he carried set battalions in motion, started artillery barrages, or sent further orders down the line to hold ground regardless of losses. Hitler felt perfectly satisfied with the comparative comfort and the vicarious satisfactions his job afforded. In fact, he felt perfectly satisfied with the war. For the first time in his life Hitler could experience some feeling of security and status. Fighting for *Kaiser und Vaterland* like a true German son no doubt brought him a sense of identification with strength he had often fantasied but never before possessed. Heroic fantasies were further encouraged by his reading of the soldier's pocket editions of Nietzsche and the heroic sagas of German literature. The German soldier became for him the Superman of a new order which could be achieved only by proving one's worth in battle, like the heroes of old. We later find traces of this philosophy in *Mein Kampf* and it was to become the basic philosophy of the SS-police state under Hitler. One of his doctors (Dr. Brandt) and his lawyer (Hans Frank) communicated to this biographer the certainty that Hitler's Superman obsession became fixated during his World War I service, while reading Nietzsche in the trenches of the German front. And Hitler himself told the world how grateful he was to be alive at a time when his country was proving its right to mastery by heroic combat.

He was wounded in 1916 and suffered an inflammation of the eyes from a gas attack just before the end. There is some evidence that Hitler's helplessness as a result of this gas attack was largely on a hysterical basis. The intermittent blindness he suffered as a result of the attack, while German manpower was being decimated, and the sudden complete recovery after the Armistice ran true to form for hysteria. Not the least secondary gain was the opportunity this afforded for an undistinguished soldier to be recommended for the Iron Cross. The decoration was not actually awarded until the war was over. The authenticity of the award and the question of hysteria can only be guessed at, for Hitler eventually had the records destroyed.

While in the hospital at the end of the war, Hitler received the news of the defeat and revolution with tortured sobs of frustration, while, by his own description, the blindness momentarily recurred. The bitter humiliation of Germany's defeat, the Kaiser's flight, the plight of a people left to the enemy's mercy, constituted a psychological trauma which Hitler would never forget until avenged. An implacable obsession took root in an ego wounded by frustration in his identification with power: *Germany must wipe out its defeat by military victory or die in the attempt!* Even Goering later admitted to the writer that it was undoubtedly Hitler's obsession to make up for the defeat and disgrace of 1918 that compelled him to insist on a military solution to Germany's aspiration for *Lebensraum*. To this Frank added his studied opinion that Hitler had been obsessed with the fantasy of leading Germany's armies to victory ever since his days as a corporal underling in the German army of World War I. This obsessive fantasy was to persist undiminished for twenty-five years until his country was once more immersed in bloodshed to prove its superiority.

First Political Activities

Postwar Chaos.—After the Armistice Hitler lost no time resolving his frustration with the same paranoid device he had resorted to previously; the plutocratic-bolshevik conspiracy of World Jewry had stabbed Germany in the back on the very threshold of victory. It was this message that Hitler began to preach to other veterans of the defeated army as a paid political stooge of the District Army Command, his first postwar job. To his gratification, he found that this ego-salving device could win him attentive audiences. His old friend Greiner heard him once in Munich after the war and was amazed to see the enthusiastic reaction evoked by the same old arguments that had bored and annoyed the boarders at the Männerheim. Apparently defeat and social tension had rendered the masses more suggestible to this kind of demagoguery.

Hitler decided to enter actively into politics and to try to "make something of himself" once more, by bringing this message to a people equally torn by economic chaos and frustration. The Treaty of Versailles provided an ideal springboard for such propaganda. The guilt clause, the Polish Corridor through Prussia, and the impossible reparations could all be cited as "proof" of a conspiracy to crush Germany spiritually and economically. Hunger and inflation were creating political agitation throughout Germany. The only trouble was that this could serve the propagandistic purposes of the left and the right, the "ins" and the "outs," the "higher-ups" and the "down and outs," equally well. Militarists, capitalists, monarchists, Socialists, Communists, nationalists, internationalists, Protestants, Catholics, Jews, Prussians, Bavarians, foreigners—all were denounced in turn and in varying combinations. Millions of Germans responded to the slogans of "workers of the world"; millions more to nationalistic and religious hatreds. Secret military organizations and political murder groups were being formed even while outraged veterans were tearing the epaulets off the shoulders of Prussian officers. Everywhere people were looking for scapegoats on whom to vent the aggression born of economic frustration. At the same time there was an almost universal stirring among the masses of Europe and the circles vaguely labeled "intellectual" for much-needed social reform; for an end to the politico-economic systems that repeatedly brought wars, depressions, inflation, and starvation. The necessity for some form of socialism seemed hardly debatable to most of the progressive political intellectuals of postwar Germany; only the means and extent of such reforms differentiated the programs of the multiplicity of embryonic socialistic splinter parties.

One of these was the German Workers party (*Deutsche Arbeiterpartei*), founded in Munich in 1919 by Anton Drexler and Gottfried Feder on a frankly socialistic platform with Pan-Germanic nationalistic overtones. The principal points of the original party program—state control of industry, abolition of capital interest, abrogation of the Treaty of Versailles, building of a Greater Germany—were hardly such as to have created any misgivings among patriotic Germans who shared the popular socialistic leanings; but few such parties were immune from the scapegoat hysteria that fed on popular socioeconomic frustration. An apparently irrelevant anti-Semitic plank was written into the platform as a sure-fire support-builder in the atmosphere of rekindled prejudices in the Munich of 1919.[6] But it was precisely this racial scapegoat psychology that appealed to Hitler's politically conditioned aggressions. Nor was he alone in this. Every fifth person in Bavaria seemed to want to start a new party, a new revolution, or a counterrevolution. The direction of these splinter movements (left or right) and their selection of scapegoats varied according to the backgrounds and

---

[6] Hermann Goering, Hans Frank, and Alfred Rosenberg informed the writer that impetus had been given to the anti-Semitic plank by the short-lived *Räterepublik,* a Communist group which had its turn at terrorizing Munich, in which some of the leaders were Jews. Goering and Frank considered this an unfortunate coincidence which had gotten Hitler off on the wrong tangent; Rosenberg still felt it was evidence of an international conspiracy.

social values of the leaders; the degree of extremism, according
to their personality pathology. But the purposes were pretty
much the same: to break the deadlock of economic chaos and
"to amount to something" in the process.

Hitler exemplified this psychology of status-striving and
resolution of frustrations through group hostilities only too well.
(It was no mere coincidence that the phrase "amount to something" was to appear repeatedly in connection with his father's
and his own aspirations in *Mein Kampf*, in a setting replete
with projected inferiority and group hatreds.) To be sure, his
inordinate need and range of aggressions included just as many
hatreds in common with the extreme left as with the extreme
right. The inconsistencies and incompatibilities in his political
attitudes, which he never overcame, were but an expression of
the ambivalence which had plagued him ever since childhood
in his need for identification and self-assertion. But the social
values which he had already developed in his craving for ascendancy predetermined the direction his aggressions would take in
the political melee of postwar Germany. The decisive difference
for him was that the leftist agitators denounced militant German
nationalism and the heroic racial myth, while he had become
more and more fanatically ego-involved in these biases from
early adolescence. Thus, when the German military pressure
group sought to encourage political parties which would supply
other than military scapegoats, Hitler could serve their purposes
with all the fanatic conviction of his own basic psychological
needs. But the militarists were traditionally identified with the
nobility and class privilege, and a corporal who continued to
run errands for them could never aspire to membership in the
in-group of the Junker officers' clique. The latter group, of
course, had their own conceptions of who was born to rule a
proud people with a great manifest destiny. Hitler was already
inextricably entangled in the unending vicious circle of aggressive aspiration with partial identification, ambivalence, mutual
rejection, and more aggression. It was soon obvious that the
erstwhile corporal could serve the military elite and share their
aspirations, but he could not be one of them. By the time the
military clique had regained a measure of political influence and

control under the guise of democracy in Prussia and Bavaria, Adolf Hitler, the perpetual rebel, decided he had to strike out into politics on his own to gain his ends. The German Workers party, whose platform he had helped to formulate, seemed ideally suited for this purpose.

Hitler's formal entrance into politics took place at the first big political rally of the German Workers party at the Hofbräuhaus in Munich in 1920. Here he took it upon himself to present the party's program to the public for the first time. Some of his army acquaintances put up a sufficient show of force to assure him a chance to speak without too much opposition; his passionate appeal to resurgent nationalism did the rest. By the end of the evening he could feel that "A fire had been kindled in whose glow Siegfried's sword would be forged anew to regain freedom for the German nation. And in this coming resurrection I could feel the implacable goddess of Revenge marching to atone for the treachery of November 9, 1918." (33, chap. xii.) Hitler's paranoid and aggressive resolutions of frustration had struck a responsive chord. Other Germans were also amenable to the suggestion of replacing defeat by victory, economic weakness by military strength, inferiority by superiority, and of venting their aggressions on the scapegoats of their misery. Adolf Hitler's inordinate drive for dominance through social conflict could thus become politically channelized.

The "Old Fighters."—By 1921 Hitler had taken over leadership of the German Workers party from its less aggressive founders. He wanted to rename it the German National Revolutionary party but was persuaded not to scare off the timid bourgeoisie. The National Socialist German Workers party (NSDAP) gave better expression to his nationalist leanings without giving up the semantic appeal to the proletariat. This confusion of values and purposes at the very outset of the National Socialist movement was, as we have seen, largely determined by the multiplicity of Hitler's aggressive needs and ambivalent group identifications. It also accounted for the extreme variety of personalities and motives among the followers, rendering any categorical judgments on the character of "the

Nazis" (if taken to mean any who held party membership at any time) extremely unreliable.[7] To the socialistically inclined idealists who joined the party out of patriotic zeal (and there were many such in the early years), national socialism represented a defensible conciliation of the needs for national recovery and social reform. The party platform and even some of Hitler's early speeches gave ample reason to justify such hopes. In a culture long inured to group and class hostilities and the absolute values of nationalism, it was not easy even for such "idealists" to recognize or properly evaluate the incompatibilities in Hitler's propaganda. Nor has psychological astuteness in politics ever been sufficiently well advanced to recognize what is so clear in retrospective analysis: Hitler's identification with Germany's frustrated "common man" was far too ambivalent and too contemptuously weighted with the disowning projection of his own inferiority feelings to have taken root in any truly humanitarian ideals.

On the other hand, those who were inspired by more antisocial and ulterior motives found in Hitler's aggressive rebellion and contempt for all established social institutions a source of steadfast leadership for *action*. The most active of these was a group of revolutionary zealots called the "Old Fighters." This old guard of the frustrated and disinherited found status and common purpose in Hitler's revolutionary movement. The revolution became for them rather a psychological end than a means to any socialistic ideal. It was this group from whom Hitler drew his chief support for his acts of aggression and his Fascist *Weltanschauung* from the very beginning, and with whose support he fought his way to power.

By the end of 1922 the spearhead of the revolutionary old guard had already met and made common cause with Hitler in Munich. Julius Streicher, a Bavarian schoolteacher who was in ill repute because of his pornographic obsessions, had tried his hand at political demagoguery and had found his master in

---

[7] The failure of the American Military Government to recognize the difference between Nazi party membership and "Nazi-mindedness" created serious inequities in the de-Nazification procedures after World War II.

Hitler. Obsessed with projected anxiety over the rape of Christian girls, like his master, he found that Hitler's movement gave his pornography free rein and his mediocre intellect a successful outlet under the guise of patriotic propaganda. A graduate architect named Alfred Rosenberg had fled to Munich from Baltic Russia after the Revolution. Being unable to find work, and having read some books outside of his field, he sought to peddle an antibolshevik, anti-Catholic, anti-Semitic political philosophy with mystic racial overtones. He found sympathy and leadership under the Hitler banner and became editor of the official party newspaper, the *Völkischer Beobachter,* giving the party propaganda a pseudointellectual air. Another foreign-born student of political philosophy at the University of Munich, an inadequate and highly suggestible personality by the name of Rudolf Hess, also satisfied his craving to "belong" by sharing the language of group hatreds that Hitler had already mastered. A former Luftwaffe officer named Hermann Goering, having returned from his postwar wanderings with a rich wife and a zest for combat, thought he could find what he was looking for in Munich. This aggressive egotist hated no one in particular and didn't much care whom he beat up or killed for laughs or loot. Hitler gave him the opportunity of discharging his aggressions by putting him in charge of his uniformed ruffians in brown shirts, the Storm Troops. At the same time a homosexual captain of the Reichswehr, Ernst Roehm, showed Hitler that he could count on his boys in any show of force against the established order—provided there was something in it for him too. A chemist by the name of Robert Ley was getting into trouble with his employers because of his alcoholism and emotional instability. He too found refuge and status among Hitler's disinherited.

Each according to his needs and abilities helped to build up the propaganda machine or the militaristic strong-arm of the party—that combination of verbal and active aggression which had proven so effective ever since the party's first big rally. Day after day Rosenberg and Streicher poured out their incitement to racial, religious, national, and class hatreds in their journals, leaflets, and mass rallies. At the same time Roehm's freebooters and Goering's Storm Troopers "kept order" at Nazi meetings while breaking up their rivals' meetings with a fair show of zest for bloody assault.

Hitler proved himself worthy of leadership in aggression of any variety during the early stormy years of Munich. In 1922 he was sentenced to three months' imprisonment for one of the bodily assaults he directed in person against one of his political enemies. He served one month in Stadelheim prison, having the remainder of the sentence suspended on the promise that he would stop resorting to violence. A new socialist government in Munich, which had replaced the communist extremists, was seeking to keep order in Bavaria while the national government attempted to have the oppressive Versailles Treaty modified by peaceful negotiation. But peaceful reform was anathema to Hitler's revolutionary spirit, for while it might accomplish his alleged patriotic purposes without bloodshed, it would fail to fulfil the heroic fantasies by which alone he could resolve his deep-seated inferiority feelings. Even while promising to forswear violence, Hitler loudly proclaimed that he was being crucified by Jewish lawmakers, conspiring both in the guise of communism and capitalism to ruin Germany, and that he would crush this conspiracy with blood and steel. He was no sooner out of jail on "good behavior" than he set about plotting his revolution to bring vengefully aggressive heroic fantasies to fruition. For Hitler's aggressive compulsions were only beginning to find political expression. After all, how could a man who had grown up full of hatred for his drunken old father keep any promise to respect established authority—or to give up his obsession to crush and replace that authority?

The Munich *Putsch*.—By November, 1923, five years after "the treachery of 1918," Hitler decided the time was ripe to stage his "revolution" and rescue Germany from her enemies. In spite of his heroic obsession, his revolutionary plot was not entirely devoid of reality-testing in his social milieu. As we have pointed out, Hitler was only one of many *Putsch*-planners and intriguers in the politically explosive climate of postwar Bavaria, and he had some reason to expect support from various quarters. His Storm Troops under Goering had grown to a small army. They were a motley crew of idealists and sadists, but they were inspired with a revolutionary zeal spurred on by skyrocketing inflation. With aggressive leadership and good luck they might become the vanguard of a people's army of restless German nationalists rallying to the cry of "Down with Versailles!" There were even certain elements in the Bavarian government itself which might be sympathetic to an uprising against the current republican government in Berlin for reasons of their own. But while these anti-Prussian conservatives and monarchists of the Bavarian Catholic Center were restrained by their bourgeois inhibitions against violence, Hitler's ambitions were not similarly encumbered. Nor were they encumbered by any confusion as to his real purposes and loyalties. As Goering later explained to the writer, "Don't forget the Bavarians themselves were in cahoots with us, because they wanted to pull their own brand of revolution. Of course, what they wanted was separatism from North Germany,[8] and a kind of Catholic Alliance with Austria—but we Greater Germany patriots wanted just the opposite. So we strung them along with the idea of getting rid of the present government first and letting us get in —but naturally, we had no idea of breaking up Germany for their Catholic Alliance." (22)

Thus, with a little shrewd calculation on combined high treason and treachery, a little actual striking power, and a great deal of obsessive heroic fantasy, Hitler embarked on his Munich *Putsch* of November 8-9, 1923. The World War hero, General Ludendorff, was inveigled into the scheme on the assurance that the Reichswehr had agreed to support the revolution—the substance of which lay entirely in Hitler's susceptibility to autosuggestion. Assured of nonintervention by the police commissioner and his Nazi-minded deputy, Wilhelm Frick, Goering and Roehm seized certain key points in the city. They then converged on the beer hall where the Bavarian minister-president, police chief, etc., were holding a political rally in full

---

[8] An issue that dated from the Thirty Years War and was supposedly settled by Bismarck's overthrow of the Bavarian monarchy and unification of Germany under Prussian rule.

strength. Thereupon Hitler himself broke up the meeting with his little armed band of Old Fighters. Nervously jumping to the speaker's rostrum, he fired a pistol at the ceiling and announced that the revolution was on. Then he contrived to get the leaders of the Bavarian government to resign on the spot and join him in a new government. The Bavarian minister-president, Von Kahr, was intimidated into acquiescing in Hitler's demand for a new Bavarian government, virtually at pistol point. Hitler then told the crowd of beer-drinkers and Storm Troopers that a new government had been formed, though he knew that Von Kahr was acquiescing under duress and Ludendorff was under a misapprehension about the commitment of the Reichswehr. Nevertheless, the bluff appeared to work by its own suggestive power. The crowd cheered and Hitler's "ministers" in turn reacted to the apparent popular sanction of the move. Speeches were made, and the crowd went home convinced that a real revolutionary coalition government had been formed in Munich under Hitler to take over the national government next day. Any agreement, any strong leadership was welcome. Hitler was in ecstasy. The bold bluff had worked on everybody, including himself. All that remained was for the Reichswehr to fulfil his fantasy by rising against the government behind General Ludendorff and the country's savior. But the fantasy failed to materialize. The next morning, when Hitler and his band of Old Fighters, Storm Troopers, and hangers-on marched on the Feldherrnhalle to take over the government of Bavaria, they were simply dispersed by the first shots of the armed Bavarian police. Hitler dropped to the ground, then fled. Goering was wounded and twenty-four minor Nazis were killed. The Berlin Reichswehr had even been alerted to crush his "revolution" if it materialized, but their precautions were superfluous. There had really been no revolution—just an abortive "beer-hall *Putsch*" based largely on bluff.

Hitler, Hess, Streicher, and several of the other Old Fighters were arrested and tried for treason against the Republic. Goering had escaped to Italy as an outlaw, nursing a wounded thigh. One bit of testimony in this trial is of some psychological significance—the statement of the Munich psychiatrist who was among the witnesses of the beer-hall *Putsch:* "I saw Hitler close up for the first time. Face and head, receding forehead indicate poor racial stock. . . . Facial expression not that of self-control, but of insane excitement. . . ." The report is interesting, not for its psychiatric acumen, but for its probable effect on Hitler. *Poor racial stock!* A drunken sot of a father of questionable background, a mother who died of cancer, three siblings who died in childhood, a half-brother who had already been sentenced to jail twice, and now he himself was on trial for treason. Poor racial stock? Traitor? The trial and testimony could only have intensified his obsession to prove his racial superiority and patriotic heroism.

Even while on trial for treason Hitler's heroic obsession enabled him to represent himself as a martyr to the cause of German nationalism. Though somewhat cowed and defensive at first, he soon rallied with emotional vituperation and ended with another ringing denunciation of Germany's enemies and pacifism.

> The maintenance of world peace cannot be the purpose and aim of the policy of a State. . . . [Germany] can maintain itself only when it places a power-policy ruthlessly in the foreground. . . . The army which we have formed grows from day to day; from hour to hour it grows more rapidly. Even now I have the proud hope that one day the hour is coming when these untrained bands will become battalions, when the battalions will become regiments and the regiments divisions, when the old cockade will be raised from the mire, when the old banners once again will wave before us. . . . The Court of History will judge us . . . who as Germans have wished the best for their people and their Fatherland, who wished to fight and to die. You may declare us guilty a thousand times, but the goddess who presides over the Eternal Court of History will smilingly tear to pieces the charge of the State prosecutor and the judgment of the court: for she will declare us guiltless. (34)

Poor racial stock indeed!

The German press received the speeches variously: some as the rantings of a demagogue, some as the moving oratory of a great patriot. The court itself seemed ambivalent. Ludendorff was exonerated as a patriot beyond reproach, and Hitler was given the minimum sentence of five years' imprisonment. The *London Times* commented laconically: "The trial has at any rate proved that to plot against the Constitution of the Reich is not considered a serious crime in Bavaria."

Political Integration of Attitudes.—We may pause at this first major milestone in Hitler's revolutionary career to consider how it reflected as well as influenced his personality development and behavior patterns.

To begin with, we have already seen how the imprisonment of 1922 and 1924 merely helped to structuralize his own heroic fantasies and feelings of persecution into a politically systematized messianic complex. We find him now in Landsberg prison with his fellow-revolutionists, plotting his political comeback through more effective hate propaganda, in order to rescue Germany from her enemies. The identification of this persecuted German son with the destiny of the nation was to be unshakable from this time on. Hitler and Germany would prove their superiority or die in the attempt. The obsession of ultimate victory in war keeps his spirit alive and reconciles him to his present frustration. He even designs a Victory Arch while in jail to eclipse in grandeur the Arch of Triumph in Paris. He will take a terrible revenge for "the disgrace of 1918" that will shake all of Europe! We can read Hitler's fantasies of revenge for Germany's (i.e., his) persecution quite readily, for they are projected into every chapter of the book he is writing about his *Kampf* (fight), thinly camouflaged by historical and geopolitical rationalizations. The Victory Arch is to remain a symbol of unresolved frustration—a true symbol of the vengeful war obsession which underlies his glowing plans to "rebuild Germany." At present it is only a symbol of heroic fantasy. But years later, when the Nazi juggernaut is crushing Europe, Hitler will betray his obsession with the cryptic remark to his architect and war production chief, Albert Speer: "How hard Fate makes it for me, to have to wage war in order to put my building plans into effect!" [9] For how else will he ever build the Victory Arch he

---

[9] "Wie macht mir's das Schicksal schwer, dass ich Krieg führen muss, um meine Baupläne verwirklichen zu können."—Reported to the writer by Albert Speer in Nuremberg, and confirmed by Hitler's physician, Dr. Karl Brandt.

is designing in Landsberg prison while writing *Mein Kampf,* except by first seizing power, then waging and winning a war of revenge? The better to prepare himself for his role of tribal heroic Superman, Hitler rereads Nietzsche and the British pro-German anti-Semite, H. S. Chamberlain. Objective history, economics, and sociology do not conform to his purposes or educational limitations, and after a brief attempt (through the reputable German historian, Leopold Von Ranke) are rejected. Later Hitler sums it up by telling Frank: "Landsberg was my college education at State expense. I recognized the correctness of my views in the long run throughout the history of the world and of nature, and was convinced of the contradictory and hypo-critical 'intellectualizing' of the professors and high priests of the Universities. Anyway, will-power is greater than knowl-edge. If God had only 'known' the world and had not 'willed' it, there would still be only Chaos." (18) Hitler would not be found wanting in will-power either.

Secondly, we already have a clear indication of the pattern of Hitler's behavior in achieving his purposes. As Hans Frank explained, the Munich *Putsch* set the pattern for all of Hitler's subsequent moves in seizing and using his political power: First he decided the time was ripe for a desperate gamble to achieve a daring goal. The balance of his own strength and the enemy's weakness (chiefly through divided self-interest) entered into the calculation of the opportune time to strike. But he counted as much on propaganda slogans, bluff, sheer luck, and the sug-gestive power of his own fanaticism as on any calculation of relative material strength. Any deceit that served his purposes, even a temporary alliance with enemies who would eventually have to be betrayed, was lightly undertaken, for morals played no part whatever in his system of values. He then staked every-thing, including his followers' lives and fortunes, on his des-perate gamble for supremacy. The intimidative power of his boldness could be counted on for at least initial success. If no resistance was offered and his adventure succeeded, he could stand forth as a man of destiny, a genius who could succeed by the sheer force of his will, giving the lie to all conservatives and experts; if the gamble failed, he was then only a persecuted patriot who had been "stabbed in the back" by traitors and cowards. The "traitors and cowards" in this case were both the leaders of the Reichswehr, who had shamefully failed to fulfil his fantasy of a national uprising under his leadership, and the conservative monarchists of the Bavarian government, who had failed to remain intimidated by his bluff. Hitler's distrust of the officers corps and the aristocracy was to be implacable from this time on.

This brings us to the third aspect of Hitler's early revolutionary behavior: the fixation of the chosen objects of his aggression. If Hitler thought about the psychological reasons for his failure—something he was quite capable of doing intuitively rather than rationally—he must have sensed that his multiplicity of hatreds was an obstacle in convincing some of the groups in power that their loyalties and purposes were not incompatible with his own. At any rate, we find in *Mein Kampf* and in his speeches after the Munich *Putsch* a gradual narrowing down and intensification of his *expressed* hatred to the safest objects. This is not to question the genuineness or universality of his hostilities, but merely to indicate a prudent selectivity in his public declarations thereof. The three principal scapegoats are now: the hostile Allies with their oppressive Treaty of Versailles, the "threat of world bolshevism," and the conspiracy of "World Jewry," which becomes the root of all evil.

Hitler's loudly proclaimed hatred of the Allies and the Treaty of Versailles requires no further explanation. This was a natural and universal postwar phenomenon in Germany. His anti-bolshevist fanaticism was also in keeping with his rightist leanings. But further explanation is required for his selection of "World Jewry" as the universal scapegoat of all his aggressions, when anti-Semitism was only one of many current prejudices among the German population. We already know that Hitler's anti-Semitism was the more virulent Eastern variety acquired during his Vienna experience and intensified by long-smoldering psychosexual conflicts. But something new came into his life about 1922 to give further political structure to this particular prejudice. This was a political tract, the so-called *Protocols of the Wise Men of Zion*. This often-exposed forgery had been "planted" by the intriguing secret police of czarist Russia to justify their own terror tactics. It purported to show that there was an actual conspiracy of "International Jewry" to gain control of the world by infiltration into positions of power and influence in all countries, resorting to any form of terror and deceit to gain their ends. This tract had been published in Russian and might have been forgotten after the Russian Revolution if Alfred Rosenberg had not picked up a copy in Munich.[10] In his political naïveté and need for hostile group identification, Rosenberg took it to heart and published it in German (1923), after calling it to Hitler's attention. Nothing could have suited Hitler's needs more perfectly. Here at last was proof of what Hitler had known intuitively all along. Had not Jews risen out of the slums of Vienna into positions of respectability and influence? Were there not Jews in positions of power in every country of the world, especially among the Allies who were persecuting Germany? Were there not some among the revolutionists who had stabbed the Fatherland in the back and in the government that sentenced him to jail in 1922 and 1924 to prevent his salvation of Germany? Were they not even now planning Germany's extinction in Moscow and Wall Street? Was there not, in fact, a World Zionist Organization to provide the façade for this conspiracy? The incongruous forms in which the universal scapegoat was conjured up merely gave convenient identification to his multiplicity of aggressions. The fact that the *Protocols* were supposed to be a forgery was readily disposed of: "The mere fact that the Jews claim them to be a forgery is the best proof that they are genuine." The fact that men of all religious backgrounds were to be found on both sides of the political fence, that Zionism could have nothing to do with even the alleged conspiracy, and that many liberal Jews were indifferent or hostile to Zionism anyway—all provided further proof of the diabolically deceptive cunning of the conspiracy (*Mein Kampf,* chap. ii). Hitler was

---

[10] Contrary to some historians, Rosenberg denied having brought it to Germany from Russia, but said he had come across it accidentally in Germany, and it proved to be an "eye-opener." He had known that it was supposed to be a forgery when he published it, but said that it *sounded* genuine.

perceiving his world in terms of his own needs and purposes and understanding its meanings by selective association. This, of course, is in the very nature of prejudice.

But by 1924 Hitler's frustrations were intensifying his prejudices and integrating them into his ego-involved political frame of reference. In the deceit and terror of the "Wise Men of Zion" he recognized at least semiconsciously his own pattern of political behavior, as we see in parts of *Mein Kampf.* ("The greater the lie, the more readily will the people accept it," etc.) But he appears to rationalize it all as merely a matter of beating "World Jewry" at its own game. Here we can again see the old vicious circle of ambivalence of group identification and rejection. In this case it was a mythical group, which he used for the projection and introjection of a lust for power. The conspirators of Zion were real to Hitler because they *had to be* to satisfy these mechanisms. At the same time the master-race myth *had to be* a biological reality to sever the intolerable ambivalence of his group identifications and his obsessive need for superior status. Finally, the fantasy of rescuing the pure German motherland, by slaying her enemies and erecting a Victory Arch over their dead bodies, *had to become a reality* or he would die in the attempt.

In short, by this time we find the beginnings of true paranoid tendencies in an unmistakably neurotic personality seeking an outlet for his aggressions through political power.

FROM *Mein Kampf* TO DICTATORSHIP

Politics and Propaganda.—Such was the mental state of the man who was released from Landsberg prison in December, 1924, after serving less than a year of his sentence for plotting to overthrow the government. With him he had the manuscript of the first part of *Mein Kampf* and a determination to complete it and put it into practice. The party had been banned, but that did not deter him. Politico-economic chaos still reigned, and Germany was still waiting for its savior. As a matter of fact, his revolutionary behavior and imprisonment had proved his leadership and had given him that aura of martyrdom on which paranoia could thrive. He must only pursue doggedly his determination to get his message across to the people and to force the march of events with his indomitable will.

The more or less autobiographical first part of *Mein Kampf* was published in 1925. The second part, containing his program for action, was published in 1926. He left no doubts about his intentions or methods of fulfilment: The party and eventually the entire state must be organized on the pattern of the Prussian army, on the principle of leadership with a hierarchy of authority. Parliamentarism, tolerance of opposition, majority rule, and other inventions of degenerate democracy must be done away with. Strong leadership would once more take over the reins of government, vanquish all enemies from within and from without, wipe out the disgrace of Versailles, and restore Germany to her pristine glory.

This use of the heroic appeal, so potent in the authoritarian cultural lag, requires further explanation. This was, after all, a time of democratic revolt in Central Europe. The conflict between democratic and authoritarian government had had its special impact on Hitler ever since his own frustrations had aroused his political interest in Vienna. Both there and in Munich, the increasing clamor for democratic self-government —proportional representation, freedom, and equal rights—had become associated in his mind with the clamor of the "inferior foreign element" for equal status. All of German history and legend, on the other hand, was written in terms of heroic leadership and ethnic solidarity against enemy outsiders. Still there was no gainsaying the powerful appeal of democratic self-government to the new masses of Germany. Hitler made a simple compromise. He distinguished between "Jewish democracy" and "Germanic democracy." The former he defined as government by a parliament of irresponsible weaklings and opportunists, slavishly following their respective party lines, making it all the easier for those who pulled the strings (the Jews, of course) to do their dirty work. "In contrast to that," he stated in *Mein Kampf,* "there stands the true Germanic democracy of free choice of a leader, who takes over all responsibility for his deeds and omissions. Here there is no voting of a majority for each and every question, but only the choice of one man, who must then stake his life and fortune on his own decisions. If one should object that under these conditions it would be hard to find anyone who would dedicate himself to such a perilous task, then I have only one thing to say: Thank God that therein lies the very essence of Germanic democracy . . . that the very greatness of the responsibility frightens off incompetents and weaklings. . . . The climb to the Pantheon of History is not for slackers, but for heroes!" (33, chap. iii.)

The would-be dictator's typically deceptive compromise between autocratic government and parliamentary chaos, appealing to the heroic symbolism of his culture, is all too transparent here. Only Siegfried had been able to brave the flames to escape Brünhilde; only Frederick the Great had had the greatness to lead the Germanic people to glorious conquest. These things did not have to be said in so many words (though Hitler soon cast off all restraint in doing so). Heroic championship and authority, ethnic solidarity for aggressive defense against enemies were symbols that had been embedded in his thinking and that of his Germanic *Volksgenossen* since earliest childhood. They would provide the needed panacea for the resolution of current socioeconomic frustration. Social unrest and the authoritarian cultural lag were working in his favor.

What Germany needed now, Hitler insisted, was heroic leadership with a bold, aggressive program; not a wrangling government of treacherous republican pacifists. Just a month before the Munich *Putsch* he had shouted to a cheering gathering:

> How are States founded? Through the personality of brilliant leaders and through a people which deserves to have the crown of laurel bound about its brows. Compare them with the "heroes" of this Republic! Shirkers, deserters, and pacifists: these are its founders and their heroic acts consisted in leaving in the lurch the soldiers at the front, in stopping reinforcements; in withholding munitions. . . . This revolution has dishonored the old heroes on whom the whole earth had looked with wonder; it allowed the scum of the streets to tear off their decorations and to hurl into the mire all that was sacred to the heroes of the front line. . . . (34)

In *Mein Kampf* Hitler reiterated his charge, and thus the "stab-in-the-back" legend became a vital corollary of the appeal to heroic championship. It was a potent appeal to millions of World War I veterans and the national pride that had been sorely wounded by the defeat. The symbols of good and evil were clearly personified: the heroic German fighter for the Fatherland; the Jewish-democratic pacifist who had stabbed him in the back. Hitler well knew the power of such propaganda in times of social unrest.

His entire program was structured around these key symbols. First, all true Germans must rally around their heroic leaders to cast out the villains who had led them astray. Under such strong leadership Germany must then rearm to seize her lost territories and to expand her *Lebensraum.* "Let us be clear about one thing: the regaining of our lost territories is not to be achieved by solemn prayers to God Almighty or by pious hopes of a League of Nations, but by the force of arms." Sooner or later, he warned, Germany must destroy her deadly enemy, France, checkmate the scheming British, and expand to the wide open spaces of the East, for which heaven seemed to have prepared the way with a crippling bolshevism. Germany's strong leadership would naturally have to crush World Jewry in the process, for the racial struggle was at the very core of the struggle for national survival. The ultimate goal was clearly if immodestly stated in the concluding remarks on the last page of Volume II: *"A State which dedicates itself to the cultivation of its best racial elements in this era of race pollution must one day become the master of the earth."*

His program finally recorded and his party once more legitimized in 1926, Hitler set out once more on his quest for power. There is no denying his strength of determination—a determination growing out of the deeply rooted paranoid obsession we have already described—for at this point he had little else to drive him on. In the German press and public opinion Hitler's sensation-value had become rather played out, and even many of the most ardent nationalists regarded him as a fanatic whose demagoguery was already somewhat passé. The publication of *Mein Kampf* only served to emphasize this impression. The

myths which were so real to Hitler were somehow not taken
so seriously by the majority of the people; his politico-economic
ideas rejected by the very authorities whose ideas Hitler thought
he was incorporating into his new *Weltanschauung*. Professor
Karl Haushofer, whose "geopolitics" filtered into the work only
through the confused mind of Rudolf Hess, recalled later : "The
book *Mein Kampf* I saw for the first time when the first edition
was already in print. I refused to review this book because it
had nothing to do with geopolitics. For me at that time it
seemed to be one of the many ephemeral publications for purposes of agitation. It is self-evident that I had no part in its
origin." (63)

There was now even a rival leader in the party who felt that
the emphasis must be on socialist reform of German economy,
rather than racial dogma and revolution. He was Gregor
Strasser, a retired pharmacist of Bavaria, a better-educated and
more sophisticated economist than Hitler, whose arguments were
winning Socialist adherents all over Germany. But the revolutionary zeal of Hitler's Old Fighters continued unabated. With
nothing to lose, they staked all on the success of the party as
a *revolutionary* party with Hitler as their acknowledged leader.
Among this group a strong emotional bond had grown up,
sealed in the blood of the Munich *Putsch* and in the "persecution" some of them shared with Hitler in prison, and continually
strengthened by their common need for aggression. Whereas
some of the more faint-hearted had already lost faith in Hitler's
revolutionary leadership, some of the more aggressively inclined
young hangers-on of the party were devoting themselves ever
more fanatically to Hitler's cause. Chief among the newcomers
to the front ranks of Old Fighters were Joseph Goebbels, an
intelligent but unsuccessful writer with a clubfoot, and Hans
Frank, an equally intelligent unemployed lawyer. Goebbels was
appointed district leader in Berlin, more or less "bought" by
Hitler to weaken Strasser's competition. He devoted his considerable talents for propaganda to the task of winning over
Berlin's leftists to the cause of Hitlerian fascism. Hans Frank
quickly became the party's leading defense counsel in its numerous lawsuits and one of its most passionate electioneers.

Streicher and Rosenberg continued their propaganda activities in Bavaria, while Robert Ley took up the cudgels in the Rhineland and Frick pulled his political strings in Thuringia. The command of the Storm Troops was taken over by Captain Ernst Roehm, and the organization began to spread all over Germany. By 1927 the party showed sufficient signs of life to induce Goering to return to the fold from his aimless existence in Scandinavia. Hitler was once more in the saddle with his coterie of Old Fighters, and the party experienced a meteoric rise for the next five years.

Hitler was determined not to risk another abortive *Putsch* but to enlist support from all classes of German society for a well-planned campaign against well-chosen enemies. In fact, just like the "Wise Men of Zion" he would use the interests of entrenched power and constitutional government to overthrow both. To begin with, it was obvious that too much socialistic talk of expropriating the holdings of the landed aristocracy for the good of the workers was not consonant with the continuation of the best source of financial support for a would-be fascist dictator. When that issue came to a head as early as 1925, Hitler, with Goebbels' help, beat the overzealous social-reformist, Gregor Strasser, over the party's decision on the issue. Hitler's support from that quarter continued. His opposition to the separatist movement in Bavaria and his support of Prussian militarism also rendered him more palatable to the Prussians. The party's opposition to "capitalist domination" did not have to be an insurmountable obstacle to the support of industrialists and bankers, for he was only attacking "foreign Jewish capital" —Wall Street; if any of these foreign capital interests were apprehensive of what he might represent in Germany, he was, of course, only fighting communism.

Nevertheless, his aggression found numerous objects out of which he could safely make political capital. In speeches all over Germany he led the way in vitriolic attacks on his selected enemies, instigating physical violence against Jews, communists, and "appeasers" of the Allies. Any attempt to ameliorate the terms of Germany's defeat (like the Dawes Plan) was treated as an attack on Germany's honor; any failure to do so (the repeated vain attempts of the Weimar Republic chancellors) was greeted as a vindication of his warlike policy.

Even the processes of legal democratic government provided their outlets for aggression. The numerous local and national elections did not merely provide an election (*Wahl*) but an election fight (*Wahlkampf*), and did, in fact, frequently provide opportunities for street brawls for his eager followers. Far from being chastened by his recent encounter with the law, Hitler continued to flout it while at the same time using it for his own purposes of indirect aggression. Legal altercations constituted his favorite indoor sport in those years—a kind of relaxation from the more arduous outdoor aggressions of the *Kampfzeit* (period of struggle to power). As Hans Frank informed us (18), Hitler made the most meticulous use of civil rights in his own behalf, whenever he felt his own "honor" threatened, though he secretly hated the laws of society as such. "The terrible thing about Adolf Hitler was that he enjoyed the protection of the law in those years, but later showed only contempt for the law and the whole judicial system." The clemency extended by the sympathetic Bavarian Minister of Justice had merely increased his contempt for the weakness of legal government in handling revolutionary upstarts, and he was determined that he would never make that mistake when he came to power. In the meantime, it suited his purposes to be the very soul of legality. When indicted for his attacks against his enemies, he took refuge by defending himself on the grounds of freedom of speech, press, and assembly. When his oversensitive ego was wounded by attacks of his opponents, he did not hesitate to bring suit for libel or slander, or to seek court injunctions. He was not only incapable of tolerating criticism, but actually found some satisfaction in these perpetual legal altercations. Altogether Frank represented him in some 150 court actions, mostly as "plaintiff." When he was not directly involved in a lawsuit himself, he was not averse to appearing as a witness in defense of any of his overzealous followers who may have committed mayhem or murder to curb an opponent's freedom of speech.

On one occasion (the Leipzig trial of 1930) a judge asked Hitler if he was not being dangerously aggressive and defying the law by constantly threatening to take revenge on his enemies if he ever came to power. With a grandiloquent gesture to the press gallery, Hitler swore that he would use only legal means to come to power—though traitors' heads might roll thereafter, in accordance with Nazi conceptions of justice. This tongue-in-cheek concession to law and order satisfied the demand for strong leadership out of chaos, while lulling the bourgeois' fear of revolution. The effect was so salutary on the sympathetic or doubtful segments of the press, and created such a sensation generally, that Hitler warmly thanked lawyer Frank for giving him the opportunity to use the trial for Nazi propaganda. Even the hostile reaction was good publicity.

In his numerous speeches and press interviews, Hitler was no less adroit in appealing to all possible segments of domestic and foreign opinion. When a delegation of national women's organizations called on him to gain assurance that he did not intend to abrogate women's constitutional rights, he replied that he was less concerned with the political meddling of idle society women than with providing every real German woman a real German man. This theme was repeated over and over again at mass rallies, to the ecstatic jubilation of the women in the audiences.

To the youth of the nation he preached the homely virtues of obedience, strength of character, patriotism; to the girls he held out the prospect of proud motherhood; to the boys, the glory of emulation for heroic leadership.

In his interviews with foreign press representatives, he was particularly careful to emphasize that he had no intention of taking such radical steps as the expropriation of property. Foreign and domestic capital could rest assured: all he wanted was economic stability. "My Party is not a movement of despair but a movement of hope. When we come to power, our watchword will be to give the world that which is really due to it, and to give to the German people as a sovereign people what it needs for its livelihood. We want nothing else. Our Monroe Doctrine is and will ever be 'Germany for the Germans.'" (34)

In dozens of speeches and interviews, Hitler assured the German worker that the original purpose of the National Socialist German Workers party had never been lost sight of: ". . .

the meaning and purpose of the State are through this form of organization to assure the livelihood of the people." To all peace-loving Germans he reiterated his assurance that even though his aim was a revolutionary clean sweep of the parliamentary chaos, his means to that end would be strictly constitutional. The ultimate goal must necessarily be the security and prosperity of the German people.

Through the persistent use of such appeals, Hitler gradually began to succeed in his attempt to become all things to all men: a champion of heroic patriotism and national pride to all good nationalists, especially the veterans of the World War; a guarantor of security to the German worker, as well as a fighting anti-communist to the industrialist; a symbol of passionate hope to women, and of high aspiration to youth—in short, the man with the authoritarian panacea.

Private Life.—While Hitler's aggressive ascendancy needs were thus finding expression through political demagoguery, it is important to consider how his adult life experiences were shaping his emotional drives at the psychodynamic level. There is unfortunately less reliable information available about Hitler's private life during this period than about his public life. We have obtained some data, however, on his personal habits and interpersonal relationships through some of the Old Fighters who were closest to him at this time.

In the psychosexual sphere, his attachments to his Old Fighters were certainly stronger than any heterosexual love he may have experienced. This is not to confirm the more sensational stories of overt homosexuality and perversion ascribed to Hitler. But the inordinate passionate devotion which some of the Old Fighters like Hess and Frank displayed during the years following their imprisonment together, and the sublime tolerance Hitler displayed for every vice except personal disloyalty—a crime which could be expiated only by death—bear some evidence to the strengthening of latent homosexual bonds during their imprisonment and struggle to power. Greiner reports that in Vienna he had been surprised to see that Hitler was not averse to associating with homosexuals, but Hitler had re-

marked dolefully, when questioned, "Don't worry, I am too tu-
bercular to be attractive either to women or to men." Hitler's
attitude toward Captain Ernst Roehm during the struggle to
power may throw some light on his barely latent homosexuality.
Hans Frank was supposed to defend Roehm against the "libel" of
homosexuality, only to discover that Roehm was a practicing
homosexual in fact. He reported this to Hitler. Hitler expressed disdain, but said that as long as Roehm didn't seduce
young boys, the matter could rest. (Hitler was himself making
a strong appeal to the nation's youth through the Hitler Jugend
at that time.) Hitler did not seem to mind Roehm's affairs with
other Storm Troop leaders, as long as all of them were passionately loyal to their Führer. As we shall see later, however, the
first suggestion of disloyalty on their part was the occasion of an
enraged orgy of bloody retaliation—the now famous "Roehm
blood purge." On the other hand, those who maintained their
loyalty and devotion were rewarded with positions of power and
a protective loyalty beyond all reason. To understand this relationship one must go beyond the obvious explanation in terms
of common purposes ; one must look to the fulfilment of psychosexual tensions (as in the case of Julius Streicher, whose "Jewish rape" stories were daily vindications of Hitler's paranoid
reaction to the frustration of his first love).

Our information gives very little indication of overt perversion, and much more of strong conflicts of an inhibitory nature,
which had a profound effect on his personal habits and interpersonal relationships. Of some significance in this connection
is the story of his relationship with his niece, "Geli" Raubal.
During these years Hitler was living with his half-sister and this
young niece in Obersalzburg, on the Austrian border. Otto
Strasser (Gregor's brother), and others who knew Hitler claim
he indulged in perverted sexual advances to his young niece. A
certain Father Stempfle had acquired and sold back to Hitler's
party treasurer a letter which was very incriminating in this respect. Otto Strasser states that Geli had told him that Hitler became enraged and locked her in her room when she refused to
submit to these perverted advances which were "scarcely credible to a healthy-minded man." However, it is no longer

possible to obtain direct confirmation of this relationship, because Geli was found shot to death on September 18, 1931 and those who knew most about it did not live very long after.

According to Otto Strasser (60) his brother Gregor had prevented Hitler from committing suicide after the latter had confessed killing Geli. A newspaperman by the name of Gehrlich had collected very incriminating evidence. Father Stempfle, Gregor Strasser, and Gehrlich were among those later murdered in the "blood purge." The death was pronounced suicide by the same Minister of Justice who had released Hitler from jail. Nevertheless, a priest gave her holy burial. Several German newspapers attributed Geli's "suicide" to the alleged perverted overtures on the part of her uncle. Hans Frank informed the writer that he stopped the stories by obtaining court injunctions in the absence of proof for the allegations, earning Hitler's undying gratitude. The real reason for Geli's suicide, as Frank understood it, was her infatuation with an officer. This might serve to dismiss the matter, if our suspicions were not again aroused by Goering's version of the story (as given in one of our last conversations with him in the Nuremberg jail). He assured the writer that the suicide had been entirely *accidental*. Geli had taken one of Hitler's pistols for self-protection in leaving the house, and had discharged it accidentally. Goering said he had arrived immediately after the event, had seen the body, and could vouch for the fact that it had been an *accidental suicide*. Just what there was behind this strange version of Goering's, we do not know. It is entirely conceivable that Goering or Himmler had orders to "shut her up." At any rate Goering unwittingly confirmed that the fatal shot came from Hitler's own pistol and that he was right at the spot after the killing.

However, the most significant part of the story is what follows. Both Frank and Goering agreed on one point: that Hitler spent two days mourning his niece and fasting in a state of almost suicidal depression (confirming Strasser's story in part), and could be prevailed upon only with great difficulty to pull himself together for a speech he had to deliver in Hamburg. Goering accompanied Hitler and stopped at a tavern overnight on the way to Hamburg. The next morning, Goering related,

Hitler suddenly refused to eat the ham which was served for breakfast. Hitler declared, *"It is like eating a corpse!"* and no power on earth could ever make him eat meat again. He had made such remarks previously, but this time the idea seemed to have traumatic significance. From that day forth he never did touch meat. Here, as in countless other instances, Goering explained, once he had made up his mind about something, no power on earth could budge him and appeals to reason were of no avail.

Hitler's relationships with women continued to be somewhat abnormal, but inhibited and strained rather than perverted. From all available evidence, we conclude that Hitler had by now arrived at a state of permanent psychic impotence, if not perversion.

Just before Geli's death, Hitler had made the acquaintance of Eva Braun, the model of a Munich photographer. As far as we have been able to gather from those who knew of their relationship, it was much more superficial than many have supposed. Our notes on conversations with Baldur von Schirach and Albert Speer are appropriate in this connection. Von Schirach spoke of Hitler's peculiar unnaturalness with women. He had always noticed that Hitler was really never at ease with them, but covered this with an inordinate politeness and show of gallantry. For example, he would kiss the hand of an ordinary unmarried girl, inappropriately imitating the gesture reserved for Junkers' and ministers' wives. Von Schirach's wife (Eva Braun's friend) told us that she was sure that the relationship between Hitler and Eva Braun was not normal, and Von Schirach said he had noticed something wrong about it himself. He did not think that there was a normal, healthy sex relationship between the two. He thought that Eva Braun was more of a puppet whom he needed to make things look normal. At all events, her own diary indicated that she was rather neglected. Hitler himself gave the simple explanation: "The greater the man, the smaller the woman must be"—a Schopenhauer quote which conveniently rationalized any psychic impotence on his part.

One other incident might be mentioned in connection with Hitler's psychosexual conflicts at about this time. The news-

papers repeatedly made cryptic remarks about Hitler's "illegitimate Jewish grandfather." About the end of 1930, he received
a blackmail letter from the son of his illegitimate half-brother,
Alois Hitler, Jr., who hinted that their illegitimate Jewish ancestry should be kept secret. Hitler had known about the alimony payments to his grandmother by a Jew, but had understood
that these had merely been obtained on false pretenses. He
asked Frank to check on the legal records. The facts of the
alimony payments for the illegitimate child were confirmed, but
Hitler could not entertain the idea that the Jew in question was
his real grandfather. Having already developed his ego-
structure on the projection of his own inferiority and of all evil,
to the Jews, and having staked his whole career on racial conflict,
he could not tolerate such a possibility. To convince himself of
the utter impossibility of such a threat to his entire ego-structure,
Hitler had to fan his own hatred of all Jews—even unto the
third generation, whether baptized or not—into a murderous
fury. The question of Hitler's father's Jewish parentage would
remain an academic one, if we did not have some proof that he
was aware of it. For our discussion it is important merely to
note that Hitler was aware of the allegation, though he refused
to believe it, and it may not, in fact, have been true. It was a
sufficient threat to his ego-security for him to know that his
grandmother had been in a position to claim alimony from a
Jew, even if it was on false pretenses.

It should now be recalled that Hitler was, and remained all
his life, a total abstainer from alcohol because of a revulsion
toward his cruel and alcoholic father. After the death of a close
blood relation, Geli, with whom he had had some kind of questionable sex relationship, he refused to "eat a corpse." We also
know that Hitler claimed (in *Mein Kampf*) that the Jewish
refugees he had seen in Vienna had inspired a physical revulsion
which "nauseated" him, because they were not Germans like
himself, and should be exterminated like vermin. We recall
also that the prevention of "race pollution" by intermarriage
between Jews and Aryans remained a lifelong obsession, accentuated by his rejection in favor of a half-Jew in Vienna.
Now some of the pieces of the psychosexual puzzle begin to fit

together. The physical revulsion and Oedipal death wish, which grew out of his parental relationships, were apparently repressed and displaced in part to the symbol "Jew," by a process of social conditioning. Traces of this conflict remained in a tendency to psychophysiological conversion symptoms (nausea, etc.). We do not have enough information to connect all the links in this psychosexual-psychosomatic complex and to complete the clinical picture in all of its ramifications. But it is certain that somewhere in the darker recesses of Hitler's libido there lay the smoldering ashes of violent, unresolved Oedipal conflicts; that these rendered his emotional attachments to men stronger than to women, determined some negative compulsions in his personal habits, and helped to inflame his paranoid hostility toward Jews. Thus, with depth analysis as the substructure for the social level of explanation, we can see how Hitler resolved his libidinal anxieties, his feelings of inferiority, and his ambivalent ego-identifications through absolutely rigid, paranoid obsessions and aggressions. These, in interaction with his culture, determined his social values and permeated both his personal habits and his political behavior.

It was this obsessive resolution of needs which caused all who knew Hitler to agree on his "iron will-power," "absolutely unflinching determination," etc.; in short, his furious fanaticism. A mere political opportunist shifts his attitudes and loyalties with the shifting winds of political fortune, in fulfilling purposes which are largely material. A fanatic is more likely to be obsessed with attitudes, loyalties, and hostilities which have deeper motivational roots in the psychodynamics of his personality development. Even when political opportunism is superimposed on these derived motives, they betray their obsessive character by going to extremes of duration and intensity far beyond the needs of this political opportunism. Such was the case of Adolf Hitler. The rigidly obsessive displacement of aggression was to grow more and more severe until it reached a virtual rigor mortis in the final years of his destructive mania.

Political Success.—But in these years of his struggle to power Hitler was still sufficiently *en rapport* with reality to pursue with skill his policy of "all things to all men." The sheer obsessiveness of his idealized psychodynamic conflicts had a powerfully suggestive force both on his disciples and the more frustrated elements of the German public. The old politico-economic conflicts were still there, and Nazi propaganda was still winning adherents. With the increasingly desperate competition for survival in a restricted economy, scapegoat propaganda and heroic ethnocentricity were having ever stronger appeal.

Many of the elements in the social unrest of postwar Germany were very similar to those Hitler had encountered in his Viennese experience. An influx of immigration from the East, particularly of Jewish and Slavic refugees, was accentuating the economic strain. Along with them came the bearers of intense prejudices to inflame the latent hostility among the German in-group. This included not only Austrian-born Hitler, but Russian-born Rosenberg, Egyptian-born Hess, and the ideas that domestic Jew-baiters like Streicher imported from medieval anti-Semitic literature. Again the refugees, struggling for security and aspiring to assimilation, found that "you're damned if you do and damned if you don't." Those who remained identified with the rebellious underprivileged group could be attacked as "foreign trouble-makers"; those who competed successfully in accordance with the established order and began to be assimilated could be attacked as "parasite capitalist exploiters, conspiring to destroy the German people." It was now only necessary for Hitler to identify them with the makers of the Treaty of Versailles to have the perfect universal outside-enemy-figure for the appeal to hostile ethnocentricity. Even moderate Germans (and again many of the assimilated immigrant families) took up the cry of "Germany for the Germans!"

Party membership grew in direct proportion to the decline of Germany's economy. In 1928, with a comparative restoration of prosperity, there had been barely enough local strength in various parts of Germany to send twelve Nazi deputies to the Reichstag, including Hermann Goering. In 1930, as renewed depression and deflation struck Germany, and the Young Plan merely inflamed the radicals, the Nazi party won 107 seats in the Reichstag. This made Hitler's party the second largest in the country. The newly appointed Chancellor, Heinrich Brüning, continued to struggle with the growing economic chaos in a wrangling Reichstag of some twenty-three parties, and the Nazi deputies did everything possible to make the struggle even harder. For Hitler realized, in spite of his speeches to the press, that his was a solution of desperation, that a prosperous economy or a smoothly working democracy would render his demagoguery superfluous.

Year in and year out Hitler and his propaganda machine stormed against this "parliamentary chaos," while the people, in desperation, listened more and more attentively to the man with the authoritarian panacea.

In 1931 mass bank failures and unemployment swept Germany just as they did all of the Western world. Panic seized industry in all quarters, while hunger and black despair spread among the people. Now Hitler was in his element. All of Germany was in a mood to respond to the same kind of propaganda that he and the rest of the disinherited had responded to in the slums of Vienna.

Between 1930 and 1932 unemployment in Germany increased by more than 100 per cent; so did the Nazi popular vote and their representation in the Reichstag (from 107 to 232 seats).

By this time important figures in finance and industry were becoming increasingly interested in Hitler's brand of "socialism," and this is what ultimately determined his success. Unimpressed by the propaganda slogans that attracted the rabble, these sophisticated realists saw in Hitler a fanatic nationalist whose rebellion against disarmament and trade restrictions could serve their own needs. His ideology was of small consequence, as long as it did not apply to German capital and kept the public distracted by other suitable scapegoats. Munitions makers and some of the other big industrialists knew that Hitler's militaristic aspirations suited their own; that his tirades against "Communist-dominated unions" and the "tyranny of Versailles" could be used to especially good advantage. Their understandably patriotic motives could easily camouflage their ulterior motives in supporting these appeals. What could be more idealistic than to support a strong leader who would restore national pride and sovereignty by breaking the economic strangle hold of the Versailles Treaty, embarking on a huge rearmament program, and restoring an economy free of reparations, communism, trade unions, or strikes? The only question was one of Hitler's chances of success. Industrialists Alfred Hugenberg and Fritz Thyssen staked millions on that chance. The owners of I. G. Farben, the Krupp Works, and other cartels became interested. Banker Hjalmar Schacht, salesman Von Ribbentrop, banker Baron von Schroeder, and other "economic royalists" enlisted more support for Hitler's movement.

A crucial move in enlisting that support was Hitler's speech before the Industry Club in Düsseldorf, on January 27, 1932. The heroic idea was skilfully blended with the capitalist sense of values to show their common interest in fascist dictatorship:

> This whole edifice of civilization is in its foundations and in all its stones nothing else than the result of the creative capacity, the achievement, the intelligence, the industry, of individuals: In its greatest triumphs it represents the great crowning achievement of individual God-favored geniuses, in its average accomplishment the achievement of men of average capacity, and in its sum doubtless the result of human labor, in order to turn to account the creations of genius and of talent. So it is only natural that when the capable intelligences of a nation, which are always in a minority, are regarded only as of the same value as all the rest, then genius, capacity, the value of personality, are slowly subjected to the majority and this process is then falsely named the rule of the people. For this is not the rule of the people, but in reality the rule of stupidity, of mediocrity, of half-heartedness, of cowardice, of weakness, and of inadequacy. . . . An internal conflict between the representatives of the democratic principle and the representatives of the principle of authority must be the inevitable consequence, and this conflict we are actually experiencing in Germany. . . .
>
> . . . For fifty years you can build up the best economic system on the basis of the principle of achievement; for fifty years you may go on building factories, for fifty years you may amass wealth; and then in three years of mistaken political decisions you can destroy all the results of the work of these fifty years. (*Audience: "Very true!"*) And that is only natural, since political

decisions spring from another root than that of constructive economic decisions.

To sum up the argument: I see two diametrically opposed principles: the principle of democracy which, wherever it is allowed practical effect, is the principle of destruction; and the principle of authority of personality, which I would call the principle of achievement. . . .

The essential thing is to realize that at the present moment we find ourselves in a condition which has occurred several times before in the history of the world: there have already been times when the volume of certain products in the world exceeded the demand. Today we are experiencing the same thing on the largest possible scale. . . . There has arisen such an increase in productive capacity, that the present possible consumption market stands in no relation to this increased capacity. But if Bolshevism as a world-idea tears the Asiatic continent out of the human economic community, then the conditions for the employment of these industries which have developed on such a gigantic scale will no longer be even approximately realized. . . . The solution rests upon the realization that economic systems in collapse have always as their forerunner the collapse of the State and not vice versa—that there can be no flourishing economic life which has not before it and behind it the flourishing powerful State as its protection . . . there can be no economic life unless behind this economic life there stands the determined political will of the nation absolutely ready to strike—and to strike hard. . . . (34)

Stripped of its grandiose symbolism, Hitler's argument to the German industrialists was simply this: if German cartels were to survive and expand, they would have to have a strong dictator at the helm, ready to pave the way by conquest if necessary. The argument proved fairly convincing.

By the beginning of 1932 Hitler felt he had enough industrial backing and popular support to enter the contest against old Marshal von Hindenburg for the presidency of the Reich. Hitler, Goebbels, and the whole party propaganda machine outdid themselves in this supreme effort. Hitler was still second best by a wide margin, but now he thought that at least the chancellorship was his due. Instead, Von Hindenburg appointed Franz von Papen Reich Chancellor, the better to protect the interests of the defensive Junker in-group. Later Von Papen offered Hitler the vice-chancellorship in order to appease him, but Hitler could tolerate no subordinate position. Von Hindenburg then called Hitler for an audience, raising Nazi hopes for the chancellorship once more. Instead, Von Hindenburg rebuked him for breaking his promise to give the administration a chance and dismissed him summarily. The rebuke was hailed by the German press as a sign that Hitler was through.

By the end of 1932 Hitler's party had actually begun to decline in popular favor. The people were beginning to get a little tired of the perpetual revolutionist with the same old line-up of scapegoats and the ruffian entourage. The brutalities of the Storm Troopers and the scandals about their homosexual leaders were becoming ever more revolting to the respectable *Bürgertum*. Many of the anti-capitalist Party members like the Strasser brothers could already see that what Hitler represented under the guise of socialist reform was unadulterated fascist dictatorship. Otto Strasser had already broken with Hitler. In private conversation with Hans Frank, even loyal Gregor Strasser voiced his misgivings over the personalities who were costing the party much of its support: "The Party is going to the dogs. Hitler is in the power of his Himmlers (brutes) and flatterers (*seine Himmler und Anhimmler*). Goering is a brutal egotist who doesn't give a damn about Germany as long as he can amount to something. Goebbels is a crippled devil, false to the core. Roehm is a swine. And that is the Führer's bodyguard!"

Many went over to the Social Democrats. Even conservative Chancellor Von Papen won over a number of Reichstag seats from the Nazis in the late 1932 elections. Gloom mounting to panic reigned at the Nazi party headquarters in Munich and Berlin as naziism began to look like a lost cause. The talk in political circles was that "Hitler has missed the boat," "the Nazi demagogue's threat is a thing of the past," etc. When, by the end of 1932, Hitler still failed to achieve the chancellorship, a large part of the influx of fair-weather Nazis as well as disillusioned adherents switched their votes to other parties.

But there were three psychological factors that were still to be reckoned with: (*a*) Hitler's unrelenting obsessiveness; (*b*) the irreconcilable group interests and loyalties in the government itself; and (c) the fact that Hitler had finally convinced the industrialists that his purposes were compatible with their own.

On December 1, 1932, President von Hindenburg appointed General von Schleicher Chancellor, when it had become apparent that his friend Von Papen could not get enough support for the administration. Nazi strength sank rapidly. Von Schleicher tried to form a coalition of the center and right and even made some overtures to socialist and labor groups. He even offered the dissenting Nazi chief, Gregor Strasser, the post of vice-chancellor—a move which would have brought a strong socialist coalition and further decreased the influence of the more radical revolutionists in the waning Nazi party. Strasser tried to make Hitler see that this compromise was the only possibility for any socialist salvation of Germany's catastrophic plight. But Strasser had deluded himself about the place of socialism in Hitler's system of values. Thereupon Hitler, egged on by Goering and Goebbels, who knew what this move entailed, denounced Strasser as a traitor and insisted on gambling for "all or nothing" regardless of the consequences. Strasser resigned from the party and left Berlin in chagrin, unable to match Hitler's reckless egomania by taking advantage of a crisis momentarily in his own favor.

The possibility of a socialist coalition began to falter. As usual, the purposes of the socialist and labor groups were incompatible with those of the Junker and industrialist groups. Another stalemate developed. Von Papen did nothing to help his successor, secretly hoping for his downfall, for Von Schleicher was too tolerant of socialist designs on Junker class interests anyway. Banker Hjalmar Schacht helped to convince Von Papen that even Hitler would be better than a frankly "leftist" government under Schleicher and Strasser. Hitler saw his main chance. On January 4, 1933, Hitler met with Von Papen and Schacht at the home of Baron von Schroeder. He brought along the industrialist, Wilhelm Keppler, as his right-hand man, to show his own industrialist sympathies. The issue was made clear: either naziism or communism. Communism (or socialism, for that matter) meant breaking up the holdings of the landed aristocracy and drastically socializing all industry and finance. The decision had to be in favor of a man fanatically opposed to communism and unencumbered by too much respect for parliamentary majorities. Schacht again persuaded Von Papen that he would have to reconcile himself to supporting Hitler if he wanted to retain any political influence and their common class interests. Whether it was mentioned in so many words or not, it could not be overlooked that both President von Hindenburg and ex-Chancellor von Papen were part of the landed aristocracy who would be the first to suffer from any real move toward socialization. Hitler promised that if he came into the government, Junker interests would be well represented, but he would have to be top man.

In the meantime something had to be done to change the popular impression that the Nazi party was on the decline. With the financial support of the bankers, industrialists, and Junkers who were now climbing the Nazi band wagon, Hitler threw all his energies into winning the only current election. This happened to be a very minor by-election in the small state of Lippe. Hitler's campaign machinery and personal appearances easily overwhelmed the villagers of Lippe, who had never seen a major political figure before in their lives. His victory in this minor contest for a couple of Reichstag seats proved of tremendous psychological importance. It helped reverse his reputation as a "played-out demagogue." It came just in the nick of time, just as Chancellor von Schleicher was considering taking rival leader Gregor Strasser into the cabinet and Von Papen was urging Von Hindenburg to appoint Hitler before the government went leftist altogether. Hitler intensified his revolutionary threat by letting his Storm Troops openly seek clashes with Communists in the streets of Berlin. In the Reichstag, with chairman Goering's help, he connived with Communist deputies to sabotage all semblance of orderly government, since that suited the revolutionary purposes of both parties. Chaos reigned and revolution threatened from both extremes. Von Papen sounded the final alarm. Giving way to all these pressures, President von Hindenburg named Adolf Hitler Reich Chancellor on January 30, 1933, much against his better judgment. Frenzied crowds of Nazis who had almost lost faith in their Führer rejoiced and staged demonstrations all over Germany. The revolutionists' millennium had arrived!

But Von Hindenburg's better judgment was confirmed by a letter he received from his old companion-in-arms, General von Ludendorff: "By the appointment of Hitler to the Reich Chancellorship, you have put our holy Fatherland at the mercy of one of the greatest demagogues of all time. I prophesy that this unholy man will plunge the Reich into chaos, will bring unimaginable misery to the nation, and coming generations will curse you in your grave for what you have done!" In Munich, while Storm Troopers paraded, caroused, and beat up Jews on the street, a historian by the name of Oswald Spengler shook his head sadly: "It will last ten years. We will have the same line-up against us. Then Germany, which led the rise of the West, will be the cause of its decline." (18)

CONSOLIDATION OF POWER

Hitler immediately set out to complete his revolution and convert the government into a dictatorship. First he had to assure his precarious government at least a temporary lease on life. Junker and industrialist interests were appeased by the presence of Von Papen as Vice-Chancellor, Baron von Neurath as Foreign Minister, General von Blomberg as Reichswehr Minister, Hjalmar Schacht as President of the Reichsbank, and even Goering as Minister Without Portfolio.

A large proportion of the voting public were now anxious to prove that they had been ardent Nazis all the time. But Hitler and Goebbels knew that the Communists could use the same tactics to swing the fickle public their way. Something had to be done immediately to get more stable popular support and eliminate all effective opposition.

Hitler ordered Goebbels to undertake an intensive propaganda campaign to scare the public into supporting his party at the forthcoming election. The "threat of communist revolution" was the keynote of the campaign. Goebbels waged it most effectively, even climaxing it with the burning of the Reichstag building in collusion with the Berlin Storm Troops and Hermann Goering. (23) The burning of the Reichstag on February 27, 1933, was immediately blamed on a "communist plot" to overthrow the government. This brought the Nazi party some more votes in the March election, but not a majority. Still too much skepticism, democracy, and free opposition. Decisive action had to be taken. Goering secured an absolute Nazi majority in the Reichstag by the simple device of excluding the Communist representatives. An "Enabling Act" was passed, giving Hitler and his cabinet emergency powers to govern by decree. This virtually put an end to the Weimar Republic. Next, Jews were barred from civil service, which included almost all educational institutions. This provided thousands of jobs for Nazi favorites, many of whom suddenly found themselves teaching school, and mediocre men moved into important university professorships. To keep the pot boiling, Joseph Goebbels, now Minister of Public Enlightenment and Propaganda, next sponsored anti-Jewish boycotts and public burnings of "subversive" books. This momentarily helped business for "Aryan" competitors. The scapegoats who had helped the Nazis to power could still be counted on to help them retain it.

While all this was done under the guise of racial fanaticism, the Nazis' basic motive of politico-economic power was not lost sight of, and the means were ruthlessly coordinated with these ends. In the succeeding months all trade unions were abolished and German labor was regimented into a "German Labor Front," under the leadership of Old Fighter Robert Ley. The persecution of Jewish businessmen was already forcing many of them to sell out cheap to those in good standing with the party. Totalitarianism was implemented first by outlawing the Communist and Social Democratic Parties, and by the end of the year, all the rest. Finally, Himmler was given extraordinary police powers to suppress all "dangers to public security," in accordance with a new law providing the death penalty for such undefined offenses. In the meantime, business started to recover as an accompaniment of the industrialist's new-found confidence in "stable government" and rearmament orders. Unemployment was sharply reduced. The militarists, industrialists, and Junker groups were "getting theirs." As for the people, they cared little whether they had fascism, socialism, or a republic as long as they had jobs and strong leadership once more. Decent citizens, including non-Aryans, even tended to excuse the brutality of the Storm Troopers and the violent propaganda as "excesses of revolutionary zeal," which would pass in time. Those who didn't like it were allowed to emigrate with a fraction of their property and capital. Those who were too outspoken in their criticism of the government were thrown into concentration camps.

However, some of the Old Fighters who had helped Hitler to seize power soon appeared to be a threat to Hitler, Goering, and Himmler in consolidating that power along lines of their own choosing. Storm Troop Leader Ernst Roehm also had some ideas about sharing the power and spoils of victory and "amounting to something"—perhaps by wiping out the General Staff with his Storm Troops and putting himself in power as the strong arm of the state. This did not suit Himmler's or Goering's plans, and the very suggestion of disloyalty threw Hitler into a towering rage. Together they conspired to wipe out the Roehm gang at one fell swoop—and to get rid of some of their other enemies, old and new, while they were at it.

Here Hitler's personality development enters a new phase. Drunk with power and having the realization of his vengeful heroic fantasies within his grasp, he put himself to the supreme test of worthiness for his historic role: willingness to commit mass murder to gain his ends. The means of executing his will were already guaranteed by the very existence of his dictatorship and the machinery he had forged to maintain it. But the decision was necessarily a personal one. If the will to mass murder required social facilitation, his revolutionary supporters provided that too. The Old Fighters reinforced each other's aggressive fury to the required threshold. There is no telling where Hitler's nerve might have faltered if he had not had the moral and physical support of men like Goering and Himmler. Gregor Strasser was right. Hitler had created a bodyguard of cutthroats and in so doing had established his own psychopathic social norm at the top level of government. The dictatorship was ready for the first supreme test.

On the night of June 30, 1934, Hitler, Goering, and Himmler, using the police and SS forces at their command, rounded up the Storm Troop leaders, a number of Storm Troopers who "knew too much" about the Reichstag fire and other Nazi activities, and all of the principal political enemies they could lay hands on. Some of these were shot on the spot. Ex-Chancellor von Schleicher and his wife were shot down in their home. Von Schleicher was not only a rival but knew about Hitler's war record. Gregor Strasser was beaten to death. He knew too much altogether. An old score was settled even with the retired Minister-President of Bavaria, Von Kahr, whose "treachery" Hitler had never forgotten. Roehm and the SA leaders apprehended in Bavaria were thrown into Stadelheim prison to be executed. Hans Frank was Bavarian Minister of Justice with jurisdiction over executions at Stadelheim prison. A little squeamish about permitting over a hundred executions without trial and only a check list for an order (it was only the second year of the Nazi regime), Frank called up Hitler and asked him by what paragraph of German law the prisoners should be booked for execution. Hitler snapped back that he had ordered the executions to protect the safety of the Reich, and that was law enough. There was to be no more nonsense about "fair trials" in Nazi Germany. (The recent trial of the alleged incendiaries of the Reichstag fire had resulted in the acquittal of all but one, the palpable tool of the Nazis.)

For three days there was a reign of terror all over Germany as political enemies of Hitler and Goering were executed without trial or hunted down and butchered to death. Altogether over two hundred enemies, including some taken by mistake, were murdered in cold blood during this purge. Goebbels announced that seventy-nine traitors to the Reich had been executed. In preparing the announcement, he was ordered to strike out the word *standrechtlich* (according to law) and to substitute the words *auf Befehl des Führers* (by order of the Führer). There was to be no misunderstanding about who was the law, who wielded the power of life and death in Germany from now on.

Later Hitler upbraided Frank for the squeamishness he had

shown: "You and your legality.—Don't forget that every revolution demands its sacrifices! Why, if one had to ask you lawyers beforehand for permission, then there would never have been a revolution in all the thousands of years of history. Revolutions are the great forward thrusts which create upheaval and force things forwards. Many must break and bleed in the process! From the viewpoint of law every revolution is illegal, and you lawyers are only annoyed because you must learn new law when the old is overthrown! . . . Now everything depends on my authority. The laws are valid only because they bear my name! . . . Anyway, I'll soon put an end to this mess of state Ministries of Justice. The Reich commands and the states obey!" (18)

The Reich, of course, was Adolf Hitler—the identification was now complete. His enemies were Germany's enemies and his murderous fantasies could now be realized on a mass scale. Hitler's dictatorship had passed the acid test.

At this point President von Hindenburg had a clear obligation to order the Wehrmacht to wipe out the murderous clique he had always despised and to restore law and order with a new government. If high-ranking generals had urged it, he probably would have. But senile Von Hindenburg was the dying symbol of a dying order and too many of the Junker caste still thought they could "get theirs" in the Hitler regime. That particularly applied to War Minister von Blomberg, who had no regrets over the purge. Von Hindenburg was persuaded to legalize the Roehm purge as an act of "protection of the Reich." The decrees which followed virtually abolished civil liberties in Germany. People's courts were set up to dispense summary justice in accordance with Hitler's ideas of the law of the land. He was determined to brook no legal restraint on the capricious use of his power. Even Von Hindenburg could not conceal a certain admiration for Hitler's display of the good old Teutonic hardness. "Any one who wants to make history, like Hitler, must be able to let guilty blood flow, and not be soft." [11]

---

[11] This description of the Roehm purge is derived from the Frank MS. (18), from the writer's conversations with Goering and Fritzsche, and from discussions among the other Nazis overheard in Nuremberg.

About a month after the Roehm purge, the overeager Nazi revolutionists in Austria assassinated Chancellor Dollfuss. Their move was a little premature. Hitler had a little more consolidating of the dictatorship to do at home before forcing the annexation of foreign "German" territories to the Greater Reich. Franz von Papen, spared from the Roehm purge, was sent to placate Austria and maintain good trade relations until such time as Hitler was ready for foreign aggression. In the meantime, Hitler reminded the Italian dictator, Mussolini, of their mutual interest in the spread of fascism, and reassured him about his peaceful intentions toward Austria. After all, they were all good Christians and anti-Communists, and Hitler had sent to Austria the very same diplomat who had negotiated his Concordat with the Pope the year before. His war on Christianity was held in abeyance for the time being. Mussolini was placated. The "Wise Men of Zion" could not have handled the situation more adroitly.

Five weeks after the Roehm purge President von Hindenburg died. The last of the great Junkers had lived just long enough to fulfil his historic role of ushering in fascist dictatorship as the last resort of class privilege. Hitler declared himself supreme dictator of Germany, and the Wehrmacht was sworn to allegiance to their new Führer. The elaboration of the police state, with its people's courts, Gestapo, and concentration camps for all "politically unreliable" and "racially inferior" elements soon consolidated Hitler's absolute power over the life and destiny of the nation. He was now free to indulge his vengeful heroic fantasies without criticism or restraint at home and to capitalize on the secret hopes of foreign interest groups that his aggressions would suit *their* purposes abroad. Acts of aggression were to follow in quick succession, while Hitler played East against West to his own advantage.

Thus a new dictatorship came into being in Central Europe, conceived in hatred, nurtured in terror and appeasement, and dedicated to the proposition that all men are created unequal in the struggle for survival.

PART II
SELECTED CASE STUDIES

Chapter 3

THE REVOLUTIONISTS

The revolutionary nucleus of the Nazi movement, as we have seen, was the group of aggressive fanatics and adventurers who gathered around Hitler about the time of the Munich *Putsch*. These Old Fighters, who were always in the vanguard of the Nazi struggle for power, became a kind of elite in-group within the Nazi party. According to the Hitlerian system of values, they proved their heroic leadership by rebelling against decadent democracy and national persecution from the very beginning, never faltering in the fight—or hardly ever. The acknowledged leader among these heroes, of course, was Adolf Hitler himself, and it was only fitting that he should become the Leader of the New Order. He, in turn, rewarded these heroic Old Fighters with positions of power as he consolidated his tyranny over Germany and all of Central Europe. They were given several of the top ministerial posts in the government; they became governors of occupied territories during the war; they were *Gauleiters* and high dignitaries of a one-party totalitarian state. It was largely with the support of these men that Hitler reinforced and implemented his aggressive obsessions from the Munich *Putsch* to the Roehm blood purge, and beyond that to the terror of World War II. Together with Hitler, their personalities left an indelible imprint on the character of Germany's dictatorship and the history of the times.

Originally they came from every walk of life and from the ranks of the uprooted masses of several countries. But they were not just a random sampling of the population that happened to be caught in the revolutionary turmoil of postwar Munich. They had banded together voluntarily because they had found a community of purpose in united rebellion against socioeconomic frustration and the still more frustrating restraints of social convention, religion, law, and the slow, orderly process of democratic government. They shared a common interest in the satisfaction of ascendancy needs through racial identification and the persecution of scapegoats. Such men were not just "ordinary Germans," however much they reflected the cultural mores and the social unrest of the times. Pathological reactions to frustration—overaggressive and paranoid tendencies—proved to be selective factors; in effect, qualifications for membership in the exclusive club of Old Fighters. Timid pacifists, moralistic conformists, humanitarian, Jew-loving democrats, as they saw them, had no place in the heroic vanguard of their movement.

Their careers illustrated the selective nature of the group. They began as rebels against the social order; they achieved power by intensifying the social conflicts and hatreds of their culture; they maintained it by a reign of terror; in most cases they met a violent death. Some of them, like the Roehm gang, were "liquidated" by their more ruthless rivals within the ingroup itself. Others, like "hangman" Heydrich, were assassinated by the enemies they terrorized. A few, like Hitler himself, committed suicide when they could no longer stave off defeat and retribution. A number of the survivors were ultimately hanged as war criminals. This group was, in short, a cult of those prepared to live and die in violence and hatred while championing the cause of fascist reaction to democratic social change.

Our study was handicapped only by the reduced survival capacities of this group. After the suicides and assassinations during the war, two of the leaders (Himmler and Ley) committed suicide before they could be brought to trial. Other distinctions were evident at once. The only two defendants whose sanity was questioned—Rudolf Hess and Julius Streicher—belonged to this group, and so did the only drug addict, Hermann Goering. The performance of the Old Fighters on the psychological tests was on the whole more erratic than that of the other groups we studied.

There was thus psychological as well as historical foundation for the designation of this revolutionary nucleus as a social identification group.

Our selection of cases from this group is determined by our desire to present a well-rounded picture of the revolutionary nucleus around Hitler as personalities developing in social interaction. The case histories were obtained largely from the men themselves, though some research was necessary to fill in gaps and provide an objective check on the data obtained. Since psychopathology is of some significance here, we also include brief interpretations of the psychological tests administered to them before the trial. (Nonclinicians may skip these parts, which are set in solid type, without any serious handicap to their understanding of the Nazi movement.) The high lights of our twelve-month observations and their interpretation in the light of social interaction provide the basis of discussion in each case.

The case of Hermann Goering is presented in some detail, because he was unquestionably Hitler's right-hand man from the very beginning, and his history provides a first-hand account of the further development of the dictatorship. He also provides an excellent study in the psychology of aggressive political leadership. Rudolf Hess, the Führer's party deputy, and Hans Frank, the party lawyer and Governor-General of Poland, are of particular interest in further illustrating the role of psychopathology in the social interaction that makes history. The propagandists whom we studied (Rosenberg and Streicher) may be conspicuous by their absence here, but the role of propaganda has already been dealt with at some length in Hitler's case history and appears throughout all of these studies.

If the cases we now present seem to be exceptionally deviate personalities for the leaders of a government, it is not an artifact of our selection, but an actual selective factor of the group formation itself. This does not, of course, imply that the leaders of *any* revolutionary movement are apt to be abnormally aggressive personalities. We are dealing here with the kinds of characters who exploit race hatred and authoritarianism in promoting an aggressive ideological dictatorship.

HERMANN GOERING, DICTATOR NUMBER TWO

We have already mentioned that without the active support of other revolutionary spirits Hitler's movement would never have survived its early precarious existence, and the dictatorship might never have passed the test of its own terror. Most aggressive and powerful among these supporters was Hermann Goering, creator of the Gestapo and concentration camps, President of the Reichstag, czar of Germany's war potential (Four-Year Plan), Commander-in-Chief of the Luftwaffe, and deputy dictator. Nominally a member of the militarist group, he identified himself very early with Hitler's revolutionary movement, and became his most powerful ally. He was without question the most aggressive of the Old Fighters, with accent on the *fight*. The purposes that a revolutionary ideology served for this type of personality is the focus of our case study.

Life History

Early Background.—According to Alfred Adler, the earliest recollections of childhood are of particular significance in indicating the source of an individual's satisfactions and his "style of life." Hermann Goering's earliest childhood recollection was bashing his mother in the face with both fists when she came to embrace him after a prolonged absence, at the age of three. A tendency to overt aggression manifested itself very early as one of his chief satisfactions in life, as we shall see. This particular incident occurred on the occasion of his family's return from Haiti. The father, a typical stern Prussian, had been a cavalry officer under Bismarck and was Consul General in Haiti at the time of Hermann's birth. Hermann was the fourth of five children by Goering's second marriage. Hermann's mother, a woman of more humble origin (we gathered from his reluctant remarks) had returned to Germany briefly for Hermann's birth in 1893 and had then left him in the care of her closest friend, Frau Graf of Fürth, until the family reunion which opens our story.

Upon their return, the family moved to Berlin, where the father continued to serve in the foreign office for a time. Here Hermann became fascinated by the military display: the uniforms and parades, the officers barking orders at their goose-stepping soldiers. Prussian militarism appealed to his aggressive temperament in preference to the Bavarian *Gemütlichkeit* and he soon identified himself with the aspirations common to the offspring of the Prussian Junker caste. He said that there was never a moment's doubt in his mind that he would become an officer in the Kaiser's army when he grew up. The reasons were obvious. The lowliest second lieutenant, he had learned from his father, took precedence over a minister of state in the rules of protocol at the Kaiser's court—even on the grand march into the ballroom at state receptions. So at the age of five he gleefully donned the hussar officer's uniform his father had given him for his birthday, and since that time, he said, he had never been without a uniform in his life (except for the brief period of civilian dress forced on him by the vicious Treaty of Versailles). Thus his natural aggressiveness and exuberance were channeled very early into a passion for things military and bellicose by the cultural values represented by his father's circle. His childhood play was devoted almost exclusively to waging war, leading his small army of youngsters and toy cannon against imaginary enemies of *Kaiser und Vaterland*. If there was any question about his leadership (he said with his usual hearty laugh), he would bash their heads together and "let them know damn quick who was boss." For if his beautiful uniforms and his father's position of authority were not enough to establish his right of dominance over his companions, the ready use of his fists settled any doubts on that score.

When the father was pensioned and prepared to retire to the family castle at Veldenstein, Hermann was furious over having to leave his real and make-believe armies in Berlin. He cried for days. But he soon found that the castle at Veldenstein provided an excellent stage setting for his military exploits. He organized new recruits for his war games, bashed some more heads together, and stormed the castle with such dangerous recklessness that he had to be soundly thrashed by his father.

Hermann protested the unfairness of this punishment, saying
that one who exhibited such courage should not be punished for
it. The Spartan element of the Prussian militaristic code was
already shaping his ethical values at the age of six or seven,
but unlike the Spartans, he did not take punishment very
stoically.

Goering said that "the romantic surroundings of Veldenstein" provided a continual active stimulant to his early romantic fantasies. In fact, his fantasy life was so vivid that on
occasion he could actually experience life in a medieval fortress.
On one occasion that he never forgot he was looking over the
countryside from the castle tower. A smoking locomotive came
lumbering down the valley below. Suddenly the whole scene
changed, and he saw Roman chariots with plumed warriors
charging down the countryside while crowds roared. "But so
real! Just as though it was all actually there like in the story
books. I don't know how long the vision lasted. Then I ran
down all excited and told my mother and sister about it. They
only laughed. I went back several times, but that particular
vision never returned." (He was then about eight.)

His fantasies were also stimulated by his early lessons in
Teutonic history—the one subject that really interested him.
He listened avidly to stories of the Nibelungen, of Siegfried and
the Valkyrie, and of the lives of Charlemagne (a *German* hero),
Frederick the Great, and Bismarck, admiring the pictures of
their war dress and heroic exploits. As he learned to read, the
lives of the great heroes of German history became his favorite
books. Heroism, chivalry, and loyalty to the sovereign became
deeply ingrained as primary values of his culture. Aside from
such ego-involved subjects, he cared little for learning, although
he was of superior intelligence (I.Q. 138).

Goering claimed that he was also influenced by the royal
heritage represented by the portraits of his noble ancestors
hanging in the halls of the castle. But in telling this he was
probably still letting his youthful fantasies run away with him,
because Baron von Neurath assured us that Goering had no
noble ancestry, but was only an upstart brat whose chief talent
was smashing windows. The very fact that Goering sought to

impress us with an elaborately printed genealogical table taking the Goerings back to Frederick the Great, Charlemagne, and St. Elizabeth of Thüringen was more significant as a revelation of Goering's aspiration level and fantasy life than of his actual background.

Another aspect of his personality, in so far as we may extract it from the mixture of fact and fancy that Goering was willing to reveal about his early development, was an apparent love of excitement and insensitivity to danger. He boasted, "Hell, I haven't been afraid of death since I was twelve or fourteen years old!" and was able to cite several instances to support this. On one occasion he was riding along a road in the Austrian Alps when an avalanche started. Goering says he just stopped to admire the awesome spectacle of crashing rocks and snow boulders while other people were dashing around in terror, trying to avoid being crushed. One carriage was, in fact, buried under the snow a short distance in front of him. He found it all very exciting, but somehow the personal danger did not seem real to him. On another occasion he was rowing on a lake with some boys when they began to drift uncontrollably toward a waterfall at the end of the lake. The other boys were panic-stricken, but Goering says he told them: "Stop jabbering! If we go over, we die, and there's nothing we can do about it, so why get excited?" In examining his feelings about danger, Goering admitted that he just never believed that any harm could really befall him. His fantasy life, it seems, conveniently carried over to real life to protect him from the anxiety of dangerous realities. The insensitive extrovert could thus satisfy his drive for physical stimulation and excitement while acting out his fantasies as a fearless hero who scorned danger. Whatever the reasons, the early signs of aggressive leadership qualities were unmistakable.

But there was an entirely different aspect of Goering's early aggressiveness which he preferred not to discuss, but which we gather from another authentic source (29). Even as a child Goering exhibited not a little aggression of the sadistic variety. Not content with tyrannizing the boys in his neighborhood, he turned upon his sisters because their stories of adventure with the father in foreign countries excited his jealousy. Neither his mother nor his governess could control him, and the father's punishments proved to be of no avail. In fact, his obstreperousness disrupted the household so much that he had to be sent back to Fürth to continue his schooling. But here he only found new outlets for his uncontrollable aggression. He discovered the sport of Jew-baiting and took a childish delight in setting his dogs on the hapless Jewish residents of Fürth. He had to be punished again. In retaliation for the rejection he was experiencing from parents, teachers, and guardians, who showed no sympathy for his courage and playful sadism, Hermann sulked in bed, playing sick. For a whole month he remained "ill" out of spite and sympathy-seeking, recovering miraculously just before the Christmas holiday. The compulsion to sadistic aggression kept precipitating a vicious circle of more punishment, more spiteful retaliation, more rejection, and more aggression. Sending him to another school at Anspach also failed to help matters. He got into trouble again and ran away. Finally his father decided to send him to the military prep school at Karlsruhe. Though he was still a difficult child, the life of a cadet seemed to agree with his militaristic aspirations.

His mother, recognizing all his unusual qualities, declared with some trepidation, "Hermann will either be a great man or a great criminal!"

Thus by early adolescence the essential pattern of Goering's personality was already apparent: aggressive egotism which found its most desirable expression in the militaristic prerogatives of his culture; enhanced by a rich and vivid fantasy life which sometimes blurred the distinctions between reality and fancy; a tendency to domination of the environment with a combination of fancy-dress showmanship and brute force; an emotional insensitivity and perverted humor which were at once the seeds of outward physical boldness and of moral depravity. His sense of values was also pretty well fixed by this time, being drawn from the cultural complex by his early indoctrination and personal inclinations: a deeply rooted sense of loyalty and obedience to the sovereign figure of the Kaiser; a sense of the in-group loyalty and solidarity of the German *Volk,* with chivalrous hostility toward all members of out-groups; an aristocratic antidemocratic bias which recognized "inferior" and "superior" groups and the authoritarian militaristic hierarchy; and an abiding awe for historical greatness rather than humanitarian progress or ethical values as the guiding motivation of mortal existence.

It is well to bear this pattern in mind, for, like the typical psychopath, Goering never outgrew the uninhibited acting out of these infantile ego-drives. Although more wholesome environmental influences might well have directed his life into more constructive channels, he was not constituted to resist the temptations presented by the social conflicts and anachronisms of his time, but rather to exploit them with unconscionable avarice.

The Young Militarist and Revolutionary.—At the age of sixteen Goering entered the officers' academy of Lichterfelde near Berlin, the West Point of the Prussian military caste. Somewhat estranged from his family by now, he made his emotional transference all the more to the military authoritarian hierarchy with the Kaiser at the top. Although he resented his father's failure to get him into those receptions at the Kaiser's court with his classmates (for even the officer-candidates marched ahead of most of the civilians), his role as Junker-officer-in-the-making satisfied his status needs. More than that, it satisfied the heroic fantasies that had long since fixed the pattern of his desired way of life. However reluctantly he submitted to stern discipline—the religion of unquestioning obedience to superiors, of loyalty to *Kaiser und Vaterland,* the ramrod posturing and goose-stepping, the punishments for small offenses were all accepted as part of the code worthy of one who was destined to follow in the footsteps of Bismarck, Clausewitz, and Moltke. For there could be no doubt in his mind that just as he now showed rigid subservience to his superiors, he would some day be able to demand the same from his inferiors when he rose in rank, in keeping with the dual tradition of subservience and arrogance dear to the Prussian military tradition.

But there was also much in the life of a cadet which satisfied the amiable prankster in him. He dared not show the slightest disrespect for the officer-instructors at the academy, but the poor civilians who taught certain subjects were the constant butt of practical jokes and outlets for rowdiness in the classroom. The reason, Goering explained quite simply, was that the officers could punish you, while the civilians could only threaten you or, what was even sillier, appeal to your moral sense. Then there were the good old war games with real soldiers and cannon, with no father to punish you for reckless daring in storming a stronghold. On the contrary, the Kaiser liked good officer material with plenty of daring. Finally, by way of relaxation, there were the usual student pranks of carousing late at night with his buddies in the very exclusive *Kadetenkorps* to which he belonged (the *most* exclusive one, Goering assured us) and plotting to sneak past the guard to be in the barracks before reveille. All in all, a way of life made to order for the exuberant Hermann Goering.

He had hardly graduated from Lichterfelde in 1913 when his father died. The following year, with the outbreak of World War I, he was committed to the front as a lieutenant in an infantry regiment. In discussing his war career, Goering glossed over his activities as an infantry officer, saying that he was more interested in aviation. No doubt it appealed more to his individualistic and recklessly demonstrative inclinations, but he also admitted suffering from claustrophobia in a tank, submarine, or Zeppelin gondola. He became a fighter pilot in 1916, was wounded and hospitalized for three months, and then resumed his aviation career. He acquitted himself quite well as a pilot, running up a total of twenty-eight planes shot down, receiving the high decoration Pour le Mérite, and taking over command of the Richthofen squadron upon the latter's death late in the war.

Aside from the glory which his reckless physical courage earned him, Goering had little to say about his activities as an officer. Again, the reason becomes clear when we go to secondary sources on Goering's career (31). It seems that like certain other darlings of the new-born Luftwaffe, Goering found his influence in choice of planes and engines very profitable. He was not so much of a sentimentalist or devotee of Prussian incorruptibility as to resist temptations of bribery. Nor was he averse to a little business interest on the side—a partnership in a shoe factory with his fellow-officer, Prince Phillipp of Hessia, in the middle of the war. He also enjoyed for a time the gay life at the notorious headquarters of Prince Wilhelm at Charleville, where his bold conviviality no doubt endeared him further to the Junker clique.

At all events, during World War I Goering made the dangerous and fateful discovery that war could bring both glory and profit to one who was sufficiently reckless, unscrupulous, and amiable.

Germany's defeat brought an abrupt end to his heyday of glory and libertinism. The flight of the Kaiser destroyed some of the heroic illusions he had built up about this figure of supreme authority. Finding Germany a barren wasteland of hunger and ruin with the people in revolt against their own military leaders, he used his aristocratic connections to roam the greener fields of Denmark and Sweden. In Sweden he met and married the rich aristocrat, Baroness Karin von Kantzow, overlooking her epileptic affliction in the interest of financial security. He returned to Germany around 1921, taking up brief studies at the University of Munich in political science—a new interest growing out of the troublesome times.

He described his own political attitudes and ventures in the seething unrest of postwar Munich and his meeting with Adolf Hitler as follows:

> The idea of a democracy was absolutely repulsive to me.—Who ever heard of a new Head of State every few years and elected representatives to tell the President what he should do and couldn't do? It was only the election of Hindenburg that made the Republic even half-way tolerable.
>
> Anyway, I had tried to found a revolutionary party myself among the officer veterans. I remember a meeting at which they were discussing getting meals and beds for veteran officers. "You damn fools!" I told them, "Do you think that an officer who is worth his salt can't find a bed to sleep in, even if it happens to be the bed of a pretty blonde? Dammit, there are more

important things at stake !" Somebody got fresh and I banged him over the head.—Well, of course the meeting broke up in an uproar. I never did get anywhere in trying to get a following for my revolutionary party. . . .

Then I remember the first time I saw Hitler. That was in 1922. There was a protest meeting in Munich against the demand to extradite some of our generals. Some little nationalistic parties were represented, and Hitler was just one of the audience. I was there too, because I considered it outrageous that Germany should be so humiliated as to have to hand over its generals to foreigners. They were making nationalistic speeches—I should say bourgeois-nationalistic. Every once in a while somebody would run up to Hitler and ask him if he wanted to speak, but he said he didn't want to. I asked who he was, and somebody told me that was Hitler, leader of the National Socialist party, who was against Versailles, etc. That interested me immediately and I asked where I could hear him speak. They told me I could hear him Monday at the Cafe Neumann. So I went there the following Monday. I just sat unobtrusively in the background. I remember Rosenberg was there. Hitler explained why he didn't speak at the other meeting. He said he didn't want to disturb the unity of the other meeting, but he did not approve of such weak protests. No Frenchman is going to lose sleep over that kind of harmless talk, he said. You've got to have bayonets to back up your threats. Well, *that* was what I wanted to hear. He wanted to build up a party that would make Germany strong and smash the Treaty of Versailles. "Well," I said to myself, *"that's* the party for me ! *Down with the Treaty of Versailles,* goddammit ! That's my meat !"

So a few days later I go down to party headquarters—quite modestly—and fill out a membership application. Well, of course there is something of a sensation when they see who I am, because I can say without vanity that among the young officers I was still something of a leader.—You know, I succeeded Baron von Richthofen—we were classmates at Lichterfelde.—Anyway, somebody tells me that Hitler would like to see me immediately. He tells me that it was a stroke of fate that I should come to him just as he was looking for somebody to take charge of the SA. He wanted an energetic young veteran officer and I was just the man he was looking for. We agreed to postpone the announcement a month, but I started right in to train the SA as a military organi-zation.—Military !—I'll tell the world it was military ! [1]

---

[1] Unpublished entry in the author's Nuremberg diary, dated February 3, 1946.

Goering's motives in joining the Nazi party were quite uncomplicated: it sounded like a good chance to satisfy his aggressiveness, greed, status-strivings, and militant nationalistic ego-involvement all at once. In his words, "For men like me it was a chance to wipe out the disgrace of Versailles—the shame of the defeat, the Corridor right through the heart of Prussia.—It was pure patriotic idealism." On a less idealistic plane, it meant a chance to restore the power, glory, and material gains of military ascendancy which he had tasted during World War I. But, as much as anything else, it was the very revolutionary nature of Hitler's program that attracted this restless, aggressive psychopath. "I joined the party precisely because it *was* revolutionary, not because of the ideological stuff. Other parties had made revolutions, so I figured I could get in on one too!" These were the purposes that suited his own.

The truth is that Goering had neither the intellectual pretenses nor the basic convictions for a fanatic ideologist. Aside from his nationalism, the only part of the Nazi ideology about which he had any convictions was its anti-Communist stand— and that on the basis of his aristocratic and individualistic leanings. Any idea of opposing the "Jewish-Masonic world conspiracy to subjugate the master race" was the furthest thing from his mind. Not only were some of his best friends Jews, like so many of the other Nazi leaders' (in spite of his Jew-baiting he did, in fact, maintain a certain protective loyalty to a few Jews who had helped him), but he missed being ideologically ineligible for party membership by the merest chance, according to his own account. "I had a date to meet some friends to join the Freemasons in 1919. While waiting for them, I saw a pretty blonde pass by, and I picked her up. Well, I just never did get around to joining the Freemasons. If I hadn't picked up that blonde that day, it would have been impossible for me to get into the Party, and I wouldn't be here [in jail] today."

There is perhaps an additional explanation on a psychodynamic basis. After the defeat and flight of the Kaiser, Goering's essentially infantile emotional dependence was left without an authoritarian figure to cling to. In Hitler he recognized such a potential figure—one who stood for dictatorial authority and rule by force, a chieftain of the German tribal in-group, who would restore the national strength and pride and provide Hermann with real soldiers, guns, and airplanes to play with. Goering did not make the emotional transference at once. There was some emotional resistance to overcome toward this "vagabond from a Viennese cafe," as Goering referred to Hitler behind his back in the early days. He did not make it until he was quite sure that this Kaiser-substitute would really succeed in satisfying his ego-needs. But the need and the possibility of fulfilment were clearly present from the beginning.

Hitler, on the other hand, knew that in Goering he had a man who could not only contribute wealth and a following among the frustrated Junker-officers of the defeated Wehrmacht, but one who also relished the use of force to achieve his ends and would not be restrained by any squeamish respect for law and order. He was not mistaken. In a short time Goering's flair for showmanship, uniforms, and military discipline, as well as his penchant for bashing heads in, had whipped the Storm Troops into shape as an efficient street-fighting organization. By this means Hitler was assured of ample opportunity to hold his speeches without too much interference from opposing parties, while effectively breaking up his opponents' meetings with a respectable toll of broken heads and smashed furniture.

In 1923 Goering participated in the Munich *Putsch,* which we have already described. When Goering escaped to Italy, leaving Hitler and the other Nazi leaders to face the music, he had undoubtedly given up the Nazi venture as a lost cause. He did not return until Hitler's star was once more in the ascendant, some four years later. In the meantime, he languished in and out of hospitals in Italy and Sweden from 1923 to 1927, becoming a confirmed drug addict in the course of his convalescence. Goering admitted that he had resorted to morphine to deaden the pain of his wound, and that he continued to use drugs off and on to deaden pain. It requires very little clinical intuition to see that it was not only physical pain that made Goering resort to narcotics. Ever since childhood Goering had demonstrated his need for physical stimulation and his inability to stand punishment or frustration. All through his life he was to resort to drugs and other devices to divert his mind from anxiety-provoking situations which he did not have the moral strength to face.

In 1927 he began to take up again with the Nazis of Germany. Apparently Hitler welcomed back the prodigal son because he could still use him, after exacting a pledge of undying loyalty to the Führer in the future. Since his wife's money and his own popularity were assets not to be overlooked, Goering was put up and elected Nazi representative to the Reichstag in 1928. The party was proving to be a "good bet" after all, and Goering's status-needs were already being fulfilled. The aggressive revolutionist in him, however, still craved satisfaction and Goering henceforth devoted himself to that goal with renewed zeal. The motivation of "pure patriotic idealism," as we have seen, was better described by Gregor Strasser's statement: "Goering is a brutal egotist who doesn't give a damn about Germany, as long as he can amount to something!"

The Number 2 Nazi.—Strasser's statement was prophetic. Goering became Reichstag President in 1932 only for the purpose of hastening the death of the Weimar Republic, which he detested. His political machinations helped Hitler to power in 1933. His reward was a number of new titles and positions of power, including Reich Air Minister, Prussian Minister of the Interior, etc. In the latter post he created the Gestapo (Secret State Police) and concentration camps. The Reichstag fire and the subsequent decrees gave him and Hitler a free hand to throw all "Communists" and personal enemies into concentration camps without legal process. At the same time it assured them a rubber-stamp Reichstag which would soon pass its own death warrant. Neither of the two top leaders of the Third Reich had any use for democratic laws or representatives who could tell them what to do and what not to do.

For his part, the head-bashing problem child and gang-leader-turned-statesman lost no time clarifying his conception of statecraft. In a radio broadcast during the reign of terror following the Reichstag fire Goering blustered forth his pure patriotic idealism: *"I am not here to exercise justice, but to wipe out and exterminate!"* If the frustrated masses had regressed to the aggressive-submissive modes of behavior of their authoritarian culture, clamoring for strong-arm leadership, Goering was not one to disappoint them.

But it was the "Roehm blood purge" of 1934 that revealed Goering at his gangster best. We recall that Goering managed to include in this blood-bath a goodly number of his own personal enemies, including Gregor Strasser and those SA men who knew too much about the Reichstag fire. In describing the purge in his Nuremberg cell years later, Goering naturally glossed over his private murder motives, but could still muster a show of righteous indignation at the mention of Roehm's name:

"Roehm! Don't talk to me about that dirty homosexual swine! That was the real clique of perverted bloody revolutionists! *They* are the ones who first made the Party look like a pack of hoodlums, with their wild orgies and beating up Jews on the street and smashing windows! They would have given you a *real* demonstration of a bloody revolution! What a gang of perverted bandits that SA was! It is a damn good thing I wiped them out or they would have wiped us out!" These were, of course, the very same hoodlums whom Goering had trained in street-fighting. Now that they had served their purpose and were getting out of hand—"We had to get rid of them to build up the party and the State." In describing one personal encounter during the purge: "I made no bones about it. I went to the SA Captain and . . . found an arsenal in the cellar bigger than the whole armament of the Prussian Police Force! . . . I just told my men to take the bastard out and shoot him!" Clearly, Goering had no inhibitions about resolving any anxieties by overt aggression. As we have shown, it was from him that Hitler received the principal added impetus to mass murder in the air-tight microcosm of dictatorship which had already crystallized in Germany.

In furtherance of their mutually reinforced purposes of aggression Hitler named Goering chief of a new Luftwaffe in 1935, in open defiance of the Versailles Treaty. Goering also "made no bones" about his attitude on preparing for aggressive war: ". . . *Of course* we rearmed!" he told the writer. "Why, I rearmed Germany until we bristled!—I'm only sorry we didn't rearm still more. *Of course* I considered your treaties (just between us) as so much toilet paper.—*Of course* I wanted to make Germany great! . . . When they told me I was playing with war by building up the Luftwaffe, I just told them I certainly wasn't running a girls' finishing school! I joined the party just because it was *revolutionary,* not because of the ideological stuff. Other parties had made revolutions, so I figured I could get in on one too." [2]

In 1935, to clear up any doubts as to who was top man in the Nazi Reich next to Hitler, Goering was designated as Hitler's deputy and eventual successor. (He significantly referred to himself as the "crown prince" in describing his position in the Hitler government.) Quite incidentally, the President of the Reichstag, who wasn't interested in the party's ideology, presented the Goebbels-sponsored "Nuremberg Laws" to the Reichstag for their rubber-stamp approval that year, thus sealing the fate of Germany's Jews.

In the same year, at the height of his pomp and power, he married the attractive actress, Emmy Sonnemann. (His first wife had died four years earlier of heart failure.) With his new diamond-tiaraed queen the crown prince held court in his sumptuous palace in Prussia, called Karinhall, displaying the lavish opulence, revelry, and comic opera costumes of a Roman emperor. Not unlike the crown princes and heroes of old, he allowed his faithful subjects in Bavaria and Prussia to give him rich estates and to appropriate huge sums out of taxes for their upkeep. In the national interest and in keeping with his regal showmanship, he also became a patron of the arts—a new interest which was not without its consequences to the art collections of Europe. Although he was loved by his wife, it is doubtful whether Goering's romantic inclinations ever went beyond the narcissistic level. If this was generally true of Prussian culture, it was doubly true of Hermann Goering. In discussing his wife Goering remarked with an indulgent smile,

[2] From *Nuremberg Diary.* (22)

". . . She could have her way in the household, in getting me to do lots of things for her, but when it comes to these basic things in a man's life, it is not a woman's affair." The "basic thing" in his life, as in Hitler's, was, of course, the acting out of heroic fantasies without moral restraint or "sentimentality."

By this time his narcissism and greed had gotten completely out of control. Titles, powers, medals, and graft were amassed with truly psychopathic avarice, and he gorged himself with esoteric foods until his medal-bedecked corpulence became symbolic of the character of Germany's leadership. In 1936 his designation as plenipotentiary of the Four-Year Plan opened up new industrial fields for power and graft. Profits from the Hermann Goering Werke, bribes from industrial leaders for tax-exemption and armaments orders swelled his coffers by millions of Reichsmarks. His greed was equaled only by his lust for power. In the industrial field he could not tolerate the rivalry of even the "financial wizard" Hjalmar Schacht. Since Goering was the more ruthlessly aggressive of the two, and had fewer "bourgeois inhibitions" about war, Hitler eventually dispensed with Schacht. In the military field, not content with being Commander-in-Chief of the Luftwaffe, Goering set about plotting to gain supreme command of the Wehrmacht. In an attempt to achieve this, he plotted frame-ups to get rid of General von Fritsch and General von Blomberg, by helping to get them involved in private scandals while still posing as a friend of the Prussian militarists. (With Himmler's help, a trumped-up charge of homosexuality was brought against General von Fritsch, Commander-in-Chief of the Army. War Minister von Blomberg married a woman who turned up in police files as "a woman of ill repute.") Goering achieved the shake-up of the High Command which he sought, and which fitted in with Hitler's plans anyway; but Hitler would not entrust too much of the responsibility for the execution of his plans for aggressive war to a crony who had grown flabby with corruption and gluttony and was despised by most of the General Staff on whom he had to rely.

For Hitler's vengeful obsession of racial conflict had already been crystallized into a definite timetable for aggression, and

Goering knew that the historical stakes of military power were now the greatest in Germany's history. At a secret meeting on November 5, 1937, Hitler outlined to Goering and the other military leaders his plans to achieve proper *Lebensraum* for the German people in the near future. In terms that Goering and the other "realists" could not help but understand, he explained the material basis of the Nazi racial ideology and the practical necessity of undertaking aggression against other countries to implement it. The minutes of the meeting, as recorded by Hitler's adjutant, Colonel Hoszbach (hence referred to as the "Hoszbach document" or conference), reveal how Hitler planned to wage war two years in advance of the actual outbreak of hostilities:

The Führer then stated: The aim of German policy is the security and the preservation of the *Volk* and its propagation. This is consequently a problem of space. . . . The German people, with its strong racial root, has for this purpose the most favorable foundations in the heart of the European continent. The history of all times—Roman Empire, British Empire—has proved that every space expansion can only be effected by breaking resistance and taking risks. . . . The question for Germany is where the greatest possible conquest could be made at lowest cost.

German politics must reckon with its two hateful enemies, England and France, to whom a strong German colossus in the center of Europe would be intolerable. Both these states would oppose a further reinforcement of Germany, both in Europe and overseas, and in this opposition they would have the support of all parties. . . .

If the Führer is still living, then it will be his irrevocable decision to solve the German space problem no later than 1943-45. . . . For the improvement of our military political position it must be our first aim, in every case of entanglement by war, to conquer Czechoslovakia and Austria simultaneously, in order to remove any threat from the flanks in case of a possible advance westward. . . . Once Czechoslovakia is conquered—and a mutual frontier of Germany-Hungary is obtained—then a neutral attitude by Poland in a German-French conflict could more easily be relied upon. Our agreements with Poland remain valid only as long as Germany's strength remains unshakeable. . . .

The Führer believes personally, that in all probability England and perhaps also France, have already silently written off Czechoslovakia. . . . Without England's support it would also not be necessary to take into consideration a march by France through Holland and Belgium. . . . Naturally, we should in every case have to secure our frontier during the operation of our attacks against Czechoslovakia and Austria. . . . The annexation of the two States to Germany, militarily and politically, would constitute a considerable relief, owing to shorter and better frontiers, the freeing of fighting personnel for other purposes. . . .

Military participation by Russia must be countered by the speed of our operations; it is a question whether this needs to be taken into consideration at all, in view of Japan's attitude. . . .

Feldmarschall von Blomberg and Generaloberst von Fritsch, in giving their estimate of the situation, repeatedly pointed out that we should not run the risk that England and France become our enemies. . . .

In view of the information given by the Führer, Generaloberst Goering considered it imperative to think of a reduction of our military undertaking in Spain. . . . (36)

By cautioning against the reckless precipitation of more antagonism than Germany could handle, Von Fritsch and Von Blomberg showed that they had insufficient appreciation of Hitler's ideological statesmanship; but ideological or not, Goering showed that he was perfectly ready and willing to gird his loins for the great historical showdown. The difference in attitudes was crucial. Hitler readily took advantage of the excuse provided him by Goering and Himmler to get rid of his unimaginative war chiefs. In February, 1938, three months after the "Hoszbach conference" the shake-up of the High Command took place. Hitler took over the command of the Wehrmacht himself and retained the obedient lackey, General Keitel, as Chief of Staff. In recognition of his reliability and heroic qualities (and as a consolation prize for failing to wangle the post of commander-in-chief), the Führer's "loyal paladin" was soon elevated to the rank of field marshal, the rank of the greatest warlords of German history.

Goering continued to use the Nazi ideology as a camouflage for his own aggressive narcissism. Again and again the solidarity and "manifest destiny" of the German *Volk* proved to be a convenient springboard for his personal ambitions and private gain.

In March, 1938, Hitler's timetable went into action with the Anschluss of Austria, exercising "the German people's right of self-determination." Goering engineered the forceful Anschluss as ranking officer of the Reich in order to prevent a plebiscite —but also in the nick of time to break up the scheduled meeting of a military court of honor which would have cleared and rehabilitated his senior officer, General von Fritsch. (Goering's promotion followed and General von Fritsch was later mysteriously slain in the first days of the war.)

The Munich Pact of September, 1938, gave Goering virtual control of the Skoda munitions plants and other Sudeten industries, with the help of the loyal Sudeten Nazis. During the preliminary negotiations with President Hacha, Goering had amiably facilitated the self-determination of German racial solidarity and *Lebensraum* by stating that "it would hurt me to have to bomb beautiful Prague." To him all diplomacy was only the interplay of conflicting material national interests anyway. Did not Chamberlain and Daladier prove that at the Munich conference? With unconcealed cynicism, Goering later described to the writer the Munich Pact conference as he experienced it:

> Actually, the whole thing was a cut-and-dried affair. Neither Chamberlain nor Daladier was the least bit interested in sacrificing or risking *anything* to save Czechoslovakia. That was clear as day to me. The fate of Czechoslovakia was essentially sealed in three hours. Then they argued four more hours over the word "guarantee." Chamberlain kept hedging. Daladier hardly paid any attention at all. He just sat there like this. (Goering slumped down and assumed a bored expression.) All he did was nod approval from time to time. Not the slightest objection to anything! I was simply amazed at how easily the thing was being managed by Hitler. After all, they knew that Skoda, etc., had munitions plants in the Sudetenland, and Czechoslovakia would be at our mercy. . . . We got everything we wanted, just like that! (He snapped his fingers.) They didn't insist on consulting the Czechs as a matter of form—nothing. At the end, Ambassador Poncet said, "Well, now I'll have to convey the verdict to the condemned." That's all there was to it. The question of a guarantee was settled by leaving it up to Hitler to guarantee the rest of Czechoslovakia. Now, they knew perfectly well what that meant. (22)

It meant, as the rest of the world soon learned, the annexation of the rest of Czechoslovakia, under the guise of a protectorate. Chamberlain and Daladier could not have known, as Goering knew, how this appeasement fitted in with Hitler's timetable for aggression; but Goering did not have the slightest doubt that they had found it to their own national interest to let Germany expand toward the East at Czechoslovakia's and Russia's expense.

As Hitler and Goering built up their war machine and *Lebensraum* to achieve still more *Lebensraum* in Germany's hour of destiny, the persecution of the scapegoats served a threefold purpose: (*a*) distraction and suppression of criticism of the Nazi regime; (*b*) the conditioning of public opinion to accept an aggressive "defense against our enemies"; (*c*) material incentives for the faithful. Though far from a fanatic ideologist, Goering was not averse to letting persecution serve its threefold purpose—least of all, the third.

The organized "spontaneous uprising" against the Jews in retaliation for the slaying of bureaucrat Von Rath, two months after the Munich Pact, was strictly the handiwork of propagandist Joseph Goebbels. But it also provided Goering with a golden opportunity. As plenipotentiary of the Four-Year Plan he imposed a fine of one billion Reichsmarks on the entire Jewish population. The "aryanization" of Jewish property and business, which followed on the heels of this confiscatory measure, became a very lucrative source of graft for the entire party machinery and for Goering's interest in business and art.

But throughout all this Goering never lost his sense of humor or "patriotic idealism." He flippantly declared to Gestapo Chief Heydrich that he would have preferred the killing of two hundred more Jews during this organized pogrom to the destruction of so much property which Germany needed for her war effort. When the question of heavy insurance payments came up for the destruction of this property, Goering forbade the payments to the injured parties, but offered to let the treasury split the proceeds with the insurance companies. He exclaimed, with his ever-ready jocularity, that surely the insurance companies would

not object if a fat angel in the person of Hermann Goering
made them a present of half the legalized loot.

At the same time, Goering was enjoying other practical
jokes, like the loading of bricks instead of guns on a shipment
destined for Loyalist Spain. Later, in 1939, when President
Roosevelt's letter requesting specific assurances of Germany's
peaceful intentions was read in the Reichstag by Hitler, Goering
led the assembly in uproarious laughter until his sides shook.[3]

Still a little ambivalent about the material risk involved in
precipitating war so recklessly—he was not unaware of the
validity of Von Fritsch's objections—Goering made a rather
amateurish attempt to see if he could not negotiate another
amiable "Munich Pact" over the Polish crisis. He allowed a
Swedish businessman by the name of Dahlerus to institute feel-
ers for such a pact. When Dahlerus pointed out to Hitler the
necessity for such negotiation, after the British Foreign Office
had expressed a willingness to negotiate but not to appease
further, Hitler became furious: "Then I will build U-boats!
U-boats! U-boats! . . ." he screamed, "and I will build airplanes! airplanes! airplanes! *and I will exterminate my enemies!!*" According to Dahlerus, Goering stood by "and did
not turn a hair." (22) On the contrary, he was by that time
exhibiting such obsequious humility to Hitler, and seemed in
such "a crazy state of intoxication" over the impending war,
that he should have realized that no attempt at negotiation
could possibly have succeeded.

For Hitler had already decided that the time was ripe to
strike the final blow for hegemony in Europe, and Goering's
real soldiers, guns, and planes were poised for the biggest and
most exciting war games of all time. Even if he had had some
momentary misgivings about embarking on such a dangerous
adventure, he was psychologically incapable of rendering effective opposition to a Kaiser-figure in that authoritarian setting.
Neither did he have the moral courage that such opposition

---

[3] This scene in the Reichstag, proudly preserved by the Nazis in their
cinematic record of the New Greater Germany, was used against them at
the Nuremberg trial. When he saw it again, Goering again laughed until
his sides shook.

would have required. In the Nazi pecking-hierarchy, there was no doubt that Hitler outpecked Goering. Besides, Hitler's violently obsessive messianic complex was more than a match for Goering's heroic play acting. Anyway, the alternative of blind support of the Führer in his reckless plans for conquest, which had brought him so much power and wealth already, was far too easy and far too attractive psychologically to have caused him any real hesitation.

The war had already been made in the mind of a dictator obsessed by a need to compensate for inferiority feelings. It was now wholeheartedly supported by a Number 2 dictator who had always craved aggression for aggression's sake and had learned to satisfy his infantile needs through a show of loyalty to his sovereign.

The War Lord.—The exploits of Goering's Luftwaffe are of more historical and military significance than psychological. Suffice it to say that in the beginning Goering performed his function in the war machine aggressively and efficiently. The bombing of Warsaw, Rotterdam, and Coventry were all, in a literal psychological sense, child's play. But with these easy victories Goering grew more and more careless in his play. As Luftwaffe prisoners later revealed, Goering concentrated too much on uniforms and showmanship and not enough on meeting the enemy's technological challenge. The task of bombing London and Moscow into submission proved to be more than child's play. But Goering was already too far gone in the satisfaction of infantile needs to sacrifice it to the more arduous tasks of warfare. With uncontrollable avarice he sought still more wealth and still more titles. Art treasures from the collections of occupied Europe began to find their way to Goering's palatial estates by the carload, while their owners were frequently among those herded into concentration camps. To the newly created rank of Reichsmarschall (about a six-star general) Goering had to add President of the Reich Research Council, Head of the Reich Defense Council, etc.

As London withstood the worst that the Luftwaffe had to offer and Moscow refused to fall, Hitler's fury vented itself more and more on his errant Luftwaffe chief. "In fact, he would scream about the inefficiency and uselessness of the Luftwaffe with such contempt and viciousness, that I would actually blush and squirm and preferred to go to the front to avoid these scenes," Goering related. "But then he *ordered* me to be present at his staff conferences at GHQ just as if to say, *'Stand there and take it, damn you!'* With that kind of viciousness!" The account is undoubtedly accurate except for Goering's pathetic pretense of going to the front. Those who were familiar with the situation informed us that Goering just disappeared for long periods of time, sulking in his palace, hunting, or "doping himself up with morphine and stealing art treasures from all over Europe when Germany was in agony" (Speer).

Apparently some physical and affective deterioration had actually set in, while his intellectual efficiency functioned very sporadically under the influence of his drugs. Paroxysmal tachycardia, neuralgia, and other psychosomatic complaints plagued him more and more. Inspiring leadership turned to terrorization and brutality, for just as Hitler cursed him, he cursed and mistreated his subordinates. The peck-right of aggressive resolution of frustration asserted itself with a vengeance. In a desperate attempt to salvage his standing with the Führer, Goering punished and castigated his officers for inefficiency. He even went so far as to forbid one of his ace generals to reveal to Hitler the relative weakness of the Luftwaffe and then demoted him to a common private for doing so. At the same time he assured the Führer that secret wonder-weapons, which would turn the tide, were just around the corner. Goering's protective fantasy was still running away with him. Again, as his frustration increased, the need to escape into another fantasy world through drugs also increased. Karinhall became reminiscent of the decadence of Rome. When he did show up at meetings of the Reich Defense Council, Speer said, his speech was often so irrational that it could be explained only on the basis of a morphine jag. It became common practice for the war leaders to ignore him and do what they could to save the tottering Reich, over his head.

But there was probably another reason for Goering's panicky flight from reality: *mass extermination!* Not that Goering was one to suffer acute anxiety reactions to the murder of political rivals, the shooting of hostages, the bombing of open cities, or the starvation of conquered populations. But even his perverted sense of values had set certain limits to the aggressive acting out of his heroic fantasies. He could handle his anxieties and aggressions in the military sphere, to a certain extent. Killing enemies, bullying his underdogs, believing in wonder-weapons, all provided certain outlets and defenses; anyway, win, lose or draw, the rules of chivalry provided for considerate treatment among war lords between wars, and Goering's amiable disposition would always get him by. But genocide was something that was not even in the books—something that shattered his entire romantic frame of reference. The alternatives of being shot as a blundering fool and traitor by his own incredibly murderous Kaiser-figure on the one hand or being tried and hanged as a war criminal by the enemy on the other was too shattering to his ego-structure to contemplate. That the problem was causing him some real concern was indicated by a remark which Speer heard him make toward the end of the war: "These atrocities will cost us dearly one day." But until that day, it was better not to think about it—and so, characteristically, Goering brushed aside the dangerous reality. When it became too much for him on top of Hitler's violent attacks, the drugs provided a reliable escape.

At all events, Goering was paralyzed into inaction. Faced with a clear decision to back up his "pure patriotic idealism"— even his desire to avoid a disgraceful death himself—by overthrowing the now unmistakable maniac who was wantonly ruining his own country, he shrank into seclusion. The would-be hero, as Speer told us, failed his country in her greatest hour of need—because he was fundamentally a moral coward.

Just before the final collapse, Goering made a premature suggestion to succeed the Führer in anticipation of his death. He was arrested and ordered killed with his family for his pains. As his wife described that last scene of the war: Goering was cursing the leader who had turned on him, in the vilest language of which he was capable, while bombs were falling all around the terrified family, and SS men were deliberating over the execution order. His own regiment finally rescued him. It took a good quantity of drugs to steady his nerves.

It was in this demoralized and exhausted state that Goering surrendered to the American authorities. He was gradually denarcotized by diminishing doses of paracodeine and put on an army diet. As the prison commandant described it in picturesque lay terminology: "When Goering came to me at Mondorf, he was a simpering slob with two suitcases full of paracodeine pills. I thought he was a drug salesman. But we took him off his dope and made a man of him." He was transported to the Nuremberg jail to await trial as a major war criminal. It was there that the examiner made his acquaintance.

OBSERVATIONS AND EVALUATION

Relieved of his drugs and put on a regular army diet, Goering was once more alert and responsive, though somewhat subdued by his recent harrowing experiences. He presented a front of utter amiability and good-humored bravado to the American officers, whom he was obviously trying to win over, though he could not conceal his inordinate egotism. Rapport was easily established for the psychological testing, which was conducted while the prisoners were still in solitary confinement. This rapport was built up by the examiner for over three weeks before attempting any tests.

Test Results.—A German version of the Wechsler-Bellevue I.Q. test was improvised, omitting the parts most susceptible to cultural differences, and a retest given on the Rorschach inkblots.

I.Q. Test. Goering responded eagerly to the test challenge, behaving like a bright and egotistical schoolboy who was anxious to show off before the teacher. The memory span test immediately caught his fancy. He chuckled with glee as the examiner showed surprise at his retention of the increasingly difficult series of digits. When he failed to repeat the nine-digit series correctly, he banged his fist on the cot impatiently, demanding a third and fourth try at it, saying *"Ach,* come on, give me another one—I can do it!" When he finally succeeded, to the examiner's expressed amazement, he could hardly contain himself for pride and joy. This pattern of rapport was maintained throughout the test, the examiner urging him on by telling him how few people were able to do the next item, and Goering responding like an eager schoolboy. The results showed superior intelligence (I.Q. 138), one of the highest in the Nuremberg group. The subtests showed the quick reaction time, sensorimotor coordination, and arithmetical facility ordinarily found in successful pilots, as well as the high verbal facility associated with political-propagandistic activities. Being led to believe that he had the highest I.Q. among the Nazi war criminals he praised the excellent discrimination of American psychometric methods. When he heard that Schacht and Seyss-Inquart had outdone him, he scorned the unreliability of the test.

Rorschach. The high degree of intellectual efficiency shown on the I.Q. test was confirmed to some extent by the Rorschach inkblot test. Here, however, he betrayed the qualitative mediocrity of his intellect. The high cognitive efficiency was indicated by the presence of projected active human figures in the inkblots, the quick responses and good form of the figures seen. However, the meagerness of the performance on this task, the overdependence on the easily recognized "popular" figures, the absence of any good original interpretations of his own, the tendency to make superficial general estimates of each situation, all revealed his superficial and pedestrian realism, rather than brilliantly creative intelligence. This coincides with the general clinical impression gained in discussions with him. Direct observation and discussion showed that Goering was a sharp and cynical realist, "quick on the uptake" in any debate, but no match for Schacht, Frank, Seyss-Inquart, or several of the other Nazis as an "intellectual," regardless of I.Q.

On the affective side, the Rorschach showed depression and anxiety. There were signs of increased morbid anxiety on the retest given shortly after the beginning of the trial. This was not surprising in view of his cyclothymic affect, and the three weeks of evidence which had added a devastating burden of guilt for aggressive war and atrocities. There was a tendency to inhibit the creative projections of active human figures on the retest, to respond more morbidly to the dark inkblots, and to react more violently to color. When he encountered the red (blood) spots on Card IV, he literally tried to "brush them off," snapping at them angrily with his forefinger. During the inquiry he reinterpreted the inkblot with the sadistic response, "—maybe two doctors arguing over the inner organs of a man (laughs)," thus giving his sadism the humorous "brush-off." This was probably the most significant part of the whole test, for it betrayed the basic sadistic compulsions, the consciousness of guilt, and the need to escape it, while brushing it all off with dramatic gestures. But the bravado was as shallow as the laugh which accompanied this response. Lady Macbeth's nightmare was hardly more obvious in betraying her anxiety to rub out the "damned spot." The response to this card confirms in a striking way Speer's description of Goering as a depraved character, a blustering hero who simply brushed off his responsibilities when he had a *real* opportunity to play the heroic role in a crisis. The clinical picture presented by the tests is certainly that of the intelligent but sadistic egotist with little real ego-strength.

Goering must have sensed that he had betrayed himself somewhere on the Rorschach, because he kept asking the examiner repeatedly throughout the trial what it had revealed. When he was told at the end, it struck home sufficiently for him to leave behind with his defense counsel a note denouncing the psychologist.

Further Observations During Trial.—More revealing than the psychological tests was the direct observation of Hermann Goering's behavior as he played out the last act of his life drama. The significance of this last episode is that, under observation in the limited environment of the Nuremberg jail, he exhibited on a small scale the very same personality pattern which he had displayed on a grand scale in the life history we have reconstructed: a ruthlessly aggressive personality camouflaged by disarming amiability when it suited his purpose; cyclothymic in affect, extremely narcissistic in his ego-gratifications, but lacking the moral courage which might have given his heroic fantasies more than theatrical substance.

As soon as the trial started, Goering's domineering aggressiveness came to the fore. The challenge of acting out a new last act of the Nazi drama before the audience of the world press was as exhilarating as a shot in the arm. He immediately started to manipulate his environment by taking charge of the prisoners' dock and dictating the strategy of defense. He declared, rubbing his hands enthusiastically, that he was the captain of the first-string team and was going to give the opposition and the audience a run for their money; the second-stringers were the prisoners on the upper tiers of cells, but they were no good because they lacked leadership. The trial, like everything else in Goering's life, was still a game of play acting in which he played the aggressive leading role. Even the evidence of atrocities and other war crimes could be evaluated only for its effect on the audience. This was strikingly illustrated early in the trial, when American films of the concentration camps were shown in court. Many of the defendants broke down and cried in shame; others hotly protested their innocence of these crimes, when we saw them later in their cells. But not Goering:

> (*November 29, 1945, Goering's cell.*) As for Goering, he was apparently disturbed because it had spoiled his show. "It was such a good afternoon too, until they showed that film.—They were reading my telephone conversations on the Austrian affair, and everybody was laughing with me.—And then they showed that awful film, and it just spoiled everything." [4]

Goering continued to brush off the atrocities just as he had done previously. He urged the others to stick together and the worst that could happen to them would be exile; when this attack didn't work he made another appeal on the basis of his projected fantasies, luring them with the prospect of heroic martyrdom, including marble caskets in a national shrine, if they would stick with him in loyalty and patriotism. At the same time his humor revealed itself behind the scenes in all its crude cynicism.

> (*January 7, 1946, lunchroom.*) "It makes me sick to see Germans selling their souls to the enemy!" he fumed at lunch. ". . . I just detest anything that is undignified!" . . . Then he turned to the audience in general, and said out loud, banging his fist on the table, "Dammit, I just wish we could all have the courage to confine our defense to three simple words: *Lick my arse!*" . . . He repeated the proposed defense with great relish, telling how Goetz had said it, how another general had said it, and how he would say it.

When the time came for his defense, Goering did not display such crude cynicism, but showed himself to be a master of eva-

---

[4] All dated observations and quotations are from the *Nuremberg Diary* (22).

sion and played the role of loyal patriot for all it was worth. He had decided quite early in the trial that the best line to follow for the sake of his public and for German history was to maintain his loyalty to the Führer and to stick to it to the bitter end. He admitted quite candidly that his role in German history was more important to him than anything else, and that this was the way to play it

The Heroic Myth.—Granting the narcissistic basis of his values, the examiner asked him whether he thought that the German people would admire him for maintaining loyalty to a leader who had ruined them with mass murder and war. Goering assured us that he knew his people better than we did, and that German tradition demanded a show of loyalty to the bitter end. When we asked for further explanation of this point after one of his grandstand plays during his defense, he revealed how his youthful fantasies were still dominating his behavior: he related the story from the *Nibelungenlied,* telling how Hagen had killed Siegfried, and how Kriemhild's brothers had refused to take revenge for Siegfried's death, because Hagen had only acted out of loyalty to his king. By analogy, therefore, any murder committed at Hitler's wish was not disgraceful in German eyes.

This complete absorption with his own heroic role in German history obsessed Goering all through the last act of his drama. With dogged stubbornness he resisted any attempt to penetrate the structure of social values he had built up since his early readings of history and German legend. Further *Diary* notes record our observations as he completed his defense:

(*March 17, 1946, Goering's cell.*) His defense being almost completed, he was already moodily brooding over his destiny and speculating on his role in history. Humanitarianism has become a thorn in his side, and he cynically rejects it as a threat to his future greatness. The empire of Genghis Khan, the Roman Empire, and even the British Empire were not built up with due regard for principles of humanity, he explained with weary bitterness—but they had achieved greatness in their time and have won a respected place in history. I reiterated that the world was becoming a little too sophisticated in the 20th century to regard war and murder as the signs of greatness. He squirmed and scoffed and rejected the idea as the sentimental idealism of an American who could afford such a self-delusion after America had hacked its way to a rich *Lebensraum* by revolution, massacre, and war. He clearly would tolerate no maudlin sentimentality to crab his entrance act into Valhalla.

(*March 24, 1946, after completing his defense:*) Goering leaned on his elbow at the other end of the cot and brooded, mumbling half to himself: "No, my people have been humiliated before. Loyalty and hatred will unite them again.—Who knows but that in this very hour the man is born who will unite my people—born of our flesh and bones, to avenge the humiliation we suffer now!"

As the grandiose chords of the *Siegfried Leitmotif* reverberated among the strains of *Götterdämmerung* in his bare cell (we could almost fantasy it along with him, so vividly did he act the part), Goering could hardly be expected to experience any actual guilt feelings. The most that could be observed was skilful guilt evasion. As for the Nazi atrocities, Goering testified under oath that he had not even known about them "to that extent," because like all good Germans he had obeyed the ban on listening to the foreign radio. This argument was all the more ludicrous in view of his repeated protestations that he had not believed all the atrocity reports he had heard on the foreign radio, and the fact that the Reich Research Council actually functioned as Goering's private military intelligence agency. Besides, Goering had already given a slight but highly significant clue to his real reaction to the blood on his hands during the psychological testing.

It is not easy to interpret Goering's true reactions to the atrocities he brushed off so grandiloquently under observation. Certainly there was a degree of callous egocentricity in his behavior, such as only a narcissistic psychopath could be capable of. Goering constantly sought to impress the examiner with his chivalry, loyalty, and patriotism, even when the most gruesome atrocities were under discussion. It even behooved him to have one of his witnesses and his lawyer at the trial refer to him as "the last Renaissance figure," as a means of currying sympathy. It was clear from his personal history and from direct observation that the role Goering had acted out was that of the Robber

Baron, rather than the Knight of the Holy Grail. But it would not be quite true to our clinical impression to attribute to him the withdrawal or absence of emotional sensitivity that one finds in a schizoid personality. As we have already indicated, the mass murder of helpless women and children was something that his playfully heroic and chivalrous concepts of war had never quite envisioned. Not without some pathetic earnestness did Goering try to impress the distinction on the examiner:

> (*March 9, 1946, Goering's cell.*) "There is just one thing I want you to know.—Really—you can believe it or not—but I must say in dead earnest—I have never been *cruel*.—I'll admit I've been *hard*. I do not deny that I haven't been bashful about shooting a thousand men for reprisals or hostages, or whatever you please. —But *cruel*—torturing *women* and *children*?—*Du lieber Gott!* That is so far removed from my nature."

It would not be distorting the clinical picture too much to grant a certain amount of validity to Goering's self-characterization. But we must then ask why Goering shrank into seclusion with his drugs and treasures while all this was going on and Hitler was quite obviously bent on destroying Germany in the same ideological "fight to the finish."

We shall never know for certain what emotions possessed Goering as he drugged the atrocities out of his mind. Perhaps for the first time in his life Goering experienced fear. Not merely the ordinary fear of death, which was suddenly becoming more real to him, but the atavistic fears of unknown horrors beyond his ken—not unlike the fear of unknown destructive forces which terrifies superstitious primitive savages far more than the wild animals or tribal warriors they can see and fight; or the panic-reaction of severe neurotics, when not only their ego-defenses but their entire conscious frame of reference collapses in the face of new overwhelming conflicts. For it is altogether likely that, in helping to seal the fate of Europe's Jews and stealing the property of those who ended in suicide or concentration camps, Goering had not visualized the gas-chamber extermination of millions of naked women and children, the packing of their hair for mattresses, the extraction of their gold teeth and gold wedding rings for gold deposits in the Reichsbank. His revolutionary Kaiser-figure had turned out to be a hideous Minotaur who violated all the self-protective rules of chivalry, murdering women and children and even devouring the youth of his own tribe. Hitler and Himmler had run amok with their ideology and converted his romantic world into a *Walpurgisnacht* of unspeakable horrors, to which all exits were sealed. All except one—the drugs and the poison he kept about him. Such might have been Goering's feelings, based on our understanding of his personality and system of values, and of the total situation. We shall never know for certain, because Goering naturally refused to discuss it, though he betrayed his reactions frequently during the year in which we observed him.

In any case, we must agree with the judgment of Albert Speer, who lived through this crisis with him: Goering had passed up his biggest chance to be a hero because he was fundamentally a moral coward. A fundamental lack of real ego-strength is, of course, implicit in the inordinate need for self-display, acquisitiveness, and aggression and in the dependence on drugs for flights from reality. The physical recklessness he displayed as a child, as a war pilot and as a revolutionary leader was only the aggressive acting out of fantasies by a not-too-sensitive narcissist. They were not of the stuff that moral courage and mature leadership are made of. Not the least of human tragedies is that such artificially inflated egos collapse when faced with the supreme test of their own values of leadership.

But Goering's theatrical sense functioned to the very end. His calculated performance in court won him a good press, all things considered, and he carefully instructed his lawyer on how to interview reporters to follow up this advantage. He also coached other defendants on the proper use of evasive tactics on cross-examination and the importance of making the stuff *interesting* so that the judges and the reporters would not get bored and try to hurry the trial. Above all, he insisted that they support him in the pose of loyal patriotism. Where humorous cynicism and bravado failed, he resorted to outright browbeating. He could not bash their heads together in the present situation, but his sheer personal dominance and aggressiveness seemed to have an intimidating effect on the more submissive characters. Keeping him separated from the other defendants outside of the courtroom had a salutary effect in minimizing this intimidation.

As one after another of the defendants admitted or were forced to admit the criminal guilt of the Nazi regime and shifted the blame to the top leaders, Goering again recoiled in frustration. His anxiety was expressed in part by his old psychosomatic complaints; more of it found expression in oral and incipient overt aggression. Sweating in his cell as the trial drew to a close, complaining of sciatica and treachery, he gave vent to vile vituperation against his codefendants, as well as some more resolution of rejection-anxiety through the group-hostility technique. It was interesting to compare notes with some of the other officers who were seeing him at this time, to see how he was maligning the psychologist to the psychiatrist, the Catholic chaplain to the Protestant chaplain and vice versa, both chaplains to the psychologist and psychiatrist, and vice versa, while fawning on each in turn. In the prisoners' dock, which was the only place he could meet the others now, he repeated the same process with militarists against civilians, Prussians against Bavarians, Protestants against Catholics, and always vice versa, smiling to each in turn, but soliciting sympathy by scorning him behind his back to members of opposed groups.

He could not ask for drugs now, but we felt that he would have given his right arm for a good shot of cocaine or a big dose of paracodeine. He fairly quivered as he struck out in all directions in frustrated aggression. Finally, when Speer made his spectacular denunciation of Hitler and Goering, Goering reacted in typical gangster fashion, threatening to have Speer murdered if he ever got out of the jail alive.

Political 'Realist' or Psychopath?—From then on, Goering was most brutally frank in revealing his true social attitudes. On the issue of morality in international affairs—repeatedly brought up in court and in our conversations in his cell—Goering only scoffed:

(*June 6, 1946, Goering's Cell.*) "What do you mean, morality?
—word-of-honor?" Goering snorted. "Sure, you can talk about
word-of-honor when you promise to deliver goods in business.—
But when it is the question of the *interests of the nation*!?—
Phooey! Then morality stops. That is what England has done
for centuries; America has done it; and Russia is still doing it!
. . . *Herrgott!* When a state has a chance to improve its position
because of the weakness of a neighbor, do you think it will stop
at any squeamish consideration of keeping a promise? It is a
statesman's *duty* to take advantage of such a situation for the good
of his country! (The writer mentioned something about the
necessity of cooperation through the United Nations at this point.)
Ach, we spit on your United Nations! Do you think that any
one of us takes that seriously for a minute? Why, you see already
that Russia won't budge, and why should they? It is only your
atomic bomb that keeps them in check at all.—Just wait five years
when they have it too! England doesn't want to give in on the
Balkan issue, because then Russia threatens the Mediterranean,
and what the hell good is England without the Mediterranean?
Morality doesn't have a damn thing to do with these things. . . .

You Americans are making a stupid mistake with your talk of
democracy and morality. You think all you have to do is arrest
all the Nazis and start setting up a democracy overnight. Do you
think that Germans have gotten one bit less nationalistic because
the so-called Christian parties are securing a majority . . . And
what do the German people really think? I've already told you:
'*Whenever things are lousy, we have democracy!*' . . . No, the
next generation is being led by its own leaders, and they will see
that their own national interests are being threatened, and then
you can take your morality and your repentance and your democracy and stick it up!"

The same nationalistic cynicism expressed itself on the question of waging aggressive war. To him preventive war, aggressive war, politics, and peace were all just different aspects of
the same struggle for supremacy which was in the very nature
of things, with the rewards going to the strongest nation and
the cleverest leaders. The old "survival of the fittest" myth
suited his purposes of uninhibited aggression by reducing social
ethics to the law of the jungle. Quite obviously, the only thing
he had done wrong about the war was that he had lost it, and
he readily brushed off the guilt for war crimes as "the judgment
of the victors." But even this hostile ethnocentrism was a cynical camouflage for authoritarian egocentricity. When challenged

on the desires of the people, on whose behalf he expressed so much protective patriotic idealism:

> (*April 18, 1946, Goering's cell.*) "Why, of course the *people* don't want war," Goering shrugged. "Why would some poor slob on a farm want to risk his life in a war when the best he can get out of it is to come back to his farm in one piece? Naturally, the common people don't want war; neither in Russia, nor in England, nor in America, nor for that matter in Germany. That is understood. But after all, it is the *leaders* of the country who determine the policy, and it is always a simple matter to drag the people along, whether it is a democracy or a fascist dictatorship or a parliament or a communist dictatorship. . . . Voice or no voice, the people can always be brought to do the bidding of the leaders. That is easy. All you have to do is tell them they are being attacked and denounce the pacifists for lack of patriotism and exposing the country to danger. It works the same in any country."

This is probably as brutally frank a statement of autocratic cynicism as any made since the classical formulation of Machiavelli's *Prince*. It is probably also the only expression of such attitudes made by a powerful war lord in a situation that allowed of clinical evaluation.

To understand Goering's social attitudes, like Hitler's, we must not only recognize the psychodynamics of his aggressive drives, but we must also evaluate the cultural impact on his personality. In Hitler's case, the psychodynamics may well have been the rebellious resolution of Oedipal conflicts and inferiority feelings; in Goering's case, the gratification of exuberant, infantile narcissistic impulses. Whatever the psychodynamics of the aggression, its confirmation and appeasement by competing national and class interests merely served the purposes of that aggression. The cultural influences on these two characters overlapped, but were not identical. In Goering's case, we have seen the close identification with Junker caste and privilege, the experience of profiteering and patriotic glory in war, economic chaos and frustration in defeat; the wrangling of group interests for political advantage in the Weimar Republic, and finally the appeasement of Hitler's lawless aggression both at home and abroad. These environmental influences could not help but confirm this avaricious realist in the reality of unenlightened self-interest. Judeo-Christian moral values and democratic humanitarianism simply did not become realities in a cultural framework that lent itself so readily to the biased perceptions of an insatiable egotist. This not only suited the pathological needs of both Hitler and Goering, but even satisfied the minimum requirements of their conscious reality-testing, since neither of them was psychotic.

It is characteristic of the psychopathic extreme in the authoritarian mentality that it only grows more malignant with appeasement. This is inherent in the sadomasochistic nature of the authoritarian psychology, where compromise is regarded as a sign of weakness or inferiority.[5] Certainly the scorn with which Goering spoke of Chamberlain's and Daladier's behavior at the Munich Pact conference gave unmistakable evidence of this attitude. His contempt for Christian and democratic morality in actual practice therefore becomes more understandable, though hardly excusable.

All this adds further evidence that the antisocial or psychopathic personality, in the political sphere as elsewhere, is largely a product of social conditioning and derives its definition only from the social context. This is not to deny the existence of predisposing constitutional factors. A compulsion to overt aggression was so evident in Goering's "style of life," from earliest childhood to the last months of his life, that some such predisposition may be justifiably inferred. But the ruthless ethnocentricity and killing of enemies, the use of drugs, the unrestrained self-indulgence, the cynicism and corruption in politics—in short, all that gave his aggressive egocentricity an antisocial character—came about through a process of social conditioning.

Goering's "last act" differed from his earliest childhood recollections only by reflecting the social conditioning through which his aggressions had been channeled. His threat to murder a defendant who had denounced the sham heroism of the in-group chieftains, his intimidation of witnesses behind the

---

[5] An excellent elaboration of this concept is made by Fromm (20). The validity of the social implication has been oddly confirmed by Mrs. Roosevelt's reaction to Soviet intransigence in the UN.

scenes, while playing the amiable patriot in public, etc., were all of the same "style of life."

Goering's last weeks on earth were spent in a state of brooding despondency as he contemplated his figure in history. The trial had succeeded in unmasking the amiable patriot; his last-ditch loyalty to Hitler had been exposed as an unconscionable gesture in the light of the denunciations. Brooding in his cell, Goering admitted that his attempt to build a heroic legend had been a failure. "You don't have to worry about the Hitler legend any more," he said. "When the German people learn what has been revealed at this trial, it won't be necessary to condemn him. He has condemned himself." Implicit in that statement was Goering's admission of grave doubts respecting his own position in German history.

His suicide was, of course, his last bid for recognition in the German history books as a national hero who could outwit the enemy, brushing aside the moral issues of the trial. It was also a solution to his overpowering anxiety about facing a form of death that was particularly disgraceful according to the stereotypes of his culture. (If he had been hanged, he could not have hoped to get his picture into the German history books.) To the very end he made dark threats of resurgent German nationalism some day "avenging the humiliation we suffer now"— and vindicating the romanticized aggression by which he and Hitler had aggrandized and ultimately destroyed both themselves and their Reich.

RUDOLF HESS, THE FÜHRER'S DEPUTY

It would be erroneous to assume that an aggressive and sadistic dictatorship required personalities who were essentially aggressive and sadistic at the top executive level. On the contrary, Hitler's dictatorship seemed to thrive on the essential weakness and passive submission of his chief supporters. Hitler could not and did not tolerate more than one truly aggressive personality like Goering in his entourage (nor, for that matter, could Goering). For the rest, a great deal of passive fanatic devotion and even mediocre ability was essential, the better to reflect the authority and omnipotence of the dictator himself. An ideal supporter from this viewpoint was Rudolf Hess, the Führer's Deputy in the party and ultimately the most celebrated psychiatric case of this half-century.

LIFE HISTORY

Early Background.—Rudolf Hess was born in Alexandria, Egypt, one of four children born to a resident wholesale merchant of German descent and his German-born wife. This fact is of crucial significance in shaping his future motivation for ethnic identification. There is some evidence of psychopathology in the family history. His father's sister died in a mental hospital at an early age, and one of his mother's brothers committed suicide under circumstances that are not clear. The father lived up to the traditional German pattern of stern authoritarianism and insisted on bringing up his children with proper German discipline. Rudolf received his elementary school education at the German school in Alexandria. At the age of twelve he was sent to the Evangelisches Pädagogium at Godesberg-am-Rhein to get a proper German education.

Very little is known of Hess's youth, except that he was an earnest pupil, modest and undistinguished in his behavior or his scholarship. He showed considerable interest in science and German history. The keen interest in German history was the only educational factor that Hitler, Hess, and Goering had in common. It served as a common determining influence in spite of the diversity of their backgrounds. The teaching of history in a manner that glorified war and aggressive nationalism, defined heroism entirely in terms of military exploits, and idealized loyalty and obedience as the highest moral values had its predictable effect on Hess's personality. Since Hess was essentially a more passive personality than Hitler and Goering, the resolution of his insecurity took the form of a need for submissive loyalty to a champion of Germany's manifest destiny, rather than acting the role himself. Having been indoctrinated by his parents' attitudes and his early German schooling to begin with, his need to overcome inferiority feelings by passive identification with strength naturally led him to identify himself fanatically with the German *Volk* in spite of his foreign birth. (His special interest in the solidarity of *Volksdeutsche* and his Auslandsorganisation can undoubtedly be traced to this early ego-involvement.)

At the age of fifteen his father sent him to the École Superieure de Commerce at Neufchâtel in Switzerland. At the age of sixteen, in 1912, he went to Hamburg to serve an apprenticeship in commerce. He did not care for business, however, longing for something more grandiose like scientific discovery or politics.

At the outbreak of war in 1914, Hess promptly volunteered for the infantry. Like Hitler he performed his duties faithfully though without distinction. He was wounded twice, and just before the end of the war he was commissioned a lieutenant and transferred to the Luftwaffe. The Armistice came just a few weeks after he started active duty as a pilot. It was a source of permanent frustration that he failed to achieve any distinction as a war ace.

Hess then returned to Munich to study political science. Along with other restless veteran students, Hess became embroiled in the political gang warfare around the University of Munich, siding with the nationalistic and antileft-wing groups. He was wounded in one of these brawls in 1919. Around 1920 he came under the influence of Professor Karl Haushofer and his geopolitical theories. For a time he followed Haushofer around as an admiring disciple. About 1922 he heard Hitler make one of his passionate appeals to resurgent nationalism and denunciation of the scapegoats. The ultrasuggestible and emotionally dependent Hess immediately succumbed to Hitler's influence. He helped Hitler to take over control of the new party (NSDAP), and participated in the ill-fated Munich beer-hall *Putsch*. After the *Putsch* he escaped to the Austrian Alps, but returned to stand trial and imprisonment with Hitler. In Landsberg fortress Hitler dictated parts of *Mein Kampf* to Hess. (Hess himself was vague and inconsistent on the question of his influence in the writing of *Mein Kampf,* but there appears to be no doubt that he played his passive role in this as in most of Hitler's political activity.)

After their release from prison at the end of 1924, he devoted himself body and soul to the support of the Führer and the rebuilding of their party. He showed tendencies to hypochondriasis and mysticism, but that did not detract from the effectiveness of his fanatic zeal in supporting Hitler's rise to power. He subordinated himself completely to the political career of the martyred hero, with whom he now identified fully and shared a "blood bond." He had literally earned his membership in the sacred order of Old Fighters—the Order of Blood (*Blutorden*) of the champions of Aryan supremacy.

By 1932 his doglike devotion to his master earned him the position of undisputed Number 2 man in the Nazi party and chief supervisor of all Nazi party organizations and societies. These organizations had the aim of subjugating all political and social activities in the nation to Nazi control. With the party's seizure of power in 1933, this policy gradually took effect. Hess became extremely influential in the formulation of policies by virtue of the dual functioning of party and state and his personal devotion to Hitler. Thus he promoted the Nazi control of education, labor, and religion, transmitted the execution orders for the Roehm purge, helped formulate the anti-Semitic policies, and controlled the formation of foreign German *Bunds*. He did all this as the passive executor of Hitler's will, but with the fanatic conviction of a supersuggestible and dependent personality. In 1935 when Goering was designated as Hitler's successor as Head of State, Hess was redesignated as Hitler's deputy in the party and Goering's political successor. He also took a more active part in all legislative matters and in the plans for aggressive war.

Hess's female subordinates considered him a modest, chivalrous, well-meaning individual who was passionately devoted to his Führer and Fatherland, and literally "would not hurt a fly"; but his Nazi colleagues regarded him as "a little queer." He is known to have required the services of quack doctors and an astrologer and to have evoked the scorn of the Führer himself for his hypochondriasis. Gastrointestinal disturbances of apparently neurotic origin were manifest along with an interest in "nature healers."

War and Captivity.—Hess was intimately, though passively, involved in all the aggressions undertaken by Hitler and Goering, from the Roehm purge to the attack on Czechoslovakia and Poland. As a member of the Ministerial Council for the Defense of the Reich he shared in the advance planning of the war in 1938 and the waging of it after it had started. He undoubtedly had some misgivings about the spread of the war, naïvely assuming that the Western Allies would understand the reasonableness of German aspirations and Germany's value as a bulwark against Communist Russia.

On May 10, 1941, ten days after Hitler had secretly set forth the final plans and date for the attack on Russia, Hess made his famous flight to England. He landed by parachute on Scottish soil and fractured his leg in landing. His purpose was to make a deal with the British government through the Duke of Hamilton to stop the war with England on his terms. Investigation shows that this was clearly an irresponsible dramatic gesture, inspired by heroic fantasies—a typical Nazi symptom—and by a dream of his old mentor, Professor Haushofer. It was also inspired by belated and naïvely conceived humanitarian motives which in his mind were consistent with German plans for aggression but which provided genuine subjective motivation. The proposals he made to the British clearly represented wishful thinking previously expressed by the Führer as a solution to his dilemma, but they were made without Hitler's knowledge and in such an irresponsible manner as to infuriate him. (Our observations of the reaction of other Nazis to this question leaves no doubt on that score.) In substance, the proposal was to give England a free hand with her empire, if she would quit her "losing war" and give Germany a free hand on the Continent and "in the East."

The British did not take Hess's proposals seriously but tried to draw him out for information purposes. Frustrated in his mission, and defensive by nature, Hess became all the more secretive and evasive. Hitler's public declaration that Hess was insane and the news that the Wehrmacht was running into difficulty in Russia strained his anxiety-tolerance to the breaking point. Almost from the very beginning of his captivity, he ex-

"(I) That Germany should be given a free hand in Europe; II. That England should have a free hand in the British Empire, except that the ex-German colonies should be returned to Germany; III. That Russia should be included in Asia, but that Germany had certain demands to make of Russia, which would have to be satisfied either by negotiation or as the result of war. There was however no truth in the rumours that the Führer contemplated an early attack on Russia; IV. That the British should evacuate Iraq; V. The peace agreement would have to contain a provision for the reciprocal indemnification of British and German nationals, whose property had been expropriated as the result of war; VI. The proposal could only be considered on the understanding that it was negotiated by Germany with an English Government other than the present British Government. Mr. Churchill, who had planned the war since 1936 and his colleagues, who had lent themselves to his war policy were not persons with whom the Führer would negotiate ... these so-called „terms" were restated by Hess in a signed document dated June 10. !..."

___

② *zu S. 104*

Ich habe die Überzeugung, daß mit Hilfe des Scheinmittels nicht nur Ungarn, Spanier, Frauchen im Verlauf bolschewistisch-kommunistischer Aufstände, Briten im Verlauf des Burenkriegs, dazu gebracht wurden, Greuel zu begehen, sondern während des 1. in 2. Weltkriegs auch Deutsche.

Durch letzteres sollte Beweis geschaffen werden, die Greuelhetze gegen Deutschland insgesamt glaubhaft erscheinen zu lassen, die größten Teils durch Falsche Zeugen dargestellt, oder als Folge

STATESMANSHIP OR PARANOIA?—HESS'S TERMS TO BRITAIN

Hess's copy of the English text of the terms he laid down to Anthony Eden as the conditions on which Hitler would be willing to "spare" Britain from bloody defeat. The terms included giving Germany a free hand in Europe and against Russia in return for England's free hand in the Empire. In Point

(Continued on following page)

HESS'S "POISON FOOD" SAMPLES

These are some of the samples of "poisoned food" which Hess wrapped, sealed, and labeled during his imprisonment in England, suspecting that an "International (Jewish) conspiracy" was at work to sabotage his peace plans and to destroy his mind through poison. The upper sample is "blotting paper soaked in peach preserve probably containing *brain poison* and *corrosive acid.*" The lower samples are labeled, "to be opened only in the presence of neutral doctors."

(Continued from page 124)

VI the Nazi guilt for planning war ever since 1936 is projected to Churchill. Below the English text Hess continues in German (paragraph 2) his paranoid ruminations about the "mysterious medium" used by international conspirators to produce atrocities and poison the minds of foreign statesmen against Germany. (From a document in the author's collection.)

hibited an unbroken chain of paranoid and hysterical symptoms. He soon complained of plots to poison him or render him insane. Six weeks after his arrival, he made a demonstrative suicide attempt by plunging down a stairway, but succeeded only in fracturing his left thighbone. He continued to build up systematized delusions of plots on his life and/or sanity, naming officers who were supposedly involved and who were themselves insane. He singled out officers to bring his peace offers to the King in spite of the "Jewish conspiracy" to foil his efforts. He hid little notes about his room, sealed and labeled food samples containing "brain poison" for later analysis by neutral chemists, and even asked for containers to preserve specimens of his feces and urine.

By the end of the year (1941) the paranoid episode began to subside somewhat; but, in the meantime, marked hysterical symptoms became manifest. He developed numerous psychosomatic complaints, particularly severe abdominal cramps which caused him to double up demonstratively with the pain (supposedly caused by these same poisons). At the same time his memory became somewhat defective. By October, 1943 (when German armies bogged down at Stalingrad), he developed virtually complete amnesia and remained in that condition until February 4, 1945. During this period he could not remember his youth in Alexandria, his role in the Nazi party, or the identity of most of the people around him. On May 10, 1944, an attempt at evipan narcosynthesis was unsuccessful, and Hess refused to submit to any further treatment.

On February 4, 1945, Hess suddenly recovered his memory and declared in an agitated state that he had an important revelation to make to the world. He had discovered that the Jews had a secret power to hypnotize people and make them commit crimes against their will. Among the people so influenced were: the King of Italy, Winston Churchill, Anthony Eden, and the British psychiatrists, and of course Hess himself had been subjected to this evil influence. Later that day Hess asked for a bread knife, stabbed himself, and claimed that he had attempted suicide. The wound was a superficial flesh wound in the chest and required only two stitches to heal. It was obviously another hysterical demonstration. Later he claimed that the Jews had left the knife there to tempt him to suicide. Nevertheless, he went on a "suicidal hunger strike" for about a week until he was made to abandon it by the threat of forced feeding.

His memory and interest in the news remained normal for several more months. The delusional system continued on a tentative, rationalizing basis. Thus the explanation for the cap ture of the Remagen bridgehead was that the Jews had hypnotized the German soldiers guarding the bridge. But the defeat of Germany required more effective ego-protection, and in July, 1945, two months after the defeat and Hitler's suicide, Hess again suffered a relapse into amnesia. There was some evident conscious simulation at the beginning of this attack; but by the time he came to Nuremberg in October, 1945, the amnesia was virtually complete. It was in this state that he was examined by the writer and by international psychiatric commissions appointed by the Tribunal.

Hess remained in this state until November 30, when the decision on his competence was to be made in court. Prior to this session, the writer made a final attempt to challenge Hess by stating that he would probably be declared incompetent and sent back to his cell for good. This threat to his ego apparently helped to shock him out of his amnesia, and he later interrupted the proceedings to announce that he had recovered his memory and had, in fact, simulated amnesia all the time.

OBSERVATIONS AND EVALUATION

Test Results.—The Wechsler-Bellevue, Rorschach, and Thematic Apperception tests were administered both before and after Hess's first recovery from amnesia early in the trial. The clinical picture was essentially the same upon test and retest: a neurotic-schizoid personality with slightly above average intelligence, severely constricted in affect and creative-ideational capacity. The individual test results were as follows:

I.Q. Test. On the Wechsler-Bellevue I.Q. Test the general performance was slightly above average, but the large disparity on the subtest scores would indicate some kind of mental disturbance. Sensorimotor coordination and power of observation were about on the average adult level; comprehension and reasoning were above average adult. The span of apprehension as measured by the digit-span test fluctuated with his amnesic state, being below average during amnesia (five forward, four backward), above average during recovery (eight forward, seven backward), and far below average again upon relapse (four forward, three backward). The test of general information was above average, but showed some selective blocking during the amnesic period. The manner of response and performance during the original test showed a large element of ostentatious autosuggestive "helplessness" characteristic of the hysteric, although rapport was good. The performance was better upon retest, but the improvement could be largely attributed to the practice effect, except for digit-span. The repetition of many of the same failures ruled out his pretense of malingering on the original test. A reliable intelligence quotient cannot be given in this case, but it would lie somewhere around 120.

Thematic Apperception Test. The TAT responses were meager in the extreme, showing constriction of associative processes and of creative thinking far beyond normal limits. In spite of a good deal of prodding, he was able to give only a meager description of each picture, averaging about forty words, where the normal adult would spontaneously produce a story of 200-300 words on each picture. The material was entirely superficial and limited to the immediate situation represented by the stimuli. He proved to be incapable of projecting the situation into a continuity of past and future. When urged to try, he protested his lack of aptitude for fantasy and insisted: "I can't see any further than what is here." Because of the meagerness of production, only the slightest clues are given to the mechanism behind this rigid fixation on the immediate situation. In a few places, the situation suggests impotence, failure, escape into oblivion. Even in the realm of fantasy, Hess seemed to be forestalling frustration by not being able to think a given hypothetical situation through to its conclusion.

Rorschach. The meager Rorschach record of fifteen responses is characterized by: the lifelessness of the figures seen, showing lack of empathy and inner life; the tendency to superficial structural-whole and built-up-whole figures, indicating a tendency to superficial generalization in his outlook; the emotionally immature preoccupation with the animal and botanical world, and only lifeless details at that; emotional instability shown in the poor color control, breaking out into the hysterical "blood" response in one place, which is significantly rationalized by a built-up-whole interpretation. At the only places where a human figure and an animal figure were seen (both popular figures), they remain drawn designs rather than representations of living things. The only movement seen in the entire series is in a mechanical object. All of this bespeaks impotence and lack of vitality in his mental resources; a lack of resilience and adaptability, forcing him to break out occasionally into uncontrolled emotional reactions which are quickly rationalized. The environment consists essentially of figures without life, since there is no projection or contact in the dynamic sense.

Both the meager descriptiveness of the TAT and the lifelessness of the Rorschach show infantile regression to the precreative level. In general, the tests show erratic intellectual functioning at slightly above average-adult level, but a severely constricted personality with a most tenuous grip on reality.

Progress During Trial.—A few weeks after his sudden recovery Hess ceased to pretend to the writer that he had simulated his amnesia, but began to show signs of the old paranoid trend. On one occasion he asked the writer to sample some crackers he suspected of giving him headaches. On another he asked codefendant Albert Speer to try out some sugar and watch the effect on his bowel movements. Other prisoners began to remark on his secretive attitude about a "big revelation" he was going to make at the trial. His notes show that he intended to make a sensational revelation of the "mysterious power" exerted by the Jews to bring about the war, the atrocities, etc. In any event, as the evidence of the Nazi guilt piled up from week to week, Hess again had to retreat into his protective amnesia. Interestingly enough, in the course of his relapse, fearing that he would forget what some of his paranoid suspicions were, he jotted down reminders on the cardboard top of the writing table in his cell:

Do not take sleeping pills.
Instead of eggs ask for marmalade and bread.
Keep an empty stomach in the morning.

He showed genuine concern over his failing memory, particularly since his mental competence was an extremely delicate subject before his companions and the public press. In fact, a contributing factor to this withdrawal reaction was the testimony on his flight to England which made him look like such a fool in court that all his codefendants expressed disgust, amusement, or embarrassment. It was thus a struggle between his subconscious need for withdrawal from further frustration and his conscious desire to prove himself a worthy Nazi leader. The former proved stronger at this point, and by the beginning of March, 1946, he was once more in a state of total progressive amnesia. He forgot his entire past history once again and forgot more and more what was going on at the trial. The genuineness of the relapse was further confirmed by various circumstances in addition to direct observation: (a) the distress some of the other defendants showed at his failure to remember facts on which he had promised to testify in their behalf; (b) his repeated rereading of the same passages in the books he kept reading in the dock, calling Goering's attention to them each time as something he had just discovered; (c) his reluctant decision not to take the stand in his own defense, because he was afraid he would make a fool of himself on cross-examination. (He had thought he could get by on direct examination by reading previously prepared answers to his counsel's questions.)

In August Hess's defense counsel again raised the issue of his sanity. The Tribunal requested the writer to submit a report on his mental state with particular reference to his competence at the time of trial. We reviewed the facts of recurrent amnesia and feelings of persecution, but confirmed the psychiatrists' opinion that Hess was not legally insane. On the basis of this report the Tribunal decided that no further psychiatric examination was necessary and their original decision on his competence could stand.

But Hess's unstable behavior had not yet run its course. After complaining bitterly that he was in no condition to make his final speech before the Tribunal, he suddenly appeared in court on the last day of the trial. To everyone's astonishment, Hess pulled out some notes he had saved for the occasion and read a rambling paranoid speech about the "mysterious influence" under which he and many other political leaders had labored, the "glassy eyes" of the people so affected, etc. (These notes, like a full-dress speech he had prepared to deliver but had forgotten about, were evidently derived from the delusions he had systematized during his psychotic episode in England.) This was no doubt what was left of the "big revelation" he had been threatening all along. During the speech Hess suddenly snapped out of his amnesia once more and ended on a forthright note of Nazi fanaticism. The need to prove his mental competence in public had finally overcome the secondary gain of amnesia.

After a two-day period of active paranoid manifestations (stimulated by his recovered memory) he gradually returned to the comparatively "normal" state observed after his recovery in England and his previous recovery in Nuremberg: negativistic and seclusive in manner; mentally preoccupied with mild suspicions of persecution; but well oriented, with normal reasoning ability, fair insight, and excellent memory.

Further Observations and Discussion.—Throughout his imprisonment, Rudolf Hess was so negativistic, secretive, and amnesic, that very little information could be obtained from him directly, to evaluate his personality development and the particular appeal that Hitler's movement had for him. However, in his occasional moments of clear insight and communicative mood, he did reveal some of the confused idealism which had been a powerful motivating force among many of Hitler's followers.

In one of our first conversations after his dramatic recovery early in the trial, he revealed a curious interest in American democracy. He even pointed out that "national socialism had a good idea behind it too—doing away with class differences and making the people united."

Since it was one of the few comments he ever made about the social values of his Nazi creed, it is highly significant. The abolition of Junker privilege, the strengthening of ethnic pride and solidarity, even a paternalistic concern for the underprivileged—these provided motive enough for the passionate allegiance of the suggestible underdog, too frustrated to examine the rest of the picture. Hess said that like many of the other students in postwar Munich, he had been a man of passionately liberal ideas, opposed to war and the persecution of minorities, opposed to class privilege, and sympathetic to democratic ideas. Somewhere along the line, something had gone wrong. He admitted that racial persecution as practiced by the Nazis had defeated their idealistic intent. As for the war—well, he, at least, had tried to stop it. What did he think of Hitler in view of all that had happened? "I don't know—I suppose every genius has a demon in him. You can't blame him. It is just in him." Hess preferred not to discuss it. When the conflict became too great, he lost his memory again. In the meantime, he secretively prepared his "great revelation" about sinister forces at work in the world, while eyeing with suspicion the food that was passed to him.

The palpable psychopathology in Hess's case appeared to be directly related to this conflict of social values. Though it undoubtedly had its roots in his early emotional development, the breakdown into outright hysterical and paranoid symptoms was precipitated by social conflict: the incompatibility of humanitarian ideals and aggressive ethnocentricity, of the need for admiration and the attempt to win it by force. Hess carried to a pathological extreme some of the conflicts of ego-involvement inherent in Fascist dictatorship.

As in Hitler's case, the Nazi ideology gave Hess, the frustrated outsider, a blood-identification with the glorious race of Germans. Feelings of inferiority and rejection could be converted into the more acceptable feelings of persecution and martyrdom. These bonds had been sealed by their willingness to spill their blood for the Fatherland and by their imprisonment for their attempt to overcome the blot on the national honor. He had helped Hitler structure their vengeful heroic fantasies into a "geopolitical" framework. The heroic myth provided just as good an outlet for the gratifications of a basically passive personality like Hess, as it did for the basically aggressive Goering. There was no mistaking the difference in their personalities; yet each served the purposes of dictatorship well according to his fashion. The inherent sadomasochistic structure of authoritarianism provided each personality in the hierarchy with outlets according to his needs.

Thus Hess constantly sought and found some resolution of his anxieties along delusional-hysterical-masochistic lines, while Goering had ample outlet for his cynical realism, manipulation of the environment, and sadistic tendencies. Hess's speeches at party rallies and state functions were full of the mystic sentimentality and self-sacrifice that appealed to German women and some of the passive menfolk in that cultural setting; Goering's speeches were full of the heroic bombast and aggressiveness, even brutality that appealed to the urge for demonstrative virility among frustrated aggressors like himself. It was characteristic that at the time of the Roehm blood purge Hess merely rubber-stamped Hitler's orders for execution as a protective measure against the threat to the security of the state, while Goering went out and spilled some of the blood himself to eliminate competition for his power. It was also characteristic that after the outbreak of war Hess made a dream-inspired dramatic flight to England as a savior of Western culture while Goering was bombing open cities and looting occupied territories. And it was characteristic too that at the Nuremberg trial Hess was groping in a self-effacing fog of amnesia and persecutory feelings while Goering was trying to browbeat the defendants into helping him perpetrate a heroic fraud on the court and the press.

The acquisition of power by a passive incompetent like Hess may well have been an artifact of his loyalty to a successful dictator. But his relatively high esteem among a considerable section of the German public cannot be explained so easily. His control of party patronage and charities undoubtedly had a great deal to do with this. The somewhat paranoid nationalism and racialism which he fanatically shared with Hitler, and which was clearly enough expressed in *Mein Kampf* and in their political speeches, represented basic needs in both their personalities, but must also have struck a responsive chord in a considerable part of the German population. Much has been made of an alleged paranoid trend in German culture. which presumably placed a premium on paranoid leadership. It is true that the Nazi dictatorship behaved *as if* Germany were suffering from delusions of persecution and a neurotic need for hostile retaliation. But we must be careful not to deduce from the apparent policies of a country's government the clinical pathology of its population. Postwar politico-economic chaos and Allied intransigence over the Versailles Treaty must be granted as realities which could be played up by propaganda, while the resultant aggressions could be focused on convenient scapegoats. Response to such realities and to such suggestion may well have been within the limits of reality-testing available to the average German already culturally conditioned in that direction, and need not be regarded *ipso facto* as evidence of clinical paranoia. We must distinguish between the pseudoparanoia of cultural norms (when judged by the frame of reference of another culture), and the truly paranoid exaggerations or deviations from those norms.

The cultural frame of reference of the average German was such as to necessitate some belief in persecution of the ethnic ingroup. Hess's paranoia is a classical example of the pathological ego-involvement with and beyond the pseudoparanoid cultural norms. It will be recalled that German history, when taught to insecure anxiety-laden adolescents like Hitler and Hess, did provide an early vehicle for fantasies of persecution and grandeur, which gradually became delusionally systematized and obsessive as they faced the frustrations of adult life. Their individual paranoid tendencies reinforced each other in their own little paranoid microcosm. The projections of their aggressive impulses then fell on receptive ears among those similarly indoctrinated and frustrated. This influence spread among the masses in ever widening circles until the cultural norm was more or less passively subjugated to the paranoid aggression of the revolutionary group. It might thus be said that (*a*) some of the top leaders in the Nazi party were paranoid individuals structuring their delusional tendencies in the idiom of their culture and (*b*) *in a dictatorship* the pathology of the leaders easily becomes inflicted on the policies and destinies of a nation.

As for Hess's guilt reaction, it was clear that the very same pathology which had made him a fanatic adherent of Hitler's movement protected him from any acute guilt anxiety over its outcome. With the hysteric's *belle indifference* and the paranoiac's lack of insight, he either retreated into amnesia or waved it all aside with a blandly paranoid explanation of mysterious hypnotic influences at work in the world. The cream of the grim jest was contained in the speech he prepared to deliver to the Tribunal in which he denounced "International Jewry" for using its diabolical hypnotic influence on Hitler and other rulers to perpetrate class warfare and group extermination (!). It was a fitting denouement to an ideology that had thrived on paranoid (or pseudoparanoid) appeals ever since their first rabble-rousing speeches in Munich. Hitler, in the "political testament" he signed just before his suicide, had culminated his lifelong paranoid projection of guilt and inferiority by blaming the Jews for the war he had started and giving that as his justification for ordering their literal extermination. Hess merely went a step further: he blamed the Jews for their own extermination as well.

These culminations of lifelong paranoid tendencies may well raise the question whether Hess and Hitler were not actually insane at the conclusion of their careers, suffering from actual paranoid psychosis. Certainly, if such behavior had been encountered among leaders in our own cultural frame of reference, we should not have hesitated in declaring them psychotic, perhaps insane. But here we encounter the difficulty of distinguishing between the pseudoparanoid cultural influences (persecuted master race, etc.) and the genuine paranoid resolutions of our subjects' inferiority and guilt feelings. The *interaction* of these two influences in a dictatorship had, as we have already pointed out, intensified a latent social trend in which a certain amount of paranoia-like behavior was normal. The estimation of psychopathology is necessarily a matter of estimating the degree of deviation from that norm. In Hess's case our estimation of this allowable "cultural discount" was just sufficient to qualify his mental state as sane (i.e., legally responsible) though obviously pathological.

After he had finally returned to a comparatively "normal" state, we asked him once more whether he did not have some misgivings over Hitler's destructiveness. The context of the discussion, was one in which Hess was quite clearly aware that his Reich lay in ruins, millions of people had been killed in combat or exterminated on Hitler's order, and most of the top leaders were either dead or about to be hanged. Hess merely shrugged it all off, saying that one could not hold a man (i.e., either himself or Hitler) responsible for what he had done under the influence of drugs and hypnosis. The Führer's Deputy then began to hint at a new scheme he was formulating to save the world from further racial conflict and destruction.

—Which shows how difficult it is to draw the line between true paranoia and culturally conditioned pseudoparanoia.

HANS FRANK, DEVIL'S ADVOCATE

Any picture of the Nazi revolutionists would be seriously deficient if it did not include some representation of the satellites of the second magnitude in the Nazi constellation—especially those well-educated intellectuals who might have been presumed to have more rational frames of reference to evaluate the appeals of dictatorial demagoguery. Not all were as paranoid and obsessive as Hitler and Hess, nor as cynically avaricious as Goering. Yet their fanatic support and leadership in the movement was indispensable to the growth of the party and the final consolidation of its terror throughout Central Europe. Most revealing of the characters studied in the second rank of Nazi leadership was Hans Frank, Hitler's lawyer and later the tyrannical governor of Nazi-occupied Poland. His is a story of pathological impulses vs. *better judgment* in submitting to dictatorship in a time of socioeconomic stress, like so many of Hitler's revolutionary supporters.

LIFE HISTORY

Early Background.—Hans Frank was born in Karlsruhe, Baden, on May 23, 1900. He was the second of three children. Both parents were German-born but differed in religious background. The father was Lutheran, the mother, Old Catholic.

The children were baptized in the mother's church, in accordance with Bavarian tradition, but Hans never took any religious instruction seriously. Little is known (or could be elicited) about his youth and the parental relationships. The father, a lawyer of dubious repute, had settled in Munich the year after the birth of Hans. He was supposedly disbarred or suspended for embezzlement or some other malpractice. The details are not clear, but it is certain that Frank had great conflicts of loyalty toward the impeccable authoritarian figure who supposedly inspired him with respect for the law at an early age. Frank confided also that his father was partly Jewish in family background, a fact which both father and son had to hide during the Nazi era. There were thus at least two circumstantial reasons why Hans never fully resolved his identification with and submission to the paternal authority in keeping with the cultural norm. In view of our subject's reluctance to discuss these matters, no further information is available on just where these conflicts became acute in his development.

Frank received his education in Munich from public school right on through the university. He was apparently a bright though somewhat unstable student, revealing a hypomanic diversity of interests and flight of ideas. Much given to histrionics and emotional discourses on the arts, philosophy, politics, and law, he sought intellectual mentorship of any and all varieties. This brought him under the influence of a wide range of Munich characters, from Oscar Strauss and Oswald Spengler to Nicolai Lenin and Adolf Hitler. He entered the University of Munich to study law in 1919. As a young revolutionary spirit with a craving for social reform and status-through-aggression, he joined the German Workers party in 1919 and the Storm Troops in 1923. He took an active part in the political student brawls of postwar Munich, fighting now on the side of the left-wing Socialists, then again on the side of right-wing nationalist groups, but always with a sense of gratification that had been denied to those too young to fight for the Fatherland in 1914. He naturally took his place among the columns of student Storm Troopers who marched with Hitler during the abortive Munich *Putsch*. The failure of the *Putsch* was emotionally traumatic to this young revolutionist. However his graduation from the University of Munich that year as a junior barrister and his degree of dr. jur. (Doctor of Law) at the University of Kiel the following year provided some gratification and a new outlet for his status aspirations.

In 1925, while still studying for his bar examinations, Frank married Brigitte Herbst, a manufacturer's daughter, five years his senior. He entered into the marriage apparently more as an emotional and financial refuge than for love. Although the marriage was not a happy one, five children were born to the Franks during the succeeding fourteen years.

Frank passed the bar examinations in 1926 and opened up a law office in Munich in 1927. The postwar economic depression was still acute, and opportunities in the legal profession were extremely limited. Even his wife was in no position to get support from her side of the family. With one child already born and another on the way, Frank cast about for some way of putting his new legal license to use and promoting his political ambitions. He therefore answered an ad in the *Völkischer Beobachter* calling for volunteers to defend Nazi party members and publications against numerous suits for libel, slander, assault, treason, etc. Before embarking on this venture, he was warned by his old law professor: "Frank, take care! Political movements that begin in the criminal courts will end in the criminal courts!" But Frank was not to be deterred by notoriety. On the contrary, he flung himself into the fray with all the zest of a frustrated, intellectual-hypomanic personality. He won immediate success in getting Nazi rowdies off with light sentences. In 1928 Hess invited him to become Hitler's chief defense counsel. Seeing his big chance, Frank devoted himself passionately to the defense of the party and the Führer in and out of court. His private practice boomed as a result of the publicity this activity brought him. A gifted and experienced orator, Frank's facile argumentation won him recognition both in the courtroom and on the political platform. In 1929 he was appointed head of the legal department of the Supreme Party Directorate. The following year he was elected to the Reichstag. Frank worked feverishly to help Hitler to power even though he early recognized Hitler's contempt for law and lawyers.

When Hitler seized power in 1933, Frank expected to get the post of Reich minister of justice, but had to be content with the post of state minister of justice for Bavaria. He also became President of the German Academy of Law and Reich Leader of the National Socialist Jurists Association. His private practice continued to boom even after he had assumed his official post in Bavaria, and he made the most of his reputation as "The Führer's Counsel."

In 1934 one of the central actions of the Roehm purge took place in the prisons under Frank's jurisdiction. Frank had a slight telephonic altercation with Hitler and Hess over the legal technicalities involved, as we have seen, but he submitted to Hitler's orders to turn over Roehm and the other SA leaders to the SS firing squads. When Hitler abolished the state ministries of justice at the end of 1934 to do away with "legalistic quibbling," he appointed Frank Minister Without Portfolio instead, putting him "on good behavior." Fearing to risk the Führer's displeasure again, Frank compromised his conceptions of legal process to appease Hitler's dictatorial conceptions. Speeches and monographs appeared on "National Socialist Criminal Law" with profound rationalizations on the "protection of the State," etc.

In 1936 Frank was selected to make the first direct overtures for an alliance with Mussolini after Hitler had supported his aggression in Ethiopia. The Rome-Berlin Axis was subsequently formed. Frank continued to act as Hitler's placating messenger to Mussolini during the aggressions against Austria and Czechoslovakia in 1938 and 1939. He also enjoyed prominent participation in the state demonstrations of Axis solidarity in Berlin and Rome.

Governor-General of Poland.—When Poland was attacked, in 1939, Frank took up his reserve commission, but had no opportunity to participate in the fighting. After the *Blitzkrieg* against Poland he became Governor-General of that conquered territory. In his palace in Krakow he disported himself with the wilful cruelty and luxury of an Oriental tyrant. Never happy with his older wife, he dallied with mistresses from time to time and got immense sadistic satisfaction from the tyrannization of his Polish subjects. Hundreds of thousands of Poles were deported for slave labor; one and a half million Polish Jews were sent to concentration camps, where most were ultimately exterminated.

To the extent that any rationalization was necessary, the Nazi ideology provided a suitable ethnocentric rationale for the wilful self-indulgence that could not be squared with legalistic conceptions of social justice. He was now in complete agreement with the Führer, whose word was law, that old moral standards of religion, law, and social mores could not be considered binding on the instruments of Fate in the struggle for the survival of races. The notes of some of his first conferences as Governor-General of Poland (which he preserved in his voluminous diaries) indicate the general line that Frank laid down in applying the master-race philosophy to his segment of the New World Order:

> Fate has decreed that we are to be the masters here and the Poles our protected subjects. . . . It is not possible to give the Poles the standard of living of Germans. There must be a difference in the standard of living of the master race and the subjects. The Poles must recognize the limits of their possibilities of development. The Führer has reaffirmed, in response to my express inquiry, that they will have to keep to the limitations imposed by us. No Pole may rise above the status of labor-foreman. No Pole can be given the possibility to acquire a higher education. . . .
> As for the Jews, I tell you quite frankly, we'll have to put an end to (that problem) one way or another. The Führer once said: If organized Jewry should again succeed in letting loose a World War, then the sacrifice in blood will be suffered not merely by the nations agitated into war, but the Jews of Europe will have met their end. . . . I ask you first to agree with me on this principle: we can have sympathy only with the German people and with no one else in the world. The others never had any sympathy with us. I will therefore consider the Jews only in the expectation that they disappear. They must go. I have therefore begun negotiations to ship them to the East. . . . Gentlemen, I must ask you to fortify yourselves against any sympathetic

qualms. We must exterminate the Jews wherever we encounter them and wherever it is possible, in order to uphold the general task of the Reich here. That will of course have to take place by other (than legal) methods. . . . One cannot transpose accustomed viewpoints to such gigantic events. . . . (36)

In exercising his power as the absolute dictator of Poland, Frank got into violent jurisdictional disputes with Himmler on control over the State Police. He could not get satisfaction from Hitler on that issue. Frustrated in his exercise of power, he suddenly became violently conscientious again on the issue of legal process vs. the police state. He made several inflammatory speeches before bar associations in Leipzig, Vienna, Berlin, Munich, and Heidelberg, denouncing the police state and abolition of justice in Germany. Some of his statements reflected the highest ideals of civil liberties and constitutional government:

> Only by applying legal security methods, by administering true justice, and by clearly following the legislative ideal of law can the national community continue to exist. This legal method which permanently ensures the fulfilment of the tasks of the community has been assigned to you, fellow guardians of the law, as your mission. Ancient Germanic principles have come down to us through the centuries. (1) No one shall be judged who has not had the opportunity to defend himself. (2) No one shall be deprived of the incontestable rights which he enjoys as a member of the national community, except by decision of the judge. Honor, liberty, life, the profits of labor are among those rights. (3) Regardless of the nature of the proceedings, the reasons for the indictment, or the law which is applied, everyone who is under indictment must be given the opportunity to have a defense counsel who can make legal statements for him; he must be given a legal and impartial hearing. . . .
>
> One cannot debase law to an article of merchandise; one cannot sell it; it exists or it does not exist. Law is not an exchange commodity. If justice is not supported, the State loses its moral foundation; it sinks into the abyss of darkness and horror. . . . I shall continue to repeat with all the strength of my conviction that it would be an evil thing if ideals advocating a police state were to be presented as distinct National Socialist ideals, while old Germanic ideals of law fell entirely into the background. . . . (36)

When it suited his purposes, Frank could be the very incarnation of the spirit of constitutional government. To be sure, he had to clarify his "legal quibbling" by making it plain that his concepts of justice applied particularly to the German in-group. But there could be no sentimental compromise with legality in Hitler's dictatorship. Having again incurred the Führer's wrath, he was removed from all party and political offices in 1942, except that of civilian administrator of the Polish government. He was forced to reconcile himself to having Himmler's SS and Gestapo authority acting over his head and to cooperate in making Poland a territory subjugated to the police state of Nazi Germany.

Fearing to risk the Führer's displeasure again, he outdid himself in "cooperating" with Himmler's terror organization with sadistic delight. The diaries he kept at that time give extraordinary evidence of the maniacal brutality with which he identified with the master race and supervised over the reign of terror: "The Poles shall be the slaves of the Great German World Empire," etc. Such statements alternated with expressions of "cultural idealism" conceived in terms of the spread of the superior German culture to the benighted Slav people.

Before the Russian assault finally overran Poland in 1944, Frank escaped to Bavaria, the last stronghold of the police state where most of the Nazi officials were seeking refuge. When captured on May 1, 1945, two days after Hitler's suicide, Frank likewise attempted suicide by slashing his throat and his wrists. He recovered under American medical care and was ultimately transported to Nuremberg to stand trial as a major war criminal. Here he underwent a conversion to Roman Catholicism while awaiting trial.

OBSERVATIONS AND EVALUATION

When Frank was examined before the beginning of the trial, he was recovering from the effects of his suicide attempt and had just undergone his conversion to Roman Catholicism. The gashes across his throat and wrists were still healing, and he was in a highly agitated state of abject repentance. The tests were administered at appropriate moments after positive transference had been established. (In Frank's highly emotional state, it quickly went beyond ordinary rapport.) The tests showed him to be one of the most intelligent of the Old Fighters, as well as one of the most unstable emotionally. In view of his previous case history, we may justifiably assume that the emotional aspect was not merely a concomitant of the situation, but rather an intensification of a basic personality pattern.

Test Results.—The modified Wechsler-Bellevue was administered, as well as a retest on the Rorschach.

I.Q. Test. He achieved high-average to maximal scores on the eight subtests selected from the Wechsler-Bellevue, obtaining a total I.Q. of 130. His lowest scores were on the memory-span and the timed performance tests, probably reflecting his emotional tension. He later demanded a retest on the memory-span and improved his score from 7 digits forward and 5 backward to 8 digits forward and 6 backward. (Oddly enough, the war criminals became ego-involved in comparing their memory-span scores. However, only the original standard trials were counted, except in the special case of Rudolf Hess.) Frank suffered a genuine handicap on the block-designs test, since his left hand was still incapacitated from the slashing of his wrists, and he had to manipulate the blocks with one hand. In any case, the I.Q. of 130, which was the mode and approximate mean of the entire group of Nazi leaders studied, was probably an underestimate of his general intelligence in comparison to the others. This was inherent not so much in the test situation as in the limitations of the ordinary I.Q. test itself, which could not tap Frank's superior capacities on the level of social abstractions. He was far superior to Goering, for example, in his grasp of philosophical abstractions, artistic and literary nuances, and all social issues. It cannot be denied, however, that his insight and judgment were handicapped by his emotional impetuosity. It is noteworthy that Frank alone, of all the intelligent German leaders tested, responded to the question, "What would you do if you were in a theater and saw smoke?" by saying, "I'd holler *'Fire!'*" Frank's social insight apparently did not extend to the danger of panic in a crowded theater—or in a frustrated society.

Rorschach. The Rorschach record reveals both the creativity of Frank's intellect and the emotional distractions under which it suffered. The highly productive record of fifty vividly seen figures strikingly reflects Frank's compulsive, hypomanic flight-of-ideas, embellished with transcendental philosophical abstractions and unearthly fantasies. The impressive number of good original interpretations of the inkblots, the variety of living human and sub-human figures seen, and the use of half the cards for symbolic abstractions show vivid creative imagination. But they also reveal a too fanciful, impetuous temperament, a labile, cyclothymic affect alternating between euphoria on the verge of ecstasy and fits of abject depression. His productivity on the test fluctuated from 2 to 10 responses per card, ebbing and flowing in waves of intense feeling that were only loosely related to the usual stimulus-value of the cards. (Frank himself admitted being "such an emotional and impressionable individual, given to these sudden outbursts of emotion.")

The presence of strong precipitating conflicts in the psychosexual sphere is indicated by the way in which sexual sensuality, romantic and phallic symbolism, and ecstatic artistic creations alternated in his fantasy with objects of misanthropic repulsion and morbid masochism. Thus one inkblot suggests "woman's breasts," another "a beautiful ballerina in a white dress." Then another inkblot becomes "two ugly heads—one-eyed cyclops—horrible!" and the next one turns into "a grave . . . a symbol of death; *pieta!*" A good example of the sublimation of psychosexual tensions into mystic and religious symbolism is the interpretation of one of the inkblots as "A wonderful sword going up into the light—it comes from the fire inside the earth, through the green earth, into the sunlight— *magnificent!* . . . (on inquiry, gasps on seeing card again). . . . It is a cosmic symbol of life: we rise from the earth, through life, into the heaven above. . . ."

The perseveration of this almost paranoid symbolism is evident throughout the record and even afterward, as he continues to respond to the stirring of these tenuously resolved libidinal conflicts: "It is uncanny;—they are just inkblots, but it shows that beauty and a deeper meaning can be concealed in the most unassuming forms. . . . You know, it is terrifying! A man wants to make an inkblot—and the *ink itself* makes a symbol of life! It just shows that the spiritual world is greater than any man's will.—You psychologists are ingenious in using such methods." All of which presents an interestingly subjective interpretation of subjectivity in perception—all the more interesting in view of Frank's religious conversion and guilt reaction. The burden of his guilt (which was related to his infatuation with Hitler, as we shall soon see), was so great that it had to be borne by cosmic and supernatural forces. His own guilt feelings were somehow more tolerable when he could think of himself as only the insignificant instrument of such forces —the ever reliable *Schicksal* of German political philosophy. The reification and animism he expressed in making his interpretations were strikingly reminiscent of primitive religion. There was also a kind of infantile regression in the animal stereotypy, which was in keeping with this pattern.

Nevertheless, Frank was never quite out of contact with reality. He could see all of the commonplace "popular" figures, make normal use of the large concrete details on the inkblot cards, and show good reality-testing in the uniformly high quality of form throughout the entire series of interpretations; the sequence of whole and detail figures was loose and unsystematic, but far from confused.

All in all, the Rorschach test showed that Frank was operating on the level of the intelligent neurotic, rather than the psychotic, although the ideation had a distinctly paranoid flavoring. A combination of cyclothymic and schizoid trends could be seen in the stream of exhaustive productivity down to the smallest detail on some cards, which suddenly froze up into a sort of detached aversion to reality in his reaction to other cards. If it is possible for a man to show both manic-depressive and schizophrenic tendencies, Frank was such a man. He certainly revealed himself, at any rate, to be a man of violent conflicts, ambivalence, and disorganized psychic energies.

Further Observations During Trial.—The case history and psychological examination have already shown that Frank represented a somewhat different type of personality from the other revolutionists we have studied—a sensitive, gifted, and very cultured intellectual, highly responsive to aesthetic cultural values, but torn to distraction by violent emotional conflicts. In the nature of his conflicts, however, Frank represented a fairly large sample of Hitler's most passionate supporters among the Old Fighters. A year of close study of this particularly responsive and introspective Nazi revealed a great deal about the psychodynamics of this relationship.

We have already had evidence that Frank was quite capable of understanding what a catastrophe Hitlerism represented to

German and European culture. If he was ever confused on that score, his intellectual friends had repeatedly set him straight. His old law professor had warned him about what he was getting into at the outset. Gregor Strasser had later explained to him why the Party was "going to the dogs." And Oswald Spengler had made his prediction of catastrophe to Frank upon Hitler's seizure of power. Frank's own speeches during the Hitler regime showed that he did have some conception of the danger of subjugating law and civil liberties to one man's capricious will in a police state. And finally, under observation in Nuremberg, he was one of the few Old Fighters who showed any real conception of the social catastrophe they had brought about. Certainly his passionate denunciation of Hitler, in one of our first conversations, for all its hindsight and new-found religious fervor, revealed not a little psychological insight into Hitler's character:

> (*November 7, 1945, Frank's cell.*) "You know, there is a divine punishment which is far more devastating in its irony than any punishment man has yet devised! Hitler represented the spirit of evil on earth and recognized no power greater than his own. God watched this band of heathens puffed up with their puny power and then simply brushed them aside in scorn and amusement." Frank brushed them aside with his gloved hand. "I tell you, the scornful laughter of God is more terrible than any vengeful lust of man! When I see Goering, stripped of his uniform and decorations, meekly taking his ten-minute walk under the curious, amused eyes of the American guards, I think of how he reveled in his glory as President of the Reichstag. It is grotesque! Here are the would-be rulers of Germany—each in a cell like this, with four walls and a toilet, awaiting trial as ordinary criminals. Is that not a proof of God's amusement with men's sacrilegious quest for power?" His smile gradually froze and his eyes narrowed to slits. "But are these people thankful for these last few weeks in which to atone for their sins of egotism and indifference, and to recognize that they have been in league with the devil incarnate? Do they get on their knees and pray to God for forgiveness?—No, they worry about their own little necks and cast about for all kinds of little excuses to absolve themselves of blame! Can't they see that this is a horrible tragedy in the history of mankind, and that we are the symbols of an evil that God is brushing aside?" His voice had been raised in anger and he apologized as the guard peeked into the cell curiously.

He continued in cold, quiet anger: "If only one of us had the courage to shoot him dead! That's the one thing for which I reproach myself. What misery, death, and destruction would have been spared! I began to come to my senses in 1942, and realized what evil was embodied in him. When I protested against terror measures in public at that time, he deprived me of military rank and political power—but he let me sit as the figurehead Governor-General of Poland, to go down in history as the symbol of the crimes in that miserable country.—That was the satanical evil in him. And so here I sit—but it serves me right—I was in league with the devil in the beginning. In later years I realized what a cold-blooded, hard, insensitive psychopath he really was. That so-called fascinating look of his was nothing but the stare of an insensitive psychopath! He was moved by sheer primitive, wilful egotism, unrestrained by form and convention.—That's why he hated all legal, diplomatic, and religious institutions—all the social values that represented restrictions to his impulsive ego-expression. . . .

"No, the psychopathic hatred of form and convention was the real keynote of Hitler's personality. . . ."

Why then did Hans Frank follow Hitler through dictatorship, war, and genocide, right to the very end, never breaking with him, and attempting suicide only after Hitler had taken his own life?

As with the other Old Fighters, the reasons were both material and psychodynamic. Frank showed clear insight into his own material motives, and semiconscious awareness of the psychodynamic. The material motivation hardly needs elaboration here. *"Ambition!"* said Frank, summing it up, "that had a lot to do with it. Just imagine—I was a Minister of State at thirty; rode around in a limousine, had servants. . . ." But there were other means of acquiring status for an intelligent lawyer who might not have wanted it at Hitler's price. Why was Frank impelled to identify his aspirations with Hitler's when he had been repeatedly warned and knew better? That is where the psychodynamic side of the motivation comes into play. If we can once grasp this interrelationship of the psychodynamic and the material in their motivation, we can understand much about the forces that drew the Old Fighters together long before it was really politically opportune, and kept them together long after it was obviously bent on defeating its material purpose. Our most valuable clues lie between the lines of Frank's introspective effusions, as the following excerpts from the examiner's *Diary* show:

> (*January 10, 1946, Frank's cell.*) "It is interesting to observe one's own reactions. It is as though I am two people.—Me. myself, Frank here—and the other Frank, the Nazi leader. And sometimes I wonder how that man Frank could have done those things. This Frank looks at the other Frank and says, 'Hmm, what a louse you are, Frank!—How could you do such things?— You certainly let your emotions run away with you, didn't you?' —Isn't that interesting? I am sure as a psychologist you must find that very interesting.—Just as if I were two different people: I am here myself—and that other Frank of the big Nazi speeches over there on trial.—Fascinating, isn't it?"
>
> (Responding to the examiner's quotation from *Faust*—"Two souls, alas, dwell in my breast!"): "Yes, we do have evil in us— but don't forget that there is always a Mephistopheles who brings it out. He says, 'Behold! the world is wide and full of temptation —behold! I will show you the world!—There is just a little triviality of handing over your soul!' . . . And so it was.—Hitler was the devil. He seduced us all that way."
>
> The metaphor of seduction must have stirred something deeply latent within him, because it perseverated, and he returned to it after the conversation had gone off on another tangent. "You know, the people are really feminine.—In its totality, it is female. One should not say *das Volk* (neuter), one should say *die Volk* (feminine).—It is so emotional, so fickle, so dependent on mood and environment, so suggestible—it idolizes virility so—that is it."
>
> It was interesting that he was using the same terms in describing the *Volk* as he had used in previous conversations to describe himself. "And it is so ready to obey—" I suggested further, with obvious reference to the German *Volk*.
>
> "That, yes—but not merely obedience—*surrender*—like a woman. You see? Isn't it amazing?" He burst into explosive laughter as though tickled by projection into a lewd joke. The identification was unmistakable. "—And that was the secret of Hitler's power. He stood up and pounded his fist, and shouted, 'I am *the man!*'—and he shouted about his strength and determination—and so the public just surrendered to him with hysterical enthusiasm.—One must not say that Hitler *violated* the German people—he *seduced* them! They followed him with a mad jubilation, the like of which you have never seen in your life.—It was a madness—a drunkenness."

Latent Homosexuality.—It was this obviously projected latent homosexuality (submission to the virile authoritarian figure),[6] in addition to his ruthless ambition, which apparently drove Frank to follow Hitler to the very hell of which he spoke.

The importance of homosexuality, both latent and overt, in cementing the bonds of fanatic devotion to Hitler's cause need not be overestimated, but it did play a part among the revolutionary group. Ernst Roehm and many of his leading Storm Troopers were active homosexuals. Their rebellion against the social norms and their furious desire to prove their manhood by sadistic brutality is clinically understandable. In a similar manner, but on a more subtle and intellectualized plane, the latent-homosexual revolutionists like Hans Frank were driven by passionate devotion to the paternalistic symbol of virility and authority represented by the man who "pounded his fist and shouted, 'I am *the man!*'—and shouted about his strength and determination." Above and beyond the prevalent submissiveness to authority which can be accounted for by the authoritarian cultural lag, Frank and many like him experienced something akin to "surrender—like a woman . . . a madness—a drunkenness"—indeed, a symbolic orgasm in submitting to such overpowering strength.

In that connection, a slight clue to the meaning that Hitler's later rejection and cruelty might have had for Hans Frank is provided by his description of his last meeting with Ernst Roehm. The Storm Troop leader, as we recall, was executed in Stadelheim prison where Minister of Justice Frank exercised local jurisdiction. With tender sympathy, Frank described his last visit with Roehm in his cell. He could hardly believe that this virile-looking officer, who wielded such tremendous power, was a homosexual. But he felt that there was true gentle goodness in Roehm's soul as he faced death. Roehm's last words had been, "All revolutions devour their own children." For Frank, this long-remembered comment must have had the meaning: "He seduces us only to destroy us." At any rate, Frank said

---

[6] Hitler also projected the idea that the masses (in his culture) were like a woman, "who will submit to the strong man rather than dominate the weakling—thus the masses love the ruler . . ." (33)

that he often thought of brash but gentle Roehm, who was one of the first to suffer the Führer's wrath, as he sat on his cot in the grey cell of the Nuremberg jail, fully resigned to death.

For there was more than a realization of legal guilt in Frank's attempt to commit suicide, in his abject confessions of guilt, and in his resignation to the death sentence. Life had become intolerable after the Führer had committed suicide. The strong undercurrent of blighted homosexual drive could be seen even in the guilt expiation of his religious conversion in jail. It was as though the ruthless dictator who had seduced him only to destroy him had betrayed him by committing suicide, leaving him to bear the guilt of their sinful relationship alone. This intolerable anxiety could be resolved only by dissociation of the ego and displacement of the guilt, with an infantile regression through religion which he did not really believe.

(*December 22, 1945, Frank's cell.*) "It is such torture to sit through the trial.—Such horrible things are laid coldly before us and before the world—things we knew; things we didn't know; things we didn't *want* to know.—And one *just sinks in shame*—!" I looked him straight in the eye questioningly and the meaning of the shame became clearer as he went on. "—Oh, *ja*—the shame is devastating.—Such fine men, those judges and the prosecuting attorneys—such noble figures—the Englishmen—the Americans —especially that fine tall Englishman.—And they sit on the opposite side, and I sit here among such repulsive characters as Streicher—Goering—Ribbentrop.—Ah, well," he sighed, "there is nothing that can be done about it. . . . I am glad that you and Pater Sixtus, at least, still come to talk to me. You know, Pater Sixtus is such a wonderful man.—If you could say 'virgin' about a man, you would say it about him—so delicate, so sympathetic, so maidenly—you know what I mean. And religion is such a comfort—my only comfort now. I look forward to Christmas now like a little child.—You know, even if I sometimes wonder in my deepest subconscious, whether this belief in life after death is really only a phantasmagoria—whether life doesn't essentially end in a cold grave—and *bing! finis!*—then it is still good that one clings to the illusion to the very end.

". . . I gave those diaries so that I could rid myself once and for all of the other Frank. Those three days after Hitler committed suicide were decisive—the turning point of my life. After he had led us on and set the whole world in motion, he simply disappeared—deserted us, and left us to take the blame for everything that had happened. Can one simply disappear after all that, and wipe one's footsteps out of the sand, leaving no trace?—One realizes at a moment like that how insignificant one is—'planet bacilli,' as Hitler used to call mankind."

Renunciation.—Frank kept wavering between his need to renounce his Nazi self and his need to be still loved by his Nazi jailmates. This ambivalence expressed itself most clearly in his ambivalence toward Goering. "I don't know what to think about Goering—he can be so charming at times—really!" And as the time for his defense approached: "I don't know—is it right to denounce one's comrades and pass judgment on one's leader—give them a last kick down the stairs, so to speak?" The mass murder testimony of Colonel Hoess (Chapter 6) finally tipped the scales of ambivalence to confession and renunciation of "the evil Frank." When asked whether he felt morally guilty for the mass extermination of Jews at Auschwitz, even though it was not in his immediate jurisdiction, lawyer Frank pleaded guilty:

> (*April 18, 1946.*) "I say 'yes'. . . . I myself have never installed an extermination camp for Jews, or promoted the existence of such camps. But if Adolf Hitler personally has laid that dreadful responsibility on his people, then it is mine too, for we have fought against Jewry for years; and we have indulged in the most horrible utterances. My own Diary bears witness against me. Therefore it is no more than my duty to answer your question in this connection with 'yes.' A thousand years will pass and still this guilt of Germany will not have been erased."

Frank delivered himself of this confession of guilt, because he knew full well how vital a role the propaganda of hate had played in the murderous conspiracy, and because his new-found religious fervor demanded that he purge himself by confession before his Maker. But there was deeper motivation underlying his legal and religious confessions of guilt: the outcome of the same motivation that had driven him to follow his virile evil genius—the need to expiate the guilt of a sinful love, to put an end to the torment of identification with a hideous alter ego.

Having delivered himself of this confession, Frank felt a tremendous emotional relief, to which he gave expression in religious ecstasy. The underlying psychodynamics of this relief could be seen immediately between the lines of his reaction to his own confession, when interviewed in his cell the next day:

(*April 19, 1946, Frank's cell.*) "Well, today is Good Friday, and I am at peace because I have kept my oath [to confess]. Yesterday I stood before the black gates, and now I have passed through to the other side.—I stood before the black gates in bare feet and sackcloth with a candle in my hand like a penitent sinner—or a Vestal Virgin—and spoke once more before God and the world.—Now I have paid my bill and passed through the black gates and do not belong to this world any more. . . . Doctor, will history ever get over this degradation of human civilization that Hitler brought us to? There is no doubt that that demon Hitler brought us to this. . . . And that man wore the mask of a human being!—the Chief-of-State! . . . I am going to write you that essay on Hitler that I promised you, but do you know that he is actually repulsive to me now? Now that he is unmasked and I see what a horrible, repulsive man I have been following, I am nauseated!" He leaned on the table with his elbow, his face in his hands, with eyes squinting as if in a trance. "—It is as if Death put on the mask of a charming human being, and lured workers, lawyers, scientists, women and children—everything— to destruction!—And now we see his face unmasked as it really was—a Death's-head skeleton! Doctor, it is terrifying!—it is repulsive!"

Repeatedly Frank warned the writer: "Beware of these demagogues—these agents of Satan. It is not with a hideous face and horns sprouting out of his forehead that the Devil appears among us.—Oh, no!—Rather as a sympathetic personality with lovely grey eyes, full of compassion and winning ways."

The attraction and repulsion of his evil alter ego reached a passionate crescendo as Frank approached death. In his final plea to the Tribunal, he literally assumed the role of Devil's Advocate and pleaded Hitler's case as identified with his own —then denounced his client as the Antichrist.

Finally, as he awaited the death sentence, he feverishly divested himself of a thousand-page essay on Hitler, to aid the writer in analyzing the mysterious character who had made men like him do what they did. In this manuscript he left a record of what was for him his last communion with his evil alter ego. For us it presents a remarkable record of the last introspections of a Nazi fanatic, such as no ordinary observation could ever have elicited, and only a demonstrative, hypomanic sadomasochist would ever have recorded so fully. With a persistent passionate ambivalence he reviews the glories of revolutionary reconstruction and the catastrophe of nihilistic philosophy; the appeal to humanitarian symbols and the acts of incredible inhumanity; the patriotism that concealed unbridled ambition, and the "loyalty which camouflaged our moral cowardice." And for himself, there was the passion for legal and social justice, which had become perverted to a conspiracy in utter depravity, because of his passionate devotion to the Führer's cause. The Devil's Advocate had realized only too late that his patron was one who had no use for the laws of God or man. Describing Hitler's oath to abide by the Weimar Constitution in the Leipzig trial, Frank apostrophizes him with the mystic, passionate incantation of an ancient priest exorcising a devil:

> If thou, Adolf Hitler, canst be conjured up out of Heaven or deepest Hell, answer me! *Adolf Hitler, hast thou kept this oath,* which thou hast sworn before the highest judges of our people, and later in being sworn in as Chancellor? Adolf Hitler—thou art vanished, gone into the night, thy Reich destroyed, thy people ruined—because thou hast betrayed God in this oath!—because thy name will be forever accursed for replacing the justice of thy people by thine own sheer capricious will!

For Hitler had not only betrayed God; he had seduced and deceived his lawyer and lover, Hans Frank.

As he awaited death after the sentence had been pronounced, and he heard how Schacht and Von Papen had been acquitted only to be hounded by an outraged populace, he paused in his penitent meditations long enough to have a last hysterical laugh at the diplomats who had also made their pact with the Devil: "Hahahaha!—They thought they were free!—Don't they know, there *is* no freedom from Hitlerism! Only *we* are free of it! We got the best deal after all! Hahahaha! . . . We swore loyalty to our Führer unto death!—*That is the only way out!*—Hahahahaha. . . ."

A really tortured soul, Frank welcomed death as the only escape from the violent neurotic conflicts that had made him a fanatic Nazi.

Chapter 4

THE DIPLOMATS

We have already shown, in describing Hitler's rise to power, how a group of "sophisticated realists," representing some of the political and financial interests, helped to secure his seizure of power at a time when his movement was actually on the decline. We designate this group as "the diplomats" because they were either seasoned diplomats in fact, or were identified with that group by their aspirations to political power and their success in obtaining it. Unlike the revolutionists, the men who came to Hitler's support at this critical time did not do so out of any pathological need for outlets for aggression; they suffered from no paranoid ego-involvement with the cultural myths, nor did they follow Hitler in tormented response to libidinal urges. To understand their motives we require, for the most part, no devious excursions into the realm of depth psychology. Their motivation is quite apparent on the level of social values, group identifications or aspirations—and plain political opportunism.

Individually, they were fairly normal representatives of their culture in positions of leadership even before Hitler came to power. Unlike the revolutionists, they were *as a rule* men of good education, cosmopolitan background, and success in their chosen careers. They were the leading conformists who upheld the existing institutions of state, law, church, and capital. Paradoxically, they represented the very powers against which the revolutionists were rebelling. The expediency of the alliance for Hitler's purposes has already been made clear. But the paradox of the conformists' support of a revolutionary dictato requires a word of explanation before we proceed with our individual cases. The key to the paradox lies not only in the duplicity of Hitler's stated purposes, but in the traditional authoritarian mentality of German leadership up to modern times.

Long before either Hitler or the contemporary diplomats had come upon the scene, the history of social institutions in Germany—from the family to church and state—had perpetuated an authoritarian psychology which permeated the entire culture. The century-old traditions of autocratic rule by princes and Kaisers, of aggressive ethnocentricity, class privilege, and militant nationalism had laid a poor foundation for any ready acceptance or even comprehension of true liberal democracy. Even the churches, with their religious wars and outbreaks of fanatic sadism, had too often competed with each other and with the state as alternative arbiters of authority. Finally, as we have already seen, the pressure of economic desperation after World War I had put the newborn democratic state to a more severe test than it was capable of withstanding in such a culture, without truly inspired leadership at home and far-sighted statesmanship abroad. These conditions not only enabled a group of fanatic nationalists to "seduce" the German people into a regressive submission to authority but also enabled a group of sophisticated power-seekers to exploit the resurgent authoritarian nationalism for their own ends without doing violence to their own basic values.

Some of the politicians who had a major share in facilitating Hitler's seizure of power were aristocratic statesmen of the Kaiser Wilhelm and Marshal von Hindenburg school. They had never overcome their conceptions of authoritarian government and class privilege, and they were willing to appease a revolution for the sake of maintaining some semblance of authority for their identification group. Ex-Chancellor Franz von Papen and ex-Foreign Minister Baron von Neurath were among the personalities we had occasion to study in this group. It was such men who most clearly symbolized the authoritarian cultural lag in the political leadership of Germany. Another group was comprised of ambitious businessmen with political and aristocratic *aspirations*. Emulating the hereditary aristocracy in their desire to "belong" to the ruling group of the "best people," they were generally ambivalent toward the principles of democratic social change. Hitler provided them with an opportunity to satisfy their ambitions to belong to the ruling class by making up 'in financial support what they lacked in birth. That opportunity resolved their ambivalence. Foreign Minister "von" Ribbentrop and banker Hjalmar Schacht were among the divergent personalities in the businessmen's contingent of the "political bandwagon." For the purposes of this study, the principal Junker diplomat (Von Papen) and the most successful businessman-turned-diplomat (Von Ribbentrop) will provide the foci of our portrayal of the "political bandwagon" that helped put the revolutionists into the saddle.

Since psychopathology is secondary here, we shall subordinate it to a consideration of the social value judgments and motives of our subjects. Even without the need for excursions into the pathological, an understanding of their behavior requires the approach of psychodynamic-social interaction.

EX-CHANCELLOR VON PAPEN

The Prussian Junker caste was long identified in German history as the hard core of the ruling class from the early Prussian monarchy to the modern Greater Germany of Bismarck and the Kaisers. This caste, strictly speaking, consisted of the land-owning hereditary aristocracy of Prussia, who constituted at the same time the military elite of the realm. Traditionally the young Junkers served as officers in designated regiments, then either entered the diplomatic service or waited to retire to their estates upon the death of their fathers. By intermarriage and nepotism within their own circumscribed in-group, the Junkers maintained a firm control of the military, economic, and diplomatic power of the nation. By the time of World War I, however, this "hard core" had become rather diluted by many intermarriages and political associations with families of diverse origins, so that the term "Junker clique" could be applied only loosely to designate a militaristic-landed-aristocracy social identification group. Within this looser extension of an old ruling class would be included Franz von Papen, one-time Chancellor of the Weimar Republic under Junker President von Hindenburg. This was the Von Papen who made way for Hitler's appointment as Reich Chancellor and continued to serve in his government to the very end. It is in such a personality that we must seek some explanation for the most glaring paradox of loyalties in the strange alliance that brought Hitler to power.

LIFE HISTORY

Early Background.—"I was born on soil which has been in the possession of my family for 900 years. I grew up with conservative principles which unite a man most closely with his own folk and his native soil, and as my family has always been a strong supporter of the Church, I of course grew up in this tradition as well. As the second son I was destined for a military career. . . ." With these words of self-identification, Franz von Papen introduced himself to the International Military Tribunal before whom he was defending his career. His introduction neatly sets the pattern of Junker tradition, except that the church affiliation in Von Papen's case was Catholic, rather than Lutheran. The "native soil" to which he referred was the family estate at Werl, Westphalia (in the Saar basin, at the western end of Prussia), where he was born in 1879. His father had been an officer under Bismarck and had participated in the Franco-Prussian wars of the 1860's and 1870's. His mother was descended from the landed aristocracy of Düsseldorf. Franz was the third of five children. As far as could be determined, there were no unusual childhood diseases or behavior symptoms.

He attended the local public school (under Catholic tutelage) and was sent to a military academy at the age of eleven, then to the officers' military academy at Grosslichterfelde, in Berlin, in accordance with Junker tradition. He also served as a page-boy at the Imperial Court of the Kaiser. Thus thoroughly indoctrinated in the militaristic and aristocratic traditions of his father's identification group, Franz von Papen became a full-fledged member when he was commissioned a lieutenant in the Kaiser's Cavalry at the age of eighteen. For the next few years he enjoyed the social advantages of his station. He rode to the hounds in Leicestershire, England, mingled with the Continental aristocracy in London and Paris, and enjoyed the favors of the Kaiser's Court in Berlin.

In 1904 he married the daughter of a rich Saar industrial baron, Martha von Boeck-Gothau. "The relatives of this family brought me in contact with many French and Belgian families, and in this way I acquired an intimate knowledge of the spiritual and cultural factors of these neighboring countries, which made a very strong impression on me at the time." Five children resulted from this marriage.

Von Papen attended the General Staff Academy in Berlin from 1905 to 1910 and achieved the much-coveted appointment to the General Staff in 1913. In that year the Kaiser decided to groom him for the diplomatic service and sent him to Mexico and the United States as military attaché to the German ambassador.

With the outbreak of war in 1914, Von Papen was given the assignment of secretly contracting for the delivery of war matériel to Germany. When his activities were exposed in 1915, he was forced to leave America. From 1915 to 1917, Von Papen commanded a regiment on the Western Front. From 1917 to 1918, he was the operations staff officer of the Army Group operating in Turkey and Palestine. In 1918 he was chief of staff of the 4th Turkish Army when they were defeated by General Allenby. "When in November 1918 I was negotiating with Ataturk about the evacuation of the German troops, we received the news of the collapse of the German armies and the abdication of the German Kaiser. This fact meant for me not only the loss of the war, a whole world had collapsed for me. The German Reich had collapsed after a thousand years of development, and everything that we had believed in was shrouded in the mists of the future." Von Papen returned to his estate in Westphalia, Germany, to find "a country riddled with revolution." The royal guarantor of Junker security had fled to Holland; socialist agitation threatened to knock the very props from under the structure of landed aristocracy.

In such a crisis Von Papen, like the rest of the Junker set, tried as best he could to preserve the remnants of his old way of life, with his accustomed group identifications and social values. He sought psychological refuge and meaning in church activities and politics. Unlike Hitler's revolutionary group of the socially disinherited, Von Papen had roots in the past and ties with such symbols of authority as still remained in Germany—the battered citadels of the church, the General Staff, and aristocratic diplomatic corps. No doubt Von Papen considered himself a middle-of-the-road liberal within that conservative frame of reference. "I decided not to join the Right, the German National Party, but the (Catholic) Center party. This decision was influenced by my conviction that in this party I would be able to do much more in making adjustments in the social sphere than among the Conservatives. At the same time this party represented the principles of a Christian concept of the State." (36)

In 1922 he was elected to the Prussian Parliament as a representative of the Catholic Center party. He described his role in the political conflicts of the time as follows: "The eight years in which I belonged to Parliament were filled with struggles for the internal recovery and strengthening of the German Republic. In the Center Party I represented the conservative ideas of my agricultural electors. I endeavored to make this party, which in Prussia had formed a coalition with the Left, form a coalition with the Right also. Thus I wanted to help create an outlet for the tensions out of which National Socialism was really born. Also, into the same period fall my efforts to remove the discriminations against Germany through the numerous terms of the Versailles Treaty, and that by way of reaching a better understanding with the French people."

From Chancellor to Ambassador.—In June, 1932, when Chancellor Brüning's government collapsed, his old friend President von Hindenburg appointed Von Papen Chancellor of the Weimar Republic. As Von Papen described the situation: "Dr. Brüning, my predecessor in office, was highly esteemed by all of us and had been welcomed with great expectations. During his period of office came the great economic crisis, the customs blockades by other countries, with production and trade almost completely at a standstill, with no foreign currency for the procurement of necessary raw materials, increasing unemployment, youth out on the streets, and the economic world depression leading to bankruptcy of the banks. Government was possible only through emergency decrees; that is, by one-sided legislative acts of the President. Support of the unemployed empties the Treasury, is unproductive, and is no solution. As a result of the widespread unemployment, the radical parties were increasing. The political splitting up of the German people reached its height. In the last Reichstag election there were thirty-two parties." (36)

Amidst this conflict of group interests Von Papen was repudiated even by his own Catholic Center Party for not adhering strictly enough to their own party line—a special version of the interdependence of church and state. Von Papen was caught between the crossfires of the old Protestant Junker clique and the Catholic Church interests. His attempt to score a moral if not material victory by securing a revision of the Versailles Treaty at the Lausanne Conference in 1932 proved a failure. Inflation and unemployment continued to "proletarianize the middle class" from whom he hoped to get his backing. With the entire social structure of the nation rapidly disintegrating, Von Papen felt justified in ruling by presidential decree. This only intensified political opposition, and his government collapsed by the end of the year.

During General von Schleicher's brief chancellorship of December, 1932, to January, 1933, Von Papen began to come to terms with Hitler. Each one had endeavored to get the other's support for the post of chancellor, but Hitler's bargaining power was now enhanced by industrialist support. By the end of January, 1933, Von Papen was able to report to President von Hindenburg that if Hitler did not get the chancellorship, a Nazi revolution or civil war would break out. Von Hindenburg replied that he could not stand a revolution at his age and reluctantly agreed that it would be better to appoint Hitler chancellor than to allow the government to go further to the left.

Upon Von Hindenburg's appeal to his duty to the Fatherland (and the implicit appeal to the maintenance of the mutual class interests), Von Papen agreed to enter the Hitler cabinet as vice-chancellor.

As vice-chancellor, Von Papen was undoubtedly in an uncomfortable position, constantly compromising his own loyalties and convictions with the revolutionary acts of the Nazis. The emergency measures suspending constitutional guaranties were not sufficient cause to call for Von Papen's resignation, though he saw power slipping from the Junker clique. These first steps in the consolidation of Hitler's dictatorship were not in themselves very different from the steps he himself had been prepared to take as chancellor. He had already been convinced that strong authority was needed to run the government of Germany, and that a free democracy amounted to anarchy. The early outbreaks of persecution and riots by Nazi rowdies called forth only palliative measures, so that Von Papen could give foreign representatives assurance that these were but isolated disturbances. It was clear to Von Papen that something had to be done to preserve some semblance of civilized order in the Nazi coalition government. In an attempt to achieve this within the framework of his own system of values, he negotiated a Concordat between Hitler and the Pope six months after Hitler's accession to power. It should not be overlooked that this move likewise served to rehabilitate Von Papen's position in Catholic church circles. It soon became apparent, of course, that Hitler's negotiation of the Concordat was a cynical gesture to placate the Catholic church momentarily.

Von Papen objected to Hitler's withdrawal from the League of Nations in October, 1933, and his investment of sweeping police powers in Himmler's terror machine, but he neither resigned nor did anything to offer effective opposition to the consolidation of the dictatorship. In all fairness it must be recognized that Von Papen had no effective means at his disposal to fight force with force, and that he did put himself on record as morally opposed to the brutality of a police state. In June, 1934, he made a speech at Marburg in which he made clear how his social values were opposed to the Nazi philosophy of statecraft. After denouncing the restriction of freedom of the press and the abolition of all criticism of the government, Von Papen went on to decry the formation of a one-party system:

> Domination by a single party replacing the majority party system, which rightly has disappeared, appears to me historically as a transitional stage, justified only as long as the safeguarding of the new political change demands it and until the new process of personal selection begins to function. . . .
>
> But one should not confuse the religious State, which is based upon an active belief in God, with a secular State in which earthly values replace such belief and are embellished with religious honors. . . .
>
> Nor should the objection be made that intellectuals lack the vitality necessary for the leaders of the people. True spirit is so vital that it sacrifices itself for its conviction. The mistaking of brutality for vitality would reveal a worship of force which would be dangerous to a people. . . .
>
> Reactions to coercion are dangerous. As an old soldier I know that the most rigid discipline must be balanced by certain liberties. Even the good soldier who submitted willingly to unconditional authority counted his days of service, because the need for freedom is rooted in human nature. The application of military discipline to the whole life of a people must remain within limits compatible with human nature. (36)

This was to be Von Papen's last public statement of opposition to the Nazi dictatorship. The publication of the speech was suppressed by the same Minister of Propaganda (Goebbels) whom he denounced for suppressing freedom of the press. This affront to his dignity was at last sufficient cause for his first tender of resignation. Hitler held him off, but two weeks later, during the Roehm purge, things came to an intolerable pass, even for the ever-adaptable Von Papen. After being held incommunicado under house arrest by Goering for three days, Von Papen indignantly insisted on the acceptance of his resignation by Hitler. During his arrest his files had been confiscated and two of his assistants, including the one who had drafted the Marburg speech, had been shot. At this crisis in his career, the courage of Von Papen's moral convictions was put to the test. Von Papen failed the test. Within a few days he was writing obsequious letters to the same dictator whose regime he had criticized so boldly only three weeks earlier. In these letters he expressed admiration for Hitler's courage and greatness and requested only that amends be made to his own dignity and honor as the price for continuation of his services in Hitler's government. Von Papen had been made "safe" for the purposes of dictatorship.

Within three weeks of his arrest during the Roehm purge, Von Papen accepted the ambassadorship to Austria. His function here, as we have already seen, was to placate the Austrians after the Nazi assassination of Chancellor Dollfuss. He kept Austria placated from 1934 to 1938, while Hitler consolidated his dictatorship at home and planned the Anschluss of Austria in his own good time. Von Papen promoted political, cultural, and trade relations between Germany and Austria, not overlooking an easing of the Austrian government policy toward the rebellious Nazis. When Hitler decided that the time was ripe for the Anschluss, he recalled Von Papen and invaded Austria in March, 1938. By recalling Von Papen three weeks earlier, Hitler not only assured the smooth functioning of the Anschluss operation, but considerately saved Von Papen's face in this breach of faith over their guaranty of Austrian autonomy.

Still unwilling to retire in protest over the duplicity of Hitler's government, or to offer further resistance to Nazi terror, Von Papen accepted the ambassadorship to Turkey in April, 1939. His function here was to keep Turkey neutral during the aggressive wars which Hitler had already secretly planned. It is quite likely that Von Papen was unaware of these plans at the time, since he had allowed himself to become a tool of Hitler without enjoying his confidence. As the schedule of Hitler's aggressive plans unfolded, Von Papen confined himself to private expressions of disdain for these reckless policies. All during the violation of the Munich Pact, the invasion of Poland, the concentration camp terror, the victories and defeats of the German armies, Von Papen remained at his post. He effectively kept Turkey from joining the Allies by strengthening the support of pro-Fascist elements in the Turkish government. He did so with good conscience as "a mission of peace."

At the peak of German victory Von Papen offered to make overtures of peace to the Western Allies, realizing that a prolongation of the war would be disastrous for Germany. However, he was forbidden to do so by Foreign Minister Von Ribbentrop, acting on Hitler's orders to make it a "fight to the finish." The Junkers who plotted to get rid of Hitler in 1944 thought well enough of Von Papen to slate him for the post of foreign minister in case the assassination plot succeeded, but he himself still took no part in opposing Hitler. At the end of the war he was indicted for conspiracy in crimes against peace.

Observations and Evaluation

A Junker Among Criminals.—Though already inured to rough treatment and indignities to his person by Hitler's terror regime, Von Papen seemed to take his imprisonment as a Nazi war criminal as "the most unkindest cut of all." Here was a gentleman of good breeding, a good Christian, and a true German statesman, jailed like a common criminal along with the Nazi rabble he had always detested. Only the high purpose of revealing the truth before God and the world reconciled Von Papen to the humiliation of standing trial with the palpable criminals who had destroyed his Fatherland. His reaction to the indictment, inscribed on our copy of that document, was: "The indictment has horrified me, because of (1) the irresponsibility with which Germany was thrown into this war and the world-wide catastrophe and (2) the accumulation of crimes which some of my people have committed. The latter is psychologically inexplicable. I believe that paganism and the years of totalitarianism bear the main guilt. Through both of these Hitler became a pathological liar in the course of the years."

While waiting to exculpate himself from the guilt of Hitlerism, Von Papen alternately read his Bible, discussed international social reform with the writer, and occasionally worked himself into a frenzy of moral indignation over the pagan immorality of the Nazi ideology: "This evil suppression of individual freedom of thought! This degradation of human dignity! The perversion of youth!—The people must be re-educated—

entirely re-educated! Goebbels said, 'We must use the tactics of the Catholic church to hammer our ideology into German youth.' But how in heaven's name can one compare this evil ideology with the moral precepts of the Christian religion?— Why, the Nazi ideology was the very antithesis of everything that was moral or worthy of the dignity of man!" And Von Papen continued to talk of wanting to dedicate the remaining years of his life to leading his country back to the moral principles it had abandoned when it embraced naziism.

To many in Western political circles, where Von Papen has always been regarded as the very personification of diplomatic duplicity (40), these attitudes of high mission and offended innocence may seem to bespeak, in the face of the record, not a little sanctimonious hypocrisy. Yet it would be ignoring the very essence of the psychology of internal appeasement to attribute Von Papen's previous actions and his attitudes under observation wholly to calculated duplicity. To understand these anomalies of action and attitude we must examine more closely the complex interrelationship of social values, motives, and contemporary social realities which form the framework of rational social behavior.

To restate Von Papen's attitudes in psychocultural terms: All his life he had identified himself with the aristocratic ruling in-group of the Kaiser Wilhelm-Marshal von Hindenburg school, with its centuries of tradition upheld by men of "good family." His basic values as Junker-diplomat had been derived from the long-inbred social influences of the church, the General Staff, and the titled aristocracy, the three pillars of society in the world he knew. When this world collapsed, he had still tried to salvage the remains by continuing to identify himself with the conservative political interests. Hitler had been an obscure radical trouble-maker, threatening the very remains of the old social order. Von Papen had finally appeased him with the greatest reluctance, only to avoid utter chaos, at Von Hindenburg's behest, when no other choice remained. Certainly Allied intransigence over the Treaty of Versailles had not helped the tottering Weimar Republic weather the storm. Nevertheless, in keeping with his indoctrinated social ideals, he had sought to guarantee the Christian foundation of the state by concluding a Concordat between the state and the church, which in centuries past had helped to bring malevolent autocrats to heel.

In helping to preserve some order in a time of revolutionary change, Von Papen felt that he had subjected himself to great personal danger and the most terrible indignities. For a time during Hitler's early social and military victories it had looked as if he had not been wrong in sacrificing so much to the welfare of the Fatherland. Who would not have been proudly ego-involved in the symbol of a newer, greater Germany, taking its rightful place as the leader and promoter of European culture? True, there was much "excess of revolutionary zeal," which would have to be curbed in time. Nobody took seriously political speeches or tracts like *Mein Kampf.* Even so, national ascendancy under strong central authority had been primary in the Junker system of values ever since Bismarck, and the Nazi victories required but little restructuring of his identifications to provide the same ego-satisfactions. An old symbol had simply been rejuvenated from a most unexpected quarter. When this symbol finally began to collapse and the "excesses of revolutionary zeal" grew to a major world catastrophe, Von Papen had retreated in dismay to his original line of ego-defense—identification with the conservative political leaders who had always regarded Hitlerism as a menace to the very foundations of German society.

Von Papen no longer considered himself an exponent of the foreign policy of the glorious Third Reich, but once more a representative of the old order. By the end of the war Von Papen was thoroughly and sincerely convinced that an evil revolutionary force he had always *inwardly* opposed had betrayed his good faith, had ruined the Fatherland and the social institutions which he and his identification group had tried in vain to save. (The German term *innerliche Einstellung,* inner set or attitude, provided a perfect semantic device for this rationalization. His outward appeasement had not compromised his inner loyalties and convictions.) Certainly there was nothing in Von Papen's basic system of values that required reckless aggression against both helpless neutrals and major world powers; and the literal mass murder of defenseless civilian populations violated the most elementary concept of a Christian state. He had been deceived by a pathological liar, had never approved of Hitler's aggressions, and had certainly never even dreamed of genocide.

It was in this context of truth and rationalization that Franz von Papen presented in the Nuremberg jail the picture of a frustrated old patriot in a state of reactive depression, full of injured pride and an obsessive need to disassociate himself from the "criminal rabble" who were his jailmates.

Social Distance.—To lend further perspective to our study, let us first sketch the structure of the interpersonal relationships between Von Papen and some of his codefendants as we found them in this controlled postwar situation. These interpersonal relationships were all the more revealing because the retreat to the original psychological line of defense by the restructuring of group identifications was marked by a further refinement: the delineation of a third line of defense for the ego-fortification of the "inner circle" of the conservative in-group. These were the true aristocrats who felt they had maintained the loftiest ideals of their breed in the manner born and scorned the pretenders who had always clamored for acceptance but did not really "belong." Thus ex-Chancellor von Papen and ex-Foreign Minister von Neurath, of the Von Hindenburg cabinet and the Kaiser's court, maintained the most cordial relationship as the last representatives of the old order. They were properly contemptuous of that upstart pretender, Nazi Foreign Minister Ribbentrop (not "*Von* Ribbentrop," if you please). They were also somewhat condescending about businessman Schacht and the crass materialism he represented. Schacht was, however, far more acceptable to the aristocratic inner circle than Ribbentrop. For the sometimes-conservative ex-President of the Reichsbank at least had the professional background to justify sharing the aristocrats' contempt for Ribbentrop's political ineptness and lack of breeding. Besides, Ribbentrop's unswerving loyalty to Hitler and his well-established favoritism with the Führer had identified him much more with the very naziism from which all three conservative "elder statesmen" now had to disassociate themselves. Yet even Ribbentrop was more tolerable than a vulgar rabble-rouser like Julius Streicher, or the other boors who were unregenerate Nazis of long standing. We thus witnessed the operation of a kind of "social distance scale" emanating from the aristocratic inner circle down through several layers of increasing rejection to the most fanatic of the revolutionary Old Fighters.

At any rate, Von Papen, Schacht, and Von Neurath were duly grateful when we made them luncheon companions and separated them from the lowly Nazi rabble and "Nazi diplomat" Ribbentrop. This greatly enhanced our rapport with the "elder statesmen" and facilitated their free expression of attitudes in our presence, both at lunch and in the privacy of their cells. They did protest too much, but, in so doing, revealed their interpersonal relationships and social attitudes quite clearly.

The hostility and contempt which all three elder statesmen showed for Goering was an interesting expression of this group identification and disassociation. While the Nazi star had been in the ascendant, these three diplomats had not been averse to catering to that powerful figure, curbing their hostile rivalries, and recognizing him as one who might represent Junker interests in the new dictatorial in-group. After all, Von Papen confided, he had looked upon Goering as "a man of good family, whose father had also been a dignitary in the Kaiser's court," and who had also graduated from the Prussian military academy. Von Papen had believed that a deputy dictator reared in the Junker tradition would see to it that any new authoritarianism would be kept somewhere within the frame of reference of their mutual class interests. Apparently Goering's outspoken contempt for democracy did not unduly disturb him, any more than did Hitler's. But he had had reason to hope that Goering might still provide a useful link to power for the old ruling class, and it is quite likely that Goering shrewdly cultivated that expectation for his own purposes. As we have seen, he was fully conscious of his popularity among the Junkers, and in those circles was not above making contemptuous references to Hitler's inferior breeding.

All the more bitter was Von Papen's realization that a man of such "good family" had turned out to be a ruthless Nazi gangster like all the rest; i.e., one who rode roughshod over the Junker interests with which they had falsely identified him. For it was that same Goering of the good family who had thrown Von Papen into "protective custody" during the Roehm purge and had elbowed him out of the way as the second dignitary of the state. With unbridled hatred Von Papen heaped abuse on the head of the predatory Nazi wolf in Junker clothing and even mustered enough courage on the last day of the trial to denounce him to his face. Von Neurath likewise scorned Goering's pretense at royal descent, when he was in fact only an "upstart brat, good for nothing but smashing windows." And Schacht, pushing his identification with the representatives of German culture to the utmost, fairly spat as he spoke of a character so depraved as to *steal* indiscriminately for his own private gain. For one of the supreme values of statesmanship, as practiced by men of culture and breeding, had always been a decent respect for matters of decorum and class interest. The respectable diplomats could have forgiven the Old Fighters much: their usurpation of authority, their "excesses of revolutionary zeal," their violence to the Weimar Constitution, perhaps even their dangerously aggressive foreign policy; but their treachery to the vested interests—never!

This makes Von Papen's continued appeasement, at least his continued service in the Hitler regime, all the more puzzling. Granted that his authoritarian values and class interests had provided a basis for making his peace with dictatorship, the question naturally arises, Why did Von Papen remain even after the appeasement had defeated its own purpose?

Conflict of Principles.—Von Papen's case actually revolved around this issue. In presenting his defense to the Tribunal, he naturally stressed the incidents that had shown him to be opposed to naziism: his denunciation of Nazi terror and regimentation in his Marburg speech; his arrest and resignation during the Roehm purge. But even his codefendants recognized the shortcoming of his anti-Nazi argument long before the prosecution took it up.

His fellow elder statesman, Schacht, in protesting his own hostility to Hitler (after Hitler had dismissed him), confided to the writer that Von Papen had little justification for climbing on the postwar anti-Nazi bandwagon. "Now Von Papen wants to know why I didn't enlist his support (in the underground against Hitler). Why, how could I when he let the Nazis assassinate his own subordinates one after another and he *still* played along? After the Anschluss I thought he was through, but then he *again* accepted an ambassadorship.—Now I ask you, does that sound like a man you could plot with against Hitler? Now he wants to say that he was against Hitler too.—No, there isn't one who was against Hitler *then!*"

Even the unmistakably "real Nazi" Hans Frank commented on the obvious flaw in Von Papen's argument, in his own fashion: "Ah, that good old Von Papen. He is like a trapped fox. —Hahahaha! He tried to do his best as a good nationalist, but naturally people will say, 'Why did you stay after the way Hitler kicked you around?' Hahahaha! Up to 1934 he was perfectly in order, after he resigned—but then he came back thinking he could do some good. He wrote the drama wrong! Hahahaha! He should have written a different last act. Now it ends as a tragedy instead of a comedy! Hahahahaha!"

One may indeed give Von Papen the benefit of many doubts up to the time of his resignation in 1934. But then, as we have noted, his courage failed him and the motive of political power proved stronger than his moral principles. As for Von Papen's defense on this crucial issue, so strong was the need to disassociate himself from naziism that he actually suffered selective memory lapses in giving his testimony. This was not attributable to the normal haziness of memory in depression and senescence, nor even to artful evasion such as the alert Reichsmarschall had resorted to. Von Papen's intellectual functions were generally very much intact for his age; but in speaking for that "other Germany," not the Nazi Germany for which Goering had spoken, Von Papen actually inhibited some significant recollections that showed how deeply he had committed himself to the new order. It was precisely with respect to his new profession of faith after the Roehm purge that the superego-

censor blocked out his moral surrender to Hitlerism, regimentation and all. To Von Papen's intense embarrassment, the
British prosecutor confronted him with the letters he had written to Hitler, calling him a great leader who had been "heaven-
sent to lead Germany out of her misery," and asking only that
amends be made for the indignity he had suffered during the
Roehm purge. It was clear from Von Papen's behavior that he
had actually forgotten such incidents. As observed in our *Diary*
notes:

(*June 18, 1946, courtroom.*) Sir David proceeded to tear apart
Von Papen's motives for resigning after the Roehm purge and
accepting another post three weeks later. He read him his own
letter reaffirming his support of Hitler and hailing his masterful
consolidation of power after the "heroic suppression" of the
Roehm purge.

"You were prepared to serve these murderers as long as your
dignity was put right!" Sir David Maxwell Fyfe shot at him.
Von Papen rejected the insinuation. (But Goering snickered
from the prisoners' dock, "That's right!" and Ribbentrop agreed.)
"You knew that his prestige, especially among Catholics, was
invaluable to Hitler at a time when world opinion turned against
him, and you might have helped to ruin him by opposing him,"
Sir David continued. Von Papen answered hesitatingly that that
was right, but if he had done so he would have disappeared like
his colleagues. Sir David kept hammering to a climax: in spite
of the Roehm purge, in spite of the murder of his own assistants,
in spite of the murder of Dollfuss, in spite of a warlike foreign
policy, Von Papen still remained in the government.—Why?
Why? Von Papen could only keep replying, lamely and finally
indignantly, that it was his sense of duty.

(*In Von Papen's cell, later that night.*) Von Papen was really
bothered by those letters of his with which Sir David had confronted him. He laughed in embarrassment as I came into his
cell. "—You know, I had completely forgotten about those letters. As a matter of fact, so did my secretary.—Of course, one
sees things differently now from the way one saw them at that
time after three days' arrest.—But those questions about why did
I stay in the government—. Now I ask you again, what could I
do when war broke out?—Come back home and go to the front
as a soldier?—Emigrate and write a book?—What could I really
do?" He threw out his arms at each question to show how useless
the alternatives were.

(*Next day, in court.*) Sir David wanted to know how, two
years after the Concordat, Von Papen could have written to

Hitler, in July, 1935, a statement calling his diplomacy "the clever hand which eliminates political Catholicism without touching the Christian foundations of the German State." (Goering snickered, "Now, he's trying to figure out a good answer to that one.") Sir David then quoted the Pope in describing the persecution of the church by the Nazis. Von Papen agreed that that was so, but tried to explain that political Catholicism and the Christian basis of the state were two entirely different things. . . . As a parting shot, Sir David threw up to him once more that he had remained (in Hitler's government) after repeated murders of his own assistants, political opponents, leading statesmen, etc. Von Papen repeated heatedly that he did it out of patriotism, and that was something he could answer for to his own conscience.

(*At lunch*) Von Papen, visibly upset, said, "Sir David has no facts, so he is trying to besmirch my character. I told him that I had to stay as a good German patriot, hard as it was to do so."

Schacht consoled him. "Yes, how well I know those struggles with one's own conscience—weighing patriotism against those other things.—How well I know.—I had the same problem."

Von Papen accepted this consolation eagerly. "Naturally, I had the most terrible struggles with my conscience," he exclaimed, waving his arms and twisting his Mephistophelean eyebrows. "My God, after they shot my own assistant!—And yet I had to say to myself: 'You still have your duty to the Fatherland!'—Do you think it was easy? It was a *terrible* conflict!"

According to Schacht, who knew about such things, the terrible conflict of conscience had been made easier for Von Papen by the enjoyment of the social prestige and palatial living quarters of a German ambassador in Vienna and Ankara. Besides, Schacht confided, Von Papen was one of those run-down aristocrats who needed money and had only their family trees to bargain with. Yet, as we know, not all men of aristocratic background had found it necessary to compromise both their group interests and their principles by appeasing the terror regime of the Third Reich to the very end. There were others who had been equally well inculcated with Junker values, but had mustered the fatal courage to oppose Hitler after they had seen the handwriting on the wall: Baron Ulrich von Hassel, General von Fritsch, and General von Beck, to mention but a few. Among men of similar social background and values, there was still the personal equation of character differences to account for the difference of their reactions to the same conflicting motives. Schacht, of course, counted himself among those men of culture who had greater strength of character than Von Papen.

We recognize, with considerable reservations, Schacht's obvious attempt to identify himself with the "super-inner circle" of anti-Nazi aristocrats. Nevertheless, we must concede that Von Papen's compromise with principle from the Roehm purge to the very end of the war can be attributed largely to political opportunism and moral cowardice. Apparently, it is the rare statesman who combines well-verbalized moral values with a high threshold of resistance to political temptations, and Von Papen was not such a man. In a showdown with psychopathic aggression, a man of Von Papen's background and character could still tolerate totalitarian aggressive nationalism, especially if it provided the only remaining means of satisfying his own status requirements.

But we would be doing less than justice to Von Papen's case if we did not take cognizance of one set of arguments which he used repeatedly to justify his course of action—the social reality of foreign appeasement. This argument revolved around the persistent strengthening of Hitler's hand by foreign action and inaction, particularly by French and British leaders, culminating in the disaster of the Munich Pact. Both Schacht and Von Papen recalled how readily the Western powers had ignored the early Nazi excesses and had sent their military attachés to observe Hitler's parading of military might in violation of the Treaty of Versailles.

In defense of his own appeasement, Von Papen further pointed out that "Even Churchill himself wrote in 1937, 'If we ever lose a war, I hope we shall find a leader who will do so much to rebuild our country.' Can you expect less from a German than Churchill himself was willing to concede to Hitler?"

"Why, before the Munich Pact," Schacht declared in a mood of righteous indignation in his cell, "Hitler didn't even dare dream of getting the Sudetenland incorporated into the Reich. All he thought he *might* get was a measure of autonomy for the Sudetenland. And then those fools Daladier and Chamberlain drop the whole thing in his lap." (The reader will recall Goering's contemptuous references to the behavior of the Western diplomats at the Munich conference.)

By their testimony and that of other witnesses, it was made clear that a liberal-conservative anti-Nazi underground coalition, which had been ready to strike in 1938, had been thoroughly demoralized by Hitler's victory in obtaining the Munich Pact. Allied inaction even after the violation of that Pact had given Hitler an aura of invincibility that dismayed stout-hearted and faint-hearted anti-Nazis alike.

"Just imagine what a little plain talk would have done in 1938," Von Papen reflected in one of our lunchroom conversations. "Suppose after the breaking of the Munich Pact Chamberlain had put his foot down with the help of the other democracies and said flatly, 'Hitler has broken his solemn pledge, and we hereby break off diplomatic relationships with Hitler's government, and refuse to deal with Germany until it gets an honest leader!' Why, if they had done that, Hitler would have collapsed in a matter of days! It would have forced a showdown and the people simply would not have stood for it. As it was, the whole thing was glossed over, and one thing led to another until another war was inevitable."

All of which points to a significant sociopsychological reality: external appeasement not only encourages aggression but defeats internal opposition to that aggression.

With the recognition of these values, motives, and contemporary social realities, we return to our original thesis. It is not in the realm of abnormal psychology, but in the normal processes of social identification, aspiration, and conflict that we must seek our basic explanations for the internal appeasement of revolutionary dictatorship. Inculcated as he was with the class-conscious authoritarian values of his social background, there was little chance to begin with that Von Papen could have readily perceived in dictatorship a potentially unlimited violation of human rights. Ego-involvement of that kind must at least have distorted his moral insights and inhibited any tendency to convert them into action. His original aversion to Hitlerism had been conceived largely in terms of his own social group identifications and aspirations and his reconciliation to it had been on a similar basis. Nevertheless, the personal factor of weakness of character must enter into the equation to account for his actions. Finally, we must reckon with the concrete realities of social chaos, brute force, and appeasement, on which revolutionary dictatorships thrive. When faced with the accomplished fact of a terror regime that was actively destroying his own system of values, Von Papen had neither the courage nor the power to oppose it but maintained his status with sublime rationalizations, noting with alarm that the Nazis were up to no good.

Thus, even among the respectable leaders of the established order, men with high ideals and little courage could be found to serve the purposes of revolutionary reaction, fully convinced that they were trying to preserve fundamental social values. Von Papen was such a man. Others in this identification group were more predatory in their pursuit of self-aggrandizement, and it is to one of these that we now turn for further enlightenment.

FOREIGN MINISTER VON RIBBENTROP

On the fringes of European diplomatic circles, largely circumscribed by the ruling in-groups of the various cultures, there have always existed coteries of successful businessmen of modest origin, whose social and material aspirations motivate them into intrigue for political power. In the more rigidly structured authoritarian cultures, such aspirants are handicapped by lack of membership in the traditional in-group of aristocratic families. The more ambitious and pretentious may nevertheless contrive by devious means to become identified with that in-group; but in periods of social disorganization they may seize instead the opportunity to oppose and replace it. In Germany, as we have seen, it was the Junker in-group that became the object of identification or rebellion. Joachim von Ribbentrop was one of those political camp-followers among German businessmen who tried first the one course, then the other, as the vicissitudes of political opportunity dictated. Whereas Von Papen exemplified the in-group's compromise with revolutionary change to preserve the remains of their group interests, Ribbentrop exemplified the ready reversibility of loyalties of those political adventurers who had no basic social values to compromise. Both men admirably served the purposes of a dictator whose strategy was first to seize control of the existing governmental machinery, then to prepare his aggressions in the most deceitful and diplomatic manner possible. It was Ribbentrop, however, who signed the treaties and conducted the "peace negotiations" that invariably became the prelude to attack. The character that lent itself to such a role in international diplomacy and its function in this dictatorship again provide the focus of our interest.

LIFE HISTORY

Early Background.—Joachim Ribbentrop was born in 1893 in Wesel in the Rheinland. He was the second of three children born to a career army officer whose ancestors had been officers for many generations. This fact gave the family some social status but was not enough to identify them with the Junker clique, since this branch of the Ribbentrop family had neither aristocratic title nor property. The mother suffered from tuberculosis and Joachim knew her only as an invalid. She died when he was eleven years old. Essentially a weak, passive-dependent child who also suffered from a mild case of tuberculosis, Joachim felt the loss of his mother very keenly. It also made him more dependent on the affections of his father, whom he admired with the awe that was a German officer-father's due. The pattern of Ribbentrop's emotional need gratifications was no doubt set by the early courting of paternal affection and approval from a father with neither the time nor the inclination for demonstrations of affection. At the same time, the father's doubts as to either son's ability to carry on the family officer tradition (since both contracted tuberculosis at an early age) would necessarily create keen feelings of inadequacy in such a cultural setting. This feeling of inadequacy could be resolved only by identification with the strong authoritarian figure on whose favor the children were now completely dependent.

Joachim's education was sporadic and unsatisfactory, due largely to the father's moving about from one garrison town to another. He received elementary schooling in Kassel and Metz in Alsace-Lorraine, where he acquired some familiarity with French culture. He was considered lazy, mischievous, and not very bright as a student. However, he did show the intellectual capacity to advance in subjects which interested him, such as history and languages. He also acquired some proficiency in playing the violin. A rather personable lad, he was adept at making friendships among his neighbors and schoolmates.

The father retired as a lieutenant colonel in 1908 and remarried at about the same time. This appeared to threaten Joachim's need for paternal attention and affection and only prompted resentment of the mother-substitute. In a short time the family ties were so strained that Joachim had to be sent away to London, ostensibly to study there. He remained in London for about a year, perfecting his English and acquiring a taste for cosmopolitan living, but he never made any serious attempt to study for a career.

In 1910 he emigrated from London to Canada with his older brother, to seek his fortune in the New World. He worked there for three years, first in railroad and construction companies, later in a liquor import-export business. His contact with the German consulate in Ottawa soon provided a bridge to social contact with the Germanophile family of the Duke of Connaught, the Canadian Governor-General. His entrance into Canadian high society was facilitated by his fluent knowledge of English and French besides his native tongue, his engaging personality, and his ability to dance and play the violin at parties. A later colleague of Ribbentrop's, Dr. Paul Schwarz, who investigated the Canadian episode rather painstakingly, reports:

> Young Joachim, about nineteen at the time, was quite a success at Rideau Hall. . . . His visits to Government House became rather frequent. The highest officials invited him to their homes. This, in itself, constitutes a remarkable record for a young German on his own in a foreign country without any official status, elaborate means, or influential relatives. It was something to brag about, and in later years Joachim always let every one know that he had been the favorite of the Canadian Governor-General, his

wife, and their daughter. . . . During Ottawa's *Kermess* festival
he was to be found at costume parties in the brocaded velvet coat
and white wig of a Louis XV courtier, either kneeling before his
lady of the moment or dancing the minuet with her. (59)

Ribbentrop's exaggeration of his "favorite" status in the
household of the Canadian Governor-General is significant, ex-
pressing his need for supremacy in a situation resembling sibling
rivalry for the special affection of an authoritarian figure. The
picture of the kneeling courtier is also interesting. For in select-
ing his role in the "psychodrama" of the make-believe, Ribbentrop unwittingly gave expression to the "style of life" that he
had already adopted as a basic expression of his personality. At
all events, the Canadian episode represented Ribbentrop's first
successful venture in cosmopolitan social climbing—an ascendancy need which was to become almost an obsession in later life.

At the outbreak of World War I in 1914, Ribbentrop escaped internment as an enemy alien by traveling to New York.
Since the United States was still neutral, he had little difficulty
securing passage aboard a Dutch steamer bound for Rotterdam.
His older brother remained behind to be interned, eventually
dying of tuberculosis. Although Joachim had escaped military
service by emigrating to Canada, he now had a chance to live
up to his father's expectations by rallying to the colors with the
Fatherland at war. Within a short time after his American
escapade, he was back in Germany, in soldier's uniform.

Ribbentrop served with the army in Poland and Russia and
was eventually commissioned a lieutenant in the cavalry. However, his physical condition prevented him from seeing much
action. He was transferred to an administrative post in the
War Ministry in Berlin. Early in 1918 he was assigned to the
Ministry's office in Constantinople, but the Turkish capitulation
forced him to return.

In 1919 his linguistic ability won him an assignment as an
aide to General von Seeckt, one of the War Ministry's com-
missioners to the peace conference. The Treaty of Versailles
gave him his first bitter taste of military diplomacy on the defeated side, but it does not appear to have been an unduly traumatic experience to him personally.

The Social Climber.—Having little but his knowledge of French and English that could be put to use in postwar Germany, Ribbentrop began to cast about for a job. Since he had acquired a little knowledge of the liquor business and the trade restrictions of the Versailles Treaty, he was able to land a job as sales representative of the German champagne producer, Henkell.

Once again the struggle for status and security began. Ribbentrop made his choice among the limited possibilities in accordance with the "style of life" that was conducive to his temperament. Not being an aggressive man-of-action or an ideological fanatic, he was repulsed rather than attracted by the revolutionary turmoil. Without Junker background or money there was nothing that he could exploit to political advantage. But he could capitalize on his engaging personality, his talents as a "good mixer," and his adeptness at superficial niceties to achieve some financial and social success. Like many a demobilized officer in what remained of the old social order, his trump card was his eligibility. He played this card shrewdly and married the proprietor's daughter in 1920. Although father Henkell expressed some misgivings about Ribbentrop's character, he helped his son-in-law build up a rather flourishing liquor import monopoly.

Nevertheless, the marriage was a reasonably romantic one by European standards. The Ribbentrops never had any serious marital difficulties, unlike many of the Nazi leaders. Annelies genuinely admired her well-poised, cosmopolitanite husband. They were compatible in temperament and mutually motivated by social ambitions. At least in the beginning they had a normal family life, and they ultimately raised five children.

The pursuit of social status became more alluring after 1925, when Ribbentrop acquired the right to use the aristocratic "Von" on a legal technicality. For certain considerations (which were never paid in full), a distant relative of the "Von Ribbentrop" strain was induced to register Joachim's legal adoption. His legal right to the name *Von* Ribbentrop opened up new vistas of social identification, and raised his aspiration level accordingly. He immediately changed his firm's name to Von

Ribbentrop & Co. and thenceforth conducted himself with the dignity due his station. This bit of pretense caused considerable amusement among Ribbentrop's business acquaintances, and some embarrassment to his in-laws, who were ribbed about having "married into the nobility."

Undaunted, the "Von" Ribbentrops sedulously pursued their social ambitions. They plunged into the whirl of Berlin cafe society and gradually edged their way into diplomatic circles. Ever adept at the social niceties, Ribbentrop made generous use of cases of the "real stuff" (not easy to come by in postwar Germany) to endear himself to the "right people." Through some German officials he met the American Ambassador; the American Ambassador introduced him to the British Ambassador, and so on down the line. The Ribbentrops never overlooked any possible occasion to "leave cards" or to wangle an invitation to a reception. They traveled a great deal, "following the calendar" to mingle with the international aristocratic set during the appropriate seasons at the Riviera, London, Paris, and Switzerland. All this proved good for business as well as for social status. Ribbentrop gradually became "accepted" and prosperous by the end of a decade of feverish social activity, in accordance with the well-worn pattern of behavior for businessmen with social aspirations.

In accordance with that pattern, Ribbentrop now began to groom himself for political influence. His mansion in the fashionable Berlin-Dahlem section now became a center of social activity for the Berlin diplomatic set. However, the depression which descended upon the Western world in 1930 began to throw the entire political and industrial machinery of the country into a state of chaos. Ribbentrop was threatened not only with the frustration of any further social ambitions, but even the loss of the hard-won and dearly cherished status he already had. Lacking the ego-strength, the basic competence, or the basically sound social values to withstand any reversal in his superficial attainments, he could only fall back on the social defenses of the incompetent and insecure. Now he too sought scapegoats on whom to vent his aggression and a "dynamic" social movement with which he could identify. The Nazi party seemed to provide

both. The commander of the Berlin Storm Troops, the rene-
gade Count Helldorf, provided Ribbentrop's link to the Nazi
party and eventually introduced him to Hitler. Ribbentrop
later said of this meeting with Hitler in 1932:

> "Adolf Hitler made a considerable impression on me even then.
> I noticed particularly his blue eyes in his generally dark appear-
> ance . . . and the manner in which he expressed his thoughts.
> These thoughts and statements always had something final and
> definite about them, and they appeared to come from his innermost
> self. I had the impression that I was facing a man who knew
> what he wanted and who had an unshakable will and who was a
> very strong personality. I can summarize by saying that I left
> that meeting with Hitler convinced that this man, if anyone, could
> save Germany from the great difficulties and distress which existed
> at the time. . . . I heard with what enormous strength and con-
> viction—if you like, also brutality and hardness—he could state
> his opinion when he believed that obstacles might appear to the
> rehabilitation and rescue of his people." (36)

We note here not a little of the passive suggestibility and
introception of aggressive resolution of frustration that marked
the fanatic devotion of men like Hess and Frank. Ribbentrop's
"style of life" and group identification had kept him aloof from
the revolutionary rabble up to 1930, but social disintegration
and frustration were now producing similar reactions among
all strata of German society. In Ribbentrop's case, the meta-
morphosis to a "convinced" adherent of naziism was far easier
to undergo than was the case with aristocrats like Von Papen.
For one thing, his status in the aristocratic in-group was far
more tenuous than that of the old landed aristocracy; but more
important, the inadequate, passive-dependent, suggestible personality was far more susceptible to such dominance and intro-
jected aggressiveness. Ribbentrop's superficial ego-defenses had
started to break down at the first puff of an ill wind, revealing
once more the insecure youth courting the protection of an
authoritarian figure. The psychodynamic motivations served
at least to reinforce the shrewd calculations of the inveterate
social climber and facilitate the restructuring of his own identifications.

Incapable of overt aggression in his own right, Ribbentrop experienced a vicarious thrill in mimicking the brave revolutionary talk of his new idol. If his position presented some strange anomalies of loyalty and attitude, these gave him no pause. Without a qualm he took up the Hitlerian cry against the scapegoats of socioeconomic frustration: not only the "Bolsheviks" whom all propertied conservatives naturally condemned, but "Jewish bankers" and "Western plutocrats" as well—including many whose friendship he had always sought to cultivate as long as they suited his purpose. He suddenly conceived a passionate concern for the welfare of the masses while still clinging to the prerogatives of the socially privileged. In explaining his motives for joining the Nazi party at this time, Ribbentrop later told us, "You know, I was not an ideological fanatic like Rosenberg or Streicher or Goebbels. I was an international businessman who merely wanted to have industrial problems solved, and national wealth properly preserved and used. If Communism could do it—all right; if National Socialism could do it—all right too." Ribbentrop's practical opportunism was certainly not encumbered by any basic social convictions.

Ribbentrop placed his Dahlem mansion at Hitler's disposal and gave him the benefit of his "connections" during the critical months preceding the seizure of power. To Hitler, who had never traveled outside of his own domain, Ribbentrop represented a sophisticated man of affairs, well versed in the intricacies of international commerce and diplomacy. He could read and comment glibly on reports in London and Paris newspapers, could boast of "contacts" with many men of importance in Western political circles—and he was *salonfähig* (adept at drawing-room etiquette). In Ribbentrop's home, Hitler was thus able to pick up a few pointers on Western opinion and social etiquette, while acquiring crucial support for his accession to the chancellorship. The decisive preliminary meeting took place at banker Baron von Schroeder's house, but important discussions that paved the way and clinched the chancellorship took place in the Ribbentrop villa. He soon found he had backed a winner.

However, Ribbentrop had still to prove his right to a major share in the spoils of the New Order. He was accordingly allowed to set up an autonomous office under the auspices of the party, to study questions of foreign policy, as personal adviser to the Chancellor. The Büro Ribbentrop was not much to begin with, but it served the purpose of providing an entering wedge into international diplomacy.

Ribbentrop displayed consummate skill in the empire-building arts of bureaucracy. His new Büro soon became a beehive of activity for domestic and foreign businessmen, as well as for politicians who wanted to get action by circumventing normal diplomatic channels. Hitler, for his part, found Ribbentrop's office useful for political intrigues which were beneath the dignity of the respectable career diplomats in the German Foreign Office. The Büro also provided an opportunity for quasi-diplomatic careers for selected SS officers and party favorites who could not get into the regular diplomatic service. This enhanced his standing among the Old Fighters. Connections with various institutes of political science were also established to broaden the Büro's informational facilities and enhance its respectability. Within two or three years Ribbentrop built up a politico-economic intelligence empire with foreign agents all over the world and an intricate bureaucracy under his own direction at home. He made the most of his opportunity to marshal evidence to support Hitler's grandiose plans for expansion, and to convince him of his fanatic devotion to the cause. The dual government of party and state quickly took shape in the field of foreign affairs, as Ribbentrop eagerly lent himself to the role of Hitler's personal agent in paradiplomatic channels.

Nevertheless, Ribbentrop's aspiration level (and his wife's) was nothing less than to achieve ascendancy over all other diplomatic rivals in the foreign affairs of the Third Reich. With petulance, cajolery, and appeals to the Führer's own exalted aspiration, Ribbentrop insisted on the necessity of official diplomatic status for the most faithful exponent of the New Order.

He soon achieved the desired entering wedge into top-drawer official diplomacy in 1934, when Hitler prevailed upon President von Hindenburg to appoint him Special Commissioner for Dis-

armament Questions.   Ribbentrop promptly busied himself with
a never-ending struggle to embrace within his jurisdiction as
much of the economic life of the Third Reich as possible, while
scurrying around European capitals to make the most of his
status as an official who "enjoyed the confidence of the Führer."
But he kept up his unrelenting demand for equal status with the
foreign diplomats with whom he had to deal on disarmament
questions.   Nothing less than ambassadorial status would do
for "the Führer's favorite."   Hitler appointed him Ambassador-
at-Large in 1935.   The Roehm purge and Von Hindenburg's
death had given Hitler a free hand to plan his aggressions and
to reconstitute the government with that end in view.

Ribbentrop was not found wanting.   He immediately won
his spurs by secretly negotiating a naval treaty with England,
allowing Germany 35 per cent of British naval strength.   This
was tantamount to a recognition of Germany's rearmament in
violation of the Treaty of Versailles.   Hitler next decided to
remilitarize the Rheinland in violation of the Locarno Pact.
Foreign Minister von Neurath and the Commander-in-Chief of
the Wehrmacht, General von Fritsch, warned him against flying
in the face of military prudence and treaty obligations.   Ribbentrop, however, assured Hitler that he was right and that the
chance could safely be taken.   The sheer recklessness of this
adventure has never been in doubt (cf. Keitel).   Nevertheless,
the experts were discredited and Ribbentrop's "statesmanlike
insight" was confirmed when the Western powers failed to re-
pulse this act of defiance.   Within a few months the Rome-
Berlin-Tokyo Axis was formed and the Franco dictatorship
recognized in Spain.   Ribbentrop did not initiate these policies,
but supported Hitler's determination to line up the fascist dictatorships against the "decadent democracies."   When Foreign
Minister von Neurath demurred at signing the anti-Comintern
Pact with Japan, for fear of alienating Great Britain, Ribbentrop
readily signed the Pact as the Führer's Ambassador-at-Large.

By this time Ribbentrop had sufficiently demonstrated his
loyalty to the cause to be selected for the coveted post of Ambassador to Great Britain, without losing his special prerogatives
as Hitler's Ambassador-at-Large.   He now descended upon

London with a retinue of undersecretaries, expert consultants, SS guards of honor, military and press attachés, etc., to take up the post that marked a climax in his political and social career. The German Embassy in London was lavishly remodeled at tremendous cost and the Ambassador proceeded to outdo himself in ostentation and humorless arrogance. This reached a much-publicized climax upon his presentation to the King, when he disdained observance of official protocol and greeted His Majesty with a Nazi salute and a raucous "Heil Hitler." The world was thus put on notice that His Excellency Joachim von Ribbentrop, Ambassador-at-Large and personal confidant of the Führer of the Greater Third Reich, signer of the Rome-Berlin-Tokyo Pact, and Ambassador of aforesaid Reich to the Court of St. James, had, in more than one sense, finally "arrived"!

Hitler's "Tough" Diplomat.—With his ascendancy to exalted social status, Ribbentrop's personality underwent an external change. A new conception of his own social role evolved out of his passive identification with the aggressive Nazi leader. He was now not merely a top-ranking, wealthy, titled diplomat, but the official spokesman for a powerful dictator who was leading a great nation to its manifest destiny. As his adulation of Hitler's leadership increased, he wasted less and less civility on his social inferiors or on foreign diplomats. This change of behavior was not merely the crude tactic of a political opportunist and social climber who had "arrived"; it was a passive-dependant personality's awkward expression of the intensified sadomasochistic authoritarianism of his culture. The values of moribund Prussian militarism had been reanimated by Hitler's "dynamic new order" and the adaptive poseur threw himself enthusiastically into the role that provided admirable defenses against his own insecurity. If he had failed to measure up to the paternal tradition of militarism in adopting the "style of life" of effete café society, he could now correct any misapprehension over his fitness for his historic role. He accordingly bent every effort to impress Hitler with his "hardness" rather than his *Salonfähigkeit*. The gracious charm now gave way to a brusque, arrogant manner, punctuated with sharp demands and

threats of force. From his underlings he exacted a formal deference and discipline that would have done credit to any petty
medieval tyrant, while obsequiously courting the favor of a stern
paternalistic Führer. It was not long before Hitler granted him
a general's rank in the Elite Guard (SS), and from then on his
overbearance knew no bounds.

But Ribbentrop's newly conceived "hardness" did little to
endear him to British public opinion or the British government.
Nor did his political successes enhance his popularity in world
opinion as much as they enhanced his status in the new order as
defined by Hitler. Somehow, his achievement of security
through power was becoming increasingly incompatible with his
craving for acceptability among the international elite. On
German soil he received all the deference that his ascendancy
needs demanded; any open references to his diplomatic ineptness
or his dubious claim to a title or high military rank were strictly
taboo. Hitler called him a statesman "greater than Bismarck"
and who was there to gainsay him? But the foreign press and
public gave unmistakable signs of hostility toward Nazi Germany
and contempt for her arrogant Ambassador. Only those Britons
whose pro-German proclivities had withstood the growth of the
Nazi terror still cherished the friendship of Hitler's hard man.
If he was not mistaken, the spokesman for the new order was
actually being snubbed!

Ribbentrop conceived a violent hatred for the British in
reaction to this hostility. Like Hitler, he expected aggressive
authority to be accorded the same awesome respect abroad that
an officer-father was accorded in his culture, and he was infur-
iated when he failed to receive it. All the more did he seek to
insinuate himself into the Führer's protective good graces and to
reinforce his vengeful heroic fantasies. The passive-dependant
youth whose father's military authority had given him ego-
support in earlier years was now the tough favorite diplomat of
a dictator who could lick any other diplomat's government if
they doubted his exalted status and prowess.

In 1937 Ribbentrop was already Foreign Minister in effect
and needed only a propitious moment to become so in fact. The
secret of his meteoric rise over the heads of all career diplomats

and even his Nazi rivals has already been indicated. In a consolidated dictatorship the secret of all successful careers lies less in demonstrated qualifications for office than in convincing the dictator of one's unswerving loyalty. It would not be amiss to cite here the impression that Ribbentrop's behavior made even on the contemporary Western diplomats with whom he had to deal. The French Ambassador, André François-Poncet later described him as follows:

> Ribbentrop was less of a minister than the Führer's private secretary for external affairs. . . . Typical of the perfect courtier, he would hurl thunderbolts of flattery at Hitler without turning a hair. His method of keeping favor was very simple. It consisted in listening religiously to his master's endless monologues and in committing to memory the ideas developed by Hitler. Also, more important, Ribbentrop noted the intentions to be divined behind these ideas. Then, after Hitler had forgotten ever discussing them with Ribbentrop, the courtier passed them off as his own, unfolding them with great warmth. Struck by his concordance, Hitler attributed to his collaborator a sureness of judgment and a trenchant foresight singularly in agreement with his own deepest thought. . . . He was more Hitlerian than Hitler. By clearing up the Führer's doubts and by dissipating the Führer's occasional hesitancies, Ribbentrop excited the Führer's supreme audacity; he pushed and pulled him into ways toward which Hitler was all too dangerously inclined. . . .
>
> Yet the Minister for Foreign Affairs was neither prepared nor fitted for this office. Culturally and intellectually he was mediocre. His ignorance of historical and diplomatic questions was prodigious. His mission as Ambassador to London proved a resounding failure; his personal spite at this was to falsify his every judgment of Great Britain's material or moral resources. . . . In his contacts with chiefs of diplomatic missions he behaved in arrogant, brutal, and peremptory fashion, fancying that language of this nature was best calculated to inspire foreigners with a lofty idea of the New Germany. . . .[1] (17)

The American Under-Secretary of State, Sumner Welles, later wrote:

> Ribbentrop has a completely closed mind. It struck me as also a very stupid mind. The man is saturated with hate for England, to the exclusion of any other dominating mental influence. He is

---

[1] André François-Poncet, *The Faithful Years*, pp. 232-33, Copyright 1949, by Reynal & Hitchcock, Inc.

clearly without background in international affairs, and he was
guilty of a hundred lies in his presentation of German policy during recent years. . . . (64)

By the end of 1937 Hitler's plan for hegemony in Europe
had become crystallized into a definite time-table for piecemeal
aggression, with the calculated risk of war. Ribbentrop was
not actually present at the "Hoszbach conference" in November,
but he lost little time proving that he was present in spirit.
Within a few weeks he sent a memorandum to Hitler confirming the practicality of armed aggression. He too advocated
force to bring about a change in the European status quo and to
establish Germany's Eastern sphere of influence. Europe could
be made safe for German expansion if England were discouraged
from backing France in any possible intervention. The cold
logic of his arguments was little more than the repetition of the
strategy divulged by Hitler at the fateful meeting in November.
Foreign Minister von Neurath had expressed some misgivings
about Hitler's aggressive plans, but now Ribbentrop confirmed
their feasibility. Hitler's mind was made up. A month after
he had written the memorandum in which he showed such statesmanlike insight, the Führer's "tough" favorite diplomat became
Foreign Minister of the Greater Third Reich.

The Foreign Minister.—Ribbentrop's role in the series of
aggressions which followed in rapid succession was wholeheartedly cooperative, even if secondary to Hitler's and Goering's.
Within a few days of his appointment as Foreign Minister, he
was echoing Hitler's intimidating threats to Austrian Chancellor Schuschnigg, in preparation for the Anschluss. Two
months later he signed the decree of annexation. A short time
after Hitler had given the world his assurances that he had only
the most peaceful intentions, Ribbentrop was at work in collaboration with the whole party machinery, fomenting agitation
for a "settlement of the Sudeten problem." Hitler negotiated
the Munich Pact himself as Ribbentrop sat in rapt admiration
of his master's persuasive powers. A few months after Hitler's
solemn declaration that he "had no further territorial claims in
Europe," Ribbentrop was echoing his threats to President Hacha

to take over the rest of Czechoslovakia by force. When the threats succeeded in bringing about an "invasion by consent," Ribbentrop signed the law establishing the Protectorate of Bohemia and Moravia.

Poland was next on the list. But by now Allied forbearance was clearly at an end. The French and British governments gave Hitler clear warning that any further aggression would mean war. President Roosevelt urged peaceful settlement of any outstanding differences. Ribbentrop nevertheless confined himself to deceptive pretenses of negotiating a settlement with Poland and carefully refrained from applying any unwanted restraint to his Führer's aggressive impulses. On the contrary, he assured Hitler that he need not be deterred by England's guaranty of Poland, because the British "would leave Poland coldly in the lurch" if it came to a showdown.

As the German armies stood poised to strike, Hitler sent Ribbentrop to Moscow to negotiate a nonaggression pact which would give Germany a free hand in dealing with Poland. The pact contained a secret clause by which Russia and Germany would divide Poland between them "in case of hostilities" with Poland. Ribbentrop was apparently as little abashed at signing a nonaggression pact with Russia, after signing the Anti-Comintern Pact, as he was at taking over the rest of Czechoslovakia after signing the Munich Pact. The invasion of Poland and the declaration of war by England and France inevitably followed. Ribbentrop told us that he suffered an attack of nerves when the news of the Allied declaration of war came, but Hitler was very calm about it. However, the record shows that Ribbentrop soon overcame his attack of jitters and expressed satisfaction that the war had come, because he too thought that the problem of Germany's *Lebensraum* should be solved in the Führer's lifetime.[2] There could be no turning back from his historic mission, even if his own daring frightened him.

---

[2] About ten days before, Hitler had summoned his military chiefs to advise them that he was now ready to go to war to solve the problem of Germany's *Lebensraum*, because the problem had to be settled in the lifetime of the leader who had both the determination and the military superiority to accomplish it.

From this point on, the militarists and State Police took over the conduct of foreign affairs, but Ribbentrop had to show that he had not outlived his usefulness. The Foreign Minister could still issue official memoranda, justifying the attack on one neutral country after another, including several with which he had solemnly signed nonaggression pacts. Hitler himself took the initiative in planning these acts of aggression, but Ribbentrop certainly never deterred him. Poland, Belgium, Holland, Norway, Denmark, France fell in rapid succession, and the Balkans were overrun soon after. In June, 1941, Hitler made his fateful decision to attack Russia in an all-out offensive involving millions of troops. Ribbentrop kept urging his Axis partner, Japan, to attack Russia and to harass the United States to checkmate help from that quarter. At the end of 1941 the Japanese militarists decided they could at least attack American possessions safely.

Through all of this bloodshed and violation of solemn commitments, Ribbentrop's chief concern continued to be his share of public recognition and favor in the Führer's eyes. His quarrels with Himmler, Goering, and the General Staff over jurisdictional matters were as acrimonious as they were petty, resembling nothing so much as sibling rivalry in its most childish form. Even in the cataclysmic struggle for Germany's manifest destiny, the Führer's entourage continued to be a house of squabbling egotists competing for status and recognition.

One such dispute with Hitler in 1941 proved to be a highly significant and very traumatic experience, because Ribbentrop referred to it repeatedly after Hitler's death. Ribbentrop took his grievance over some fancied slight to his authority (he was later vague and inconsistent on this point) directly to Hitler, giving vent to petulant recriminations. Only under these circumstances, we gather, did he venture to criticize some of Hitler's policies. When the argument became heated, Hitler flew into one of his furious temper tantrums with marked psychosomatic reactions, screaming that Ribbentrop was taxing his health and menacing Germany's destiny with his petty objections. The device was not unlike that which an hysterical parent may resort to, stirring guilt panic in an ungrateful child, as a weapon of control. At any rate, the effect on Ribbentrop was precisely the same. He begged forgiveness, reaffirmed his loyalty, and promised never to provoke Fate by challenging the Führer again. It should be mentioned that Ribbentrop's father died the same year (it is not certain whether the father's death preceded or followed this scene). If anything was needed to reinforce Ribbentrop's slavish obedience to his father-surrogate throughout the critical war years, Hitler's well-timed threat of collapse turned the trick. Since the suggestible Foreign Minister fully accepted Hitler's identification with Germany's destiny, the appeal to that symbol even provided a workable rationalization for reinforced submission. In the succeeding years Ribbentrop outdid himself in supporting Hitler's most brutal policies.

Nevertheless, his anxiety over the outcome of his adventure with historical destiny continued to increase, in spite of all attempts to suppress it. He suffered increasingly from severe headaches, nervous tension, insomnia, neuralgia, and numerous other psychosomatic symptoms. He consulted various physicians and chiropractors and resorted more and more to sedatives.

Yet he continued to play his part faithfully. The occupation of conquered territories was perforce a military affair, but he showed the Führer that the Foreign Minister could also be a man of blood and steel when it came to dealing with the heads of conquered foreign countries. A German document which reports a meeting between Hitler, Ribbentrop, and Regent Horthy of Hungary gives specific evidence of this:

> (The Führer demanded more suppressive measures against the Jews of Hungary.) To Horthy's counterquestion as to what he should do with the Jews, now that he had deprived them of almost all possibilities of livelihood—he could not kill them off—the Reich Foreign Minister declared that the Jews must either be exterminated or taken to concentration camps. There is no other possibility. (36)

Ribbentrop likewise urged Italy to follow Germany's "cruel but necessary measures" to get rid of the Jews. In his dealings with occupied France, he at one time advocated the taking of 2,000 hostages; at another time he negotiated the assassination of a French general. Wherever possible, he used his good offices to expedite the recruitment of slave labor. In 1944 world-wide revulsion over the discovery of Maidanek extermination camp forced him to make timid inquiries as to whether this was all in order. Hitler reminded him sharply that those things were under Himmler's jurisdiction and none of his business. The Foreign Minister dutifully dismissed the matter from his mind.

Since Hitler was obsessed with the determination to fight the war to a finish, he flatly refused to countenance any suggestions for a negotiated peace, even as the outlook became disastrous for Germany. Hitler's faith in ultimate victory was still unshaken, and the Foreign Minister dared not suggest otherwise, or even think otherwise.

Only two weeks before the final capitulation did Hitler allow his faithful Foreign Minister to entertain the thought of defeat. When Ribbentrop asked him what he should do in such an eventuality, Hitler advised him still to seek rapprochement with England. It was therefore a severe shock to Ribbentrop to discover, after his capture, that England was not interested in rapprochement with the Nazi government, and that Hitler had not even mentioned him in his will as Foreign Minister of the defeated Reich.

OBSERVATIONS AND EVALUATION

"The Führer's Shadow."—It was an extremely confusing world in which Ribbentrop found himself after the death of the Führer. He had, of course, experienced some nervous exhaustion and a severe jolt to his ego in the collapse of the Third Reich, as had most of the Nazi leaders. But the panic and disintegration that Ribbentrop manifested as he went on trial were quite extraordinary. At times it resembled agitated or comatose depressions. His mental processes were generally so retarded and confused [3] (in spite of his high I.Q.) that he could

---

[3] On the Rorschach test he barely eked out eight uncertain and mediocre responses (about the same on retest), so that an analysis of the record would not be profitable. The I.Q. test, given at a suitable moment, yielded an I.Q. of 129, which was probably an accurate measure of his basic capacities.

hardly give a rational account of his activities. Every vestige of dignity, not to speak of pride, was gone. He pleaded with every one who came within earshot to give him advice, to explain what had happened during the "mass psychosis" of Hitlerism, and for God's sake to let bygones be bygones. Since he was one of the few who could speak English fluently, even the cell guards were not spared his importunities. He scribbled hundreds of pages of memoranda and poured out a flood of confused denials and rationalizations upon interrogation. His lying, self-contradiction, and petulant demands drove two defense attorneys to despair. He could not sleep without daily sedatives. At times he felt too incapacitated physically to come to court. As the evidence of war crimes was presented, Ribbentrop's guilt anxiety knew no bounds. He offered to be cut to pieces or thrown over a cliff if he had really had any responsibility for those things. He accosted the writer and others in terrified apprehension, pleading, swearing, protesting his innocence with wild gesticulations. As his own defense approached, his psychosomatic reaction was so severe that he tried to beg off altogether on account of illness—an illness which he described to us as "a laming of the will." Ribbentrop was clearly undergoing a severe reactive depression with intense anxiety and psychosomatic symptoms, precipitated by the fear of retribution for a guilt whose enormity he dared not face. In short, the Nazi Foreign Minister was "scared stiff."

This extreme reaction was due not only to the fact that he had good reason to be afraid, but to his complete lack of ego-defenses in this crisis. It is the latter circumstance which is particularly salient in our study of the psychology of dictatorship.

As we have already seen, the disintegration of the Nazi microcosm produced different reactions in the leading personalities of the Third Reich. The revolutionists fell back on pathological defense mechanisms similar to those that had set their world in motion; the diplomatic and military satellites retreated to their social "second line of defense." Thus Goering had his heroic acting and manipulation of the environment to the very end; Hess alternately resorted to hysterical amnesia or paranoid rationalizations; Hans Frank had another passionate conversion of faith with mystic diffusion of overpowering guilt feelings; Von Papen reidentified himself with the violated authority of church and state; the militarists, as we shall presently see, had the long, honorable tradition of Prussian militarism to fall back on. But after Hitler's death, Ribbentrop had nothing. He had neither the pathological defenses nor fanaticism of the revolutionary mental deviates, and he was cut off from the "second line of defense" of the aristocratic in-group with whom he sought to identify.

Like Von Papen, Ribbentrop had aspired to social respectability and had not been driven by a pathological lust for rebellion against the established order. But unlike Von Papen, his social aspirations were not so much the products of deeply rooted in-group values as they were the compensatory needs of an insecure personality. With his lack of basic values or ego-strength, Ribbentrop's ego-ideal had always been "status at any price"— with neither the restraint of the well-bred aristocrat nor the antisocial impulses of the psychopath. The solution for a personality so constructed, in a time of crisis, had been to identify with a dominant political leader who represented his ego-ideal, to introject *his* aggression, his social values, even his heroic fantasies and plan of action. The stratagem had worked magnificently for a time in producing the primary gain. But the inevitable secondary loss of such completely obsequious identification with the dictator had been the utter deterioration of any other ego-defenses.

In terms of group acceptance he was neither fish nor fowl; in terms of personal conviction he was a complete nonentity. The aristocrats rejected him as an unscrupulous pretender; the Old Fighters resented him as a bandwagon climber who had achieved his status without fighting for it; the militarists understandably relegated him to the genus "cheap politician"—i.e., one of those who play reckless politics to maintain their own power and then leave the soldiers to fight it out and take the blame.

As for motives and values to justify his actions, Ribbentrop was completely at a loss. All attempts to get at his basic convictions proved fruitless, for he had no basic convictions. He had attempted the impossible feat of championing the values of polite society and the Nazi new order at one and the same time and had never resolved the dilemma. When called upon to explain, let alone justify, his actions, Ribbentrop showed by his confused vacillation, suggestibility, and inane and inconsistent rationalizations that he himself had little conception of statesmanship, good or bad. He could mimic Goering's cynical realism or Von Papen's pious platitudes with equal facility and with equal lack of conviction.

With this utter lack of psychological defenses, Ribbentrop's disintegration was more complete and more pathetic than that of any of the others. The collapse of the Hitlerian system of values, which had for a time sustained and inflated an ego with no inner substance, now left a vacuum in which that ego could no longer sustain itself. If Ribbentrop was completely unable to give a forthright explanation of his policies and attitudes, it was because they had been Hitler's policies and attitudes, and Hitler was dead. There was significance in his resigned helplessness, as he moaned:

> (*March 27, 1946, Ribbentrop's cell.*) "Ah, well, it makes no difference.—We are only living shadows—the shadows of a dead era—an era that died with Hitler. . . . The old era died with Hitler—we do not fit into the present world any more. On April 30 [the day that Hitler committed suicide] I should have taken the consequences. Yes, it is a great tragedy, a great tragedy, that is certain. What can one do now?"

The full extent of his suggestibility in his reaction to the mere image of the Führer had to be seen to be appreciated. When the movies on the Nazi Rise to Power were shown in the Nuremberg courtroom, for example:

> (*December 11, 1945, courtroom.*) Ribbentrop was completely overwhelmed by the voice and figure of the Führer. He wept like a baby, as if a dead father had returned to life. "Can't you feel the terrific strength of his personality?—Can't you see how he swept people off their feet? I don't know if you can, but we can feel it. It is *erschütternd!* . . ."
>
> (*Later, in Ribbentrop's cell.*) Still half moved to tears, Ribbentrop asked me if I hadn't felt the terrific power of Hitler's personality emanating from the screen. I confessed I hadn't.

Ribbentrop talked as if he were again hypnotized by the Führer's figure. "Do you know, even with all I know, if Hitler should come to me in this cell now, and say *'Do this!'*—I would still do it. Isn't it amazing? Can't you really feel the terrific magnetism of his personality?"

Small wonder that Ribbentrop's first reaction to the war crimes indictment had been: "The indictment is directed against the wrong people.—We were all under Hitler's shadow." The Foreign Minister's personality *had* become absorbed in the dictator's shadow, and that was all that was left of it now.

Nazi Statesmanship.—Ribbentrop nevertheless made a feeble attempt to disassociate himself from the "typical Nazis," and to show that he was, after all, a cultivated statesman with a cosmopolitan outlook. But even this attempt at reidentification only emphasized how his surrender to Hitlerism had burned his psychological bridges behind him. It was a sorry spectacle to watch his feeble attempts to keep up the pose of cultured statesman, as the aristocrats closed ranks with their backs literally turned to the Führer's favorite diplomat. The following excerpt of our observations, for example, recorded his reaction to Von Papen's defense of pre-Hitlerian statesmanship:

(*June 15, 1946, Ribbentrop's cell.*) Stimulated by Von Papen's self-portrayal as a statesman and man of culture, Ribbentrop started to impress me this morning with his qualities as a statesman and man of culture too. He launched into a long, confused, and abstruse speech on "political dynamics": The dynamic of Russian one-party politics led inevitably to the spreading of communism all over Europe, just as the National Socialist dynamic naturally had to lead to the spreading of National Socialism in the conquered territories, but America, with its two-party system, had a better balanced dynamic, whereas the dynamic of the British Empire naturally led dynamically to empire politics, etc., etc. Finally he asked me if I understood what he was talking about. To avoid argument I said yes. Ribbentrop was so tickled, he started to hiccough. He obviously did not understand it himself.

Then he asked me if I had read Otto Spengler (of course, he meant Oswald). He said when he thought of Otto Spengler he just hated to think of it, because he hated to think of the future of the West, which America, of course, was part of, and we ought to think about that too. . . .

His next thought was that if America had only listened to him, the whole catastrophe would have been avoided. He had sent somebody to America in 1940 to tell the Standard Oil people and the Jewish bankers not to let America get into the war. If they had only not been so hostile toward Germany. . . .

Ribbentrop's explanation of his statesmanship actually never rose above the level of such inane palaver, either in our informal conversations in his cell or in his formal defense before the Tribunal. On such a catastrophic issue as the making and breaking of the Munich Pact, he recalled that Hitler had simply charmed Chamberlain and Daladier with his glowing personality; he was sure because he had felt it himself. Besides, the Pact had not really been broken because Hitler had established a "Protectorate"—after some "sharp talk" to be sure—but then Czechoslovakia had merely been a state created by the Treaty of Versailles, and one must not take "diplomatic language" too seriously. We sought to draw him out on some rationale for signing the Russian Nonaggression Pact after signing the three-power Anti-Comintern Pact, and then attacking Russia two years later. He assured us that he had always been in favor of rapprochement with Russia and had wanted to include her in the three-power pact. The idea of including Russia in an anti-Comintern alliance did not strike him as presenting any diplomatic difficulties. Besides, "Hitler had great admiration for Stalin. He was only afraid some radical might come in his place." (22)

In his prepared defense on the witness stand he gave no better an account of himself than he did in these spontaneously inane explanations during our informal conversations. The confused thinking, the recklessness and sheer dilettantism of Ribbentrop's "statesmanship," as it became apparent throughout his defense, caused even his codefendants to wince. His explanation of the Munich Pact and Anti-Comintern Pact made the other diplomats' hair stand on end.

(*March 29, 1496, elders' lunchroom.*) . . . Von Neurath was equally contemptuous. "You can just see by the way he talks that he did not have the faintest conception of foreign affairs, when he took over the Foreign Office. And yet at that time he puffed himself up as the big expert."

"That's right!" Von Papen interjected with a sour face. "Not the remotest conception!—You can see from the way he talks about the Munich Pact and the Anti-Comintern Pact. The man simply did not know what he was doing!"

The Anti-Comintern Pact touched on Von Neurath's tender spot. "Yes, he does not say why he was the one to sign the Anti-Comintern Pact—because I refused to!! I knew it was dangerous business.—But he slavishly did everything Hitler wanted him to, even sticking his nose into things that were none of his business. As Ambassador to England he should have absolutely minded his own business in this matter. Instead he went out of the way to give the British a deliberate slap in the face by signing this pact while he was still Ambassador there. Naturally, the British had no use for him after that."

"The most flagrant violation of diplomatic usage you can imagine!" Von Papen scowled. "And such stupid dangerous dilettantism! And such abject servility to Hitler—ready to sign anything any time, the moment Hitler even thought of it, or before, if possible."

Doenitz had been listening and finally spoke up. "I don't think that Hitler was so dull as not to have seen through his stupidity, but I imagine he purposely kept such a man as his Foreign Minister, so that he could run the show himself."

Even Goering, for all his personal malice, could not help shaking his head painfully at that "pitiful spectacle! . . . people saying, 'What kind of a Foreign Minister did you Nazis have anyway?' It makes our foreign policy look so stupid. . . . He wasn't always so stupid and weak—but I realize now more than ever that he was hiding a lot of ignorance behind that arrogant front. . . . *Ach Gott!*—it is sad—very sad!"

Propagandist Hans Fritzsche (who was later acquitted of any complicity in war crimes) was almost in tears as he remarked, "Just imagine German soldiers going to war, confidently thinking that there is a competent Foreign Minister and a responsible administration that would not send them to war unless it was necessary."

And Hans Frank, ever-ready with his belated insights, observed, "It is not that simpleton's fault that he did not know anything about foreign affairs. But it was a crime on Hitler's part to make that man Foreign Minister for a nation of seventy million people. That shows you the real weakness of a dictatorship. It cannot stand criticism. Hitler surrounded himself with such fawning yes-men to give himself an artificial appearance of strength."

If Ambassador François-Poncet's and Sumner Welles's judgments of Ribbentrop's diplomacy were a little harsh, his fellow-Nazis' opinions were certainly not less so. Even his star witness at the trial, Under-Secretary Steengracht, had to admit that the Foreign Office was a mess of wrangling bureaucracy, with Ribbentrop spending 60 per cent of his time in petty jurisdictional disputes. The best he could say in Ribbentrop's defense was that "he was completely hynotized by Hitler and then became his tool."

This was, in fact, the real key to his motivation and the role he played, as well as the disintegration that followed.

Guilt Reaction.—To analyze his guilt reaction in this state of demoralization, we must first separate the war guilt from the atrocities. Ribbentrop was spared the full impact of guilt feelings about precipitating the war by his inability to comprehend it fully. To some extent, at least, his war guilt anxiety was buried in a maze of confused rationalizations about loyalty, foreign oppression, and political "dynamics." But no amount of confused rationalization could sufficiently obfuscate his moral guilt for unprovoked mass murder. Even in those states that bordered on agitated depression, he felt constrained to make the distinction:

(*January 5, 1946, Ribbentrop's cell.*) "In the atrocities and persecution of the Jews, our guilt as Germans is so enormous, that it leaves one speechless. There is no defense, no explanation. But if you just put that aside—really, the other countries all have a share in bringing about the war. . . . I know how Germany was being strangled by the Versailles Treaty. . . . How Hitler could have done all those things later, I don't know—I just don't know."

(*May 4, 1946, Ribbentrop's cell.*) Ribbentrop is getting into an increasingly agitated state. He paced the cell, sat down, got up, paced the cell again, sat down, snapped his fingers rapidly out of sheer nervous tension, his face twitching as he spoke rapidly with wild gestures, as if in a panic over the denunciation of the Nazi leadership.

"I have been thinking over and over again the incredible things that have happened.—The future looks so black—for Europe.—If I only didn't have children.—Stalin is a tremendous power—a mighty man, greater than Peter the Great. . . . I think that is why Hitler decided to attack him. . . . But the Jewish murders— that is terrible. That is where my loyalty stops—that is the most horrible thing imaginable, there is no doubt about that. But the political questions—there is so much to be said about it; if I could only talk to a few reasonable Americans. . . ."

As the atrocity evidence multiplied, Ribbentrop's anxiety increased to panic. On that issue, at least, the impossibility of being Hitler's shadow and one of the social elite at the same time fully penetrated his consciousness. Indeed, the dilemma had now to be finally resolved with his own life hanging in the balance. The testimony of his brutal ultimatum to Regent Horthy of Hungary—"either exterminated or taken to concentration camps"—shook him even more than his threats to President Hacha of Czechoslovakia. "I *could not* have said such a thing! It is so entirely contrary to my character," he insisted. He had "violently opposed" Hitler's persecution of the Jews. Decent Germans simply don't *do* such things!

It was, indeed, rather strong talk for one who had aspired to the epitome of social respectability. Such statements, literally taken out of Hitler's mouth, might have sounded more in character coming from any one of the revolutionary psychopaths than from the genteel, would-be-aristocrat of Berlin and London salons. We have already indicated that by that time Ribbentrop had completely subjugated his mind to Hitler's. But the traumatic impact of the atrocity evidence involves something more subtle than his realization that he was being held culpable for the role of Hitler's shadow. Our observation was that Ribbentrop acted as if he had *not fully realized* that the mass exterminations were actually taking place while he was implementing the policy of genocide.

We must pause here to consider a crucial question: How was it possible for a political leader, supposedly not a criminal psychopath, however unscrupulous in his ambition, to continue for years to condone a policy of human extermination, unless he did not know that it was actually being carried out?—and how could he have failed to know it?

Let us first cite Ribbentrop's reaction to the testimony of Colonel Hoess of Auschwitz, describing how he himself had carried out this mass extermination on Hitler's orders:

(*April 20, 1946, Ribbentrop's cell.*) Ribbentrop seems to have suffered a relapse into a depression with an aphasia-like condition.

"I either can't find—the words—or I can't make the sentences. . . . I have thoughts—but I can't control—. Do you understand? . . . Tell me, I wasn't in court on Monday.—Did Hoess actually say—that Hitler had ordered the mass murders?—In 1941?—did he say that?—in '41?—in '41?—in '41?—Did he really say that? (We confirmed the testimony.)—But Hitler only spoke of transporting them to the East or to Madagascar. . . . Did Hitler really order the extermination?—in '41?—in '41?"

Ribbentrop held his head in his hand and repeated in a descending whisper, "—'41—'41—'41—My God!—Did Hoess say in '41?" (We again confirmed the details.)

"Stop! Stop, doctor!—I cannot bear it!—All those years— a man to whom children came so trustingly and lovingly.—It must have been a fanatic madness. There is no doubt now that Hitler ordered it? I thought even up to now that perhaps Himmler, late in the war, under some pretext—. But '41 he said? My God! My God!"

To understand this reaction, we must first recall that 1941 was the year in which Ribbentrop's father died, as well as the year in which the violent scene with Hitler occurred. Panicked at the threat of losing favor, or of causing the mighty Führer's collapse, Ribbentrop had given his word of honor never to question his judgment again. This had required nothing less than the complete stifling of the last vestige of independent judgment and conscience, since the actual extermination program went into full production that year. That operation was, to be sure, a carefully guarded state secret strictly under Himmler's jurisdiction; but there can be no doubt that the ubiquitous Foreign Minister had, as always, gotten ample indications of what was afoot. Indeed, it was common knowledge among higher SS officials, and one of Ribbentrop's underlings later stated that "the Reich Foreign Minister, Ribbentrop, obviously knew Hit-

ler's intention to exterminate the Jews of Europe." Nevertheless, it is a moot question just how clearly Ribbentrop allowed
the *actuality*—the *full realization*—of mass extermination to
penetrate his consciousness. The distinction is no mere academic quibble. It is the crux of our observations on the vital
question: How could the respectable conformists to the norms
of Christian civilization have apparently condoned and even
promoted the commission of such fantastic atrocities?

Our psychological reference point, of course, is the functional
gap between discrete sensations and the full realization of meaning in social context, with value judgments leading to action.
It is a psychological truism, often applied to hysterics, that
"there are none so blind as those who will not see." We know
that Ribbentrop was a passive, suggestible, inadequate personality who dared not see the evil of the man who so abundantly
fulfilled his ego-needs and whom he had sworn under traumatic
circumstances never to criticize. *But he was not a frank hysteric,* like Hess, who could conveniently blot it out of his consciousness, nor a paranoiac who could distort the reality of it
with a system of delusions. Yet he could not have done what
he did with full knowledge of the consequences, unless he was
also a sadistic psychopath, which he was not. Here again, the
traditional concepts of psychopathology fail us.

But between knowledge and ignorance there is the limbo of
arrested perceptions and inhibited insights. Between calculated
hypocrisy and hysterical dissociation there is semiconscious self-
deception. It is possible to look at things without fully perceiving them, to divert one's attention from the unpleasant to the
pleasant, from the ego-threatening to the ego-gratifying; to sus-
pend the process of rational inference in mid-air, and to distort
one's insights just enough to suppress anxiety. As Hans Frank
said, "We did not *want* to know!"—and there are none so blind
as those who would suppress anxiety by arresting insight.

The question whether Ribbentrop was fully aware of the
enormity and actuality of his guilt with respect to the atrocities
can be answered only in such paradoxical terms. We can reconcile all of our observations and evaluations only by inferring that
Ribbentrop verbalized Hitler's aggressions while blinding him-

self to their actuality; that he suppressed any full realization of his guilt in preference to sacrificing his only source of security in a chaotic world. Even when the world-wide revulsion to Maidanek in 1944 forced the reality upon him, he accepted Hitler's admonition to mind his own business and put that thing out of his mind—for that is precisely what he had been doing for several years in an attempt to resolve the incompatibility of his ego-needs. Complete self-deception was no longer possible after that, but he still sought desperately to divert his attention from any full realization of what had taken place and hoped against hope that he would never be forced to face the realities in the light of non-Hitlerian social values. It was for that reason that Ribbentrop came to Nuremberg in such a demoralized state, and the atrocity evidence struck him as with the sudden realization of murder. His moral collapse was complete even before the death sentence was pronounced. Just how abysmal this collapse was may be judged by the fact that the once proud spokesman of the new order begged the writer to intercede with the Tribunal to spare his life, so that he could write a long exposé of the Nazi regime.

The sordid end to Ribbentrop's career emphasized the dismal inadequacy of some of the leading personalities in the Nazi dictatorship—the blind passiveness of their aggression, the shallowness of their loyalties and values. This was far from the united determination of purpose, the Machiavellian craftiness, even the ruthless fanaticism one had been led to expect in Hitler's diplomats.

The distinction between the political opportunist and the ideological fanatic has already been made. But when we speak of reckless political opportunists, we must distinguish at least two extremes of personality variants: the ruthlessly aggressive psychopath who consciously pursues his self-centered goals with a cynical disdain for the social mores; and the passive-dependant, suggestible conformist, who seeks social status at any price but suppresses any insight into the incompatibility of his motives. These opposite extremes may join hands in a political conspiracy to achieve their common material goals—a conspiracy in which the morally halt lead the purposefully blind. This is particularly true in an authoritarian culture, which reaches the epitome of capricious leadership under an ideological dictatorship. In such a conspiracy, the passive, imitative, compensatory aggression of the inadequate personality may become just as disastrously effective as the aggressive lust of the most ruthless psychopath. Such, at least, was Foreign Minister Ribbentrop's function in the Nazi dictatorship.

Chapter 5

THE MILITARISTS

Among social institutions, the undisputed prototype of authoritarianism is the military hierarchy. From earliest tribal warfare to modern times, the principle of organized aggression in obedience to leaders in a hierarchy of command has been regarded as essential to the security of ethnic and national groups. The protection of that security, either aggressively or defensively, has been the chief responsibility of the warrior caste, whose status within the culture has frequently been relatively high (until the advent of modern democracy). Inevitably, the ancient guarantor of group security has represented an increasing threat to international security. Along with a growing realization of this anachronism has grown a changing attitude toward militaristic values. Certainly the ancient proverb *dulce et decorum est, pro patria mori* has not been regarded as the highest of human aspirations by modern liberalism, either in Germany or the Western democracies. On the contrary, the glorification of war and military authority have become increasingly identified with the value systems of aggressive militaristic dictatorship. Such values, rightly or wrongly attributed to Prussian militarism, have been held largely responsible for setting loose two disastrous world wars in the past thirty-five years. It behooves us to examine these values.

Hitler and Goering have eloquently stated for us the dictators' cynically aggressive conceptions of nationalism. But they were by no means the true representatives of Prussian militarism. (Their Bavarian background is irrelevant here, since we are dealing with the functional *identification* of group values.) We have advisedly put them into a distinct group of Nazi revolutionists—a group that set up its own system of values by a rebellious revision of the traditional values of their culture. It was the career officers of the Wehrmacht, particularly the officers of the General Staff and High Command, who were the true representatives of Prussian militarism.

The career officers of the General Staff and High Command constituted the most homogeneous and least pathological group among the leaders of Nazi Germany whom we studied. Although there were definite differences in origin and temperament, the homogeneity of their lifelong indoctrination and social milieu had rigidified their behavior patterns and system of values in the common mold of traditional Prussian militarism. Whatever adverse effect social conflict may have had in the selection and cultivation of political leaders, the General Staff had produced leadership of a different breed. No mere haven for frustrated neurotics or psychopathic adventurers, the General Staff had long represented the very kernel of the hard core of Junker leadership in Germany. And not without reason. An almost ascetic devotion to duty, a self-sacrificing spirit of patriotism and loyalty to the Chief of State, a rigid code of honor and personal integrity, an aloofness from extramilitary group prejudices, even a certain deference to humane (albeit self-protective) principles in the conduct of war—these were the more or less positive values derived from medieval concepts of chivalry. These values upheld the prestige of Prussian militarism within its own culture and among the militarists of the world. But this rigid asceticism had its negative aspect as well, when viewed from a broader humanitarian viewpoint—or its distinct advantages from a dictatorial viewpoint. There was the rigid obedience to superiors, regardless of right or wrong, the incentives of promotion and power, the aloofness from social responsibility even at the highest levels of authority, and an academic attitude toward preparation for war, with or without provocation. These were some of the well-indoctrinated attitudes that could serve to make the General Staff a ready tool in the hands of an aggressive dictator.

There was bound to be a conflict of loyalties among the General Staff officers when confronted with a Commander in Chief who represented a complete revolution of traditional values, just as there was among the diplomats. Certainly many of the *Gen-*

eralstäbler refused to let any militaristic values or aspirations completely abolish their sense of responsibility in the strengthening of national security. Many drew the line at reckless aggression and atrocities (Generals von Fritsch, Beck, and Oster, Admiral Canaris, etc.), and paid for this "sentimentality" with their lives. Those who rose to favor and served Hitler to the end, like those we studied at Nuremberg, were the more rigid militarists who could be moved by no broader considerations of duty to abandon the obsession of obedience or the advantages of promotion and power. It was they who most obediently served the "upstart corporal" in spite of their misgivings and who protested that their code of loyalty rendered them helpless to exercise independent value judgments on policy. It is this difference between the narrower and broader conception of patriotic duty, between rigid formality and basic adaptability of group ideals, that concerns us here.

The case of Hitler's Chief of Staff will suffice to provide a focal point for our examination of the militaristic mentality that implemented aggressive dictatorship.

FIELD MARSHAL KEITEL, CHIEF OF STAFF

Wilhelm Keitel became Hitler's Chief of Staff at the same time that Ribbentrop became Foreign Minister. The parallel was psychologically highly significant, as we shall see. But as a leading member of his professional group, the general had a way of life and a code of values that were not to be confused with that of any mere politician. These values may have been shared to some extent by other leaders who reflected the common heritage of an authoritarian culture; but it was the career officer of the Wehrmacht, especially the *Generalstäbler,* who was the very prototype of that tradition, whose entire life was dedicated to it, and who controlled the armed might of the nation to carry it forward. In the military hierarchy of Nazi Germany, there were many who might be held up as better examples of this tradition than was Field Marshal Keitel; but it was certainly Hitler's Chief of Staff who best symbolized the Prussian militarists' collaboration with aggressive dictatorship.

Life History

Early Background.—Wilhelm Keitel was born in 1882 in Helmscherode, Braunschweig. He was the older of two sons born to Karl Keitel, a descendant of one of the land-owning-officer families of North Germany, whose allegiance to Prussian militarism had been firmly established under Bismarck's iron rule. The Keitels owned the estate of Poppenburg in the former kingdom of Hanover. The father was a hale and hearty lord of the manor, who supervised the estate on horseback until he was eighty-one years old. The mother, however, suffered from tuberculosis. She died of puerperal fever after the birth of their second son. Wilhelm was then seven years old.

Aside from his mother's untimely death, his youth was uneventful. He received his early training from his father and from a private tutor. He absorbed the indoctrination that was common to all Junker youth, and grew up with the same sense of security and tradition that was rooted in the soil of the family estate. At the age of ten he was sent to Göttingen to receive his intermediate education, in preparation for a military career. His accomplishments as a scholar were indifferent, but his behavior was exemplary.

Upon graduation from secondary school at the age of nineteen, Keitel enlisted as an officer-candidate in an artillery regiment of the Prussian army. After eighteen months of grueling training in the usual tradition, he received his commission. For the next few years he performed various routine tours of duty in the peacetime Prussian army.

In 1904, two years after receiving his commission, Keitel married Lisa Fontaine, the daughter of another land-owning Hanoverian family. They had to live very modestly without children, as became a junior-officer couple, for the first few years, but a proper level of social activity had to be maintained. Family allowances supplemented the altogether too modest salary of a junior officer so that proper social amenities could be observed. Seven years after their marriage, when Keitel had been made captain, they started to raise a family. Three sons and two daughters were born to them between 1911 and 1919.

The only other event Keitel considered worthy of mention in his pre-World War I career was a fracture of the hip he sustained in a fall from a horse in 1907, while taking riding lessons at the Military Institute in Hanover. This injury continued to disturb him in later years, but did not interfere with his career.

At the outbreak of World War I Keitel was a regimental adjutant. He was wounded in the right arm shortly after the beginning of hostilities, but was nevertheless able to take command of a battery soon afterward. In 1915 he passed the highly competitive requirements for duty as a General Staff officer. He was now a full-fledged member of the in-group. From then on he served, with no particular distinction, on the general staffs at various echelons from division to corps. He was on the General Staff of the Naval Corps in Flanders when the war ended.

Like all other General Staff officers, Keitel received the news of Germany's capitulation as a severe blow. The humiliation was the more intense since many of his group were blamed for losing the war or for having started it needlessly and had their epaulets ripped off their shoulders by angry veterans in the streets of Berlin. Like the others, *Generalstäbler* Keitel's aggression vented itself against the monstrous injustice and humiliation of the Treaty of Versailles. His own family estate was not affected by the Polish Corridor through Prussia, but he shared the violent indignation of his father and all North German landowners over this emasculation of their entire socioeconomic structure. Though otherwise aloof from politico-economic issues, he never overcame his indignation at this "outrage." His recollection of his feelings during these post war years, as given to us later, was:

> "I wanted to be a country gentleman.—But I must tell you one thing, professor, an American simply cannot understand our desperation after the Treaty of Versailles. Just think: unemployment, national disgrace. Let me say it bluntly in all honor—the Treaty of Versailles was a *dirty shame!* And that is what every decent German had to feel. Just imagine ripping the heart out of Prussia to give Poland a corridor to the sea! . . . Every decent German had to say, '*Down with the Treaty of Versailles,* by any means, fair or foul!'" (22)

Between Wars.—Keitel would have preferred to retire to his family estate, but in accordance with Junker tradition he had to continue to serve as an officer at least until he inherited the estate. He accordingly availed himself of the General Staff officer's priority for duty in the Reichswehr, the 100,000-man army allowed Germany under the Treaty of Versailles. In this way the nucleus of the General Staff and Officers Corps remained intact while planning future opportunities to undo the disgrace of defeat. Keitel played a very minor role in the Reichswehr's activities for the next ten years, confining himself mostly to the border defense activities for which the Reichswehr had supposedly been sanctioned. In 1929, by dint of faithful service and seniority, he became chief of the Army Organizational Division of the Reichswehr Ministry.

In 1932 an arterial embolism and thrombosis incapacitated Keitel for some time, and he was forced to consider giving up his military career. The long-awaited opportunity to retire as a "country gentleman" came in 1934, when his father died. He did, in fact, retire to inactive status from 1933 to 1935. But by this time Hitler had come to power and things were beginning to look up for the General Staff. The opportunities in the rapidly expanding Wehrmacht were too good to overlook, especially for one who had accumulated so much seniority in the General Staff. Retirement on a modest pension in the midst of a depression, with a colonel's rank at best, and no great victories to relate to his children—this was not the most attractive prospect that his training had led him to look forward to.

On the other hand, "It was clear to me that when Hitler became Chancellor, we soldiers would undoubtedly have a different position in the Reich under new leadership, and that the military factor would certainly be viewed differently than heretofore . . . I must confess that I welcomed the plan and intention to rearm as far as possible at the time." (36)

Keitel accordingly accepted an appointment as Chief of Staff to the new Minister of War, Field Marshal von Blomberg, in 1935. His promotion to brigadier general followed soon afterward.

One of his first duties, at Von Blomberg's behest, was to have the Operations Division draw up a plan of march for the occupation of the Rheinland. He asked Von Blomberg what they were supposed to do if the French resisted. Von Blomberg told him that in that case, of course, they would have to beat a hasty retreat; but the Führer took full responsibility for the adventure, so they didn't have to worry about it. Keitel confided later that three battalions of French troops would have flicked them right off the map, and he "wouldn't have been a bit surprised." But the success of the adventure breathed new life into the General Staff. The control of iron and steel production of the Ruhr enabled Hitler to throw his rearmament program into high gear. Within a short time he was able to announce that the Versailles Treaty was dead.

The prospects of a brilliant military career were enhanced when Keitel's oldest son married the youngest daughter of the War Minister. However, his pride in this union went glimmering when Von Blomberg became the subject of a major scandal by marrying a woman of ill repute, and Von Fritsch demanded that Hitler remove this stain on the honor of the General Staff. Nevertheless, to his surprise, Keitel was given the post of Chief of Staff of the High Command, directly under Hitler, in the reshuffle that took place in February, 1938. Keitel was one of the few General Staff officers who believed Hitler's estimate of his own military genius, and applauded his taking over the post of Commander-in-Chief. As in the case of Ribbentrop, it was this obsequiousness, rather than any professional distinction, which won him the top post under Hitler. Generals von Fritsch and von Blomberg had taken exception to Hitler's aggressive plans after the "Hoszbach conference," but Keitel had listened and kept his peace. He had really done little more than follow the time-honored formula for military promotion—"Keep the old man happy, and don't stick your neck out." Thirty-five years of adherence to a rigid code of obedience had not inspired the passive militarist, who longed to be a country squire, with any sense of responsibility or independence of thought.

In accordance with Hitler's plans, Keitel delegated the preparation of plans for the invasion of Austria, Czechoslovakia, and Poland from 1938 to 1939. As far as he was concerned, plans for attack were routine academic exercises for the General Staff and did not mean that war would actually break out. In fact, the army was little better prepared for hostilities in the event of war over Czechoslovakia or Poland than they had been at the time of the remilitarization of the Rheinland. But Hitler's "clever strategy" convinced many of the General Staff and High Command that great victories could be won by bluff without shedding a drop of blood.

Keitel could not have been entirely in doubt that Hitler was serious about deliberately creating an incident to provide a "propagandistic cause" for the attack on Poland. Full mobilization was ordered, and Admiral Canaris, Chief of Counter-Intelligence, told Keitel that Himmler had asked for Polish uniforms for a secret operation. Keitel apparently sensed what was afoot but merely told Canaris not to get the Wehrmacht mixed up in it. Conscious implication in deliberate aggression, which might have disturbed his Junker sensibilities, was obviated by the simple device of denying jurisdiction and inquiring no further into the matter. Keitel later claimed that he did not even remember hearing of the "Gleiwitz incident," in which some Polish soldiers had allegedly attacked the radio station at Gleiwitz as a preparation for an attack on Germany. (The "Polish soldiers" turned out to be concentration camp victims whom Himmler had dressed in Polish uniforms and left dead at the Gleiwitz radio station.) A Chief of Staff who was busy drawing up plans for an attack did not have time to concern himself with questions of international diplomacy. The General Staff was accordingly quite shocked when England and France made good their pledges and declared war as soon as German troops invaded Poland. The mysterious death of General von Fritsch in the first days of the Polish campaign likewise shocked and mystified the entire Junker military clique. (General Jodl confirmed these reactions.) But any misgivings Keitel may have had were soon assuaged by his sense of patriotic duty and his promotion to General der Infantrie after the three-week *Blitzkrieg* in Poland.

World War II.—According to Keitel, the German generals were quite surprised by France's immobility during the early months of the war, especially during the Polish campaign, considering the vulnerability of the Wehrmacht. "From a purely military operational point of view, a French attack during the Polish campaign would have encountered only a German military screen, not a real defense. Since nothing of this sort happened, we soldiers thought, of course, that the Western powers had no serious intentions," Keitel later testified. (36) Hitler could thus assure the generals that the West was not really interested in Germany's Eastern *Lebensraum,* and they still assumed that some negotiated peace could be arranged as soon as Hitler got what he wanted.

Nevertheless, Keitel had the Operations Division, under General Jodl, prepare plans for the invasion of Norway and Denmark, knowing that it constituted a violation of Germany's nonaggression pacts with those countries and would commit both sides to a bitter fight to the finish. However, the legal and moral issues were not the concern of the General Staff as Keitel saw it. "I left those things, I must say, to those who were concerned with political matters." The same applied to the neutrality of Belgium, Holland, and Luxembourg. For purely strategic reasons, the commanding generals and General Staff did object to Hitler's eagerness to press the attack against France immediately through the neutral Low Countries. They pointed out that even if there was a danger that France might beat them to it, they were better prepared to meet such an eventuality than to undertake the offensive. Hitler upbraided Keitel for siding with the timid Old Guard of Prussian General Staff officers. However, the plans were ready, and the neutral countries were invaded in the spring of 1941. The Maginot Line was turned, and the victory over France soon followed. Keitel could only bow to his master's superior genius as he happily signed the French Armistice in the same railroad car where the Allies had received the Kaiser's generals in 1918—and then received his promotion to Field Marshal.

This historic and personal victory would have been enough to turn any German general's head. It assured him of a definite and glorious place in the annals of the German General Staff and a sure mention in the German history books for all time.

The promotion, furthermore, elevated him to the top rank of Prussian militarists—to the rank of Moltke, Clausewitz, and Von Hindenburg himself. Here was status and prestige enough to last him even in retirement for the rest of his life. Keitel confided that he did not feel worthy of being in such exalted company because he really had no conception of strategy and had not earned his laurels in the field of battle, as a field marshal should. But at the time, who was to deny the slogan *Der Führer hat immer Recht* (The Führer is always right)? Certainly not Keitel. On the contrary, he prostrated himself all the more slavishly at the feet of the military genius whose intuition proved surer than the studious calculations of the whole General Staff. It required no hysterical scene, no plea of forgiveness to assure Hitler of Keitel's unquestioning obedience from that time on. Allied indecision had played into Hitler's hands and immeasurably increased his prestige among the generals, all along the way from remilitarization of the Rheinland to the fall of France.

But then things started getting out of hand. Italy had joined the fray to share in the spoils. "We were drawn into the war against Greece and against Yugoslavia in the spring of 1941 to our complete surprise and without having made any plans. . . . There were calls on the part of Mussolini for help. . . . Therefore, by improvised means, help was rendered." (36)

It soon became apparent that the war could not end with the defeat of France, even if England had been willing. As early as the summer of 1940, a year after signing the Nonaggression Pact, Hitler had revealed to the generals his intention of attacking Russia. Keitel had accordingly assigned the task of drawing up a plan for this ambitious undertaking to Generals Jodl and von Paulus. The General Staff had no heart for such a reckless violation of the basic principle of Prussian military strategy—"under no circumstances a two-front war!" Even Keitel made efforts to dissuade Hitler from such a mad adventure—not to his face, but through the dubious offices of the Foreign Minister, who was just as little disposed to tell the Führer he was wrong. The tide of easy victories was clearly running out, and the more determined generals insisted on finishing the war in the West before extending their Eastern adventure. The aerial offensive against England was bogging down, and partisan resistance in the East was trouble enough for one war. But there was no dissuading a Commander-in-Chief convinced of his own military genius. The time was ripe for the decisive blow Hitler had promised in his own lifetime to secure Germany's Eastern *Lebensraum.*

The High Command were informed that this was to be a showdown between two ideologies and that ordinary rules of land warfare and international law were to be abandoned. Orders were accordingly given "to do away with the legal system in territories that were not pacified, to combat resistance with brutal means."

As soon as the invasion started, in June, 1941, it became clear that this meant wholesale extermination of civilian populations by Himmler's SS Commandos and wholesale execution of hostages, prisoners of war, and partisans. This was unorthodox warfare according to the standards of Prussian militarism, and Keitel had "severe conflicts of conscience." But Hitler took the responsibility, and Keitel's function was merely to sign or initial orders issued by him. Many of these merely directed commanding generals to "cooperate" with Himmler's SS (who had no compunctions about the accepted rules of land warfare) and were not directly under their command. Far from the scene of action, under direct daily pressure of Hitler's "military genius," Keitel could not see the masses who were butchered in cold blood by the grace of the directives he initialed and passed on.

In the meantime personal tragedies overcame the general who had so recently reached the pinnacle of success. His youngest son, newly commissioned a lieutenant in the army, was severely wounded and then killed on the Russian front. The two older sons, both majors, were wounded and then captured somewhere in Russian territory. His younger daughter died of tuberculosis in Switzerland in 1940.

To what extent he was demoralized by these personal losses could not be determined, but Keitel continued to issue directives surpassing in brutality all practices in the archives of the General Staff. Any aggression that his personal losses engendered was not, at any rate, directed against the Führer who had insisted on this reckless gamble. On the contrary, the Führer convinced him that the hostility and underhanded measures of resistance by the enemy justified the most Draconian countermeasures.

As resistance in all occupied territories increased, the "unorthodox" suppressive measures increased. One decree after another went out with Keitel's initials :—The *Nacht und Nebel* decree, by which dangerous civilians disappeared in the dead of night without trace, to avoid the fuss of uncertain court-martials ; the "lynch law" for enemy parachutists ; the "special treatment" of partisans ; the branding and enslavement of Russian prisoners ; the "severe measures" against families of Frenchmen fighting in Russia ; firing squads for relatives of saboteurs. In addition, he verbally transmitted "the Führer's wishes" for assassination of escaped prisoners who had excited the Führer's wrath (like Generals Giraud and Weygand), and stood helplessly by while other groups were apprehended and executed by Himmler (like the fifty Royal Air Force officers who escaped from the Sagon prison camp).

Field Marshal Keitel said he had some "misgivings" about many of these measures and thought that some of them were simply "impossible for a soldier." He even considered resigning or shooting himself (confirmed by Jodl), but his code of loyalty to a superior forbade him to think of plotting against him.

Some of the other generals, however, were taking a radically different view of their responsibility to the security of the nation. The decimation and surrender of the armies at Stalingrad and the retreat all along the Eastern and North Africa fronts proved that Hitler's recklessness and intuitive methods had gone too far. A group of top-ranking generals resumed their plot to assassinate Hitler as the only means of putting an end to the senseless slaughter incurred by the dilettante corporal. They felt out the Chief of Staff on the possibility of his cooperation, but his blind obedience and admiration of the Commander-in-Chief left any support from that quarter out of the question. Finally, after the successful Allied landings in France in June, 1944, the generals knew that the war was irrevocably lost and decided to take matters into their own hands.

On July 20 General Beck placed a bomb under Hitler's table at GHQ but in such a position that the blast was partly diverted by the heavy table-top. Keitel and Jodl suffered slight concussions, and Hitler escaped with a split eardrum and lacerations of the arm and leg. Keitel supported Hitler's fury against traitors in their midst and helped turn them over to a people's court, after depriving them of their rank. (A German general must never hang.) He required the Wehrmacht to take a new oath of allegiance to Hitler and to use the Hitler salute. Any further talk of possible defeat was to be punished as treason.

The Führer who had always been right in the beginning was by now always wrong, but Keitel would not forswear his loyalty in times of adversity. The armies were driven back with heavy losses in France, Italy, the Balkans, and Poland, uncovering scenes of incredible atrocities. Early in 1945 Hitler planned a dramatic counteroffensive with spies in American uniforms behind the lines in the Ardennes. This was Germany's last all-out effort, in command of General von Rundstedt, though he and every one else had doubts about its possibility of success. This counteroffensive also fizzled out, as Rundstedt had warned it must, and a large part of the German army was annihilated in the "Battle of the Bulge." Hitler nevertheless still insisted on fighting on to a finish. He ordered last-ditch resistance and a "scorched earth" policy on all fronts, with ruthless reprisals for any one harboring a "defeatist attitude." The "scorched earth" policy was so patently suicidal for a patently defeated nation, that some of the Nazi leaders took it upon themselves to ignore it. But not Keitel. The Führer's word was still law.

Hitler had already announced that if the German race could not prove its superiority in the struggle for its manifest destiny, it did not deserve to survive. Keitel could not think in such lofty terms, but if Hitler had ordered a scorched earth, a scorched earth it would have to be. He would not be a traitor like certain other generals. If there was anything wrong with destroying even the basis of Germany's future survival, the Führer had assumed full responsibility for it.

But to Keitel's horror, the Commander-in-Chief, who had assumed all the responsibility and had demanded such unquestioning loyalty, committed suicide to avoid capture and left him to sign the surrender.

OBSERVATIONS AND EVALUATION

"The Führer's Mouthpiece."—Field Marshal Keitel had impressed some of General Eisenhower's staff, who witnessed the signing of the surrender, as a living example of "Prussian arrogance and defiance." But his erect posture and military bearing at the surrender must have been deceptive. All the iron went out of his character with the signing of the surrender because in fact it had never really been anything but the adopted behavior pattern of his breed. As in Ribbentrop's case, there was the anomaly of shadow and substance that revealed itself when the social props were removed. In Keitel's case, it was not merely the disappearance of the commander on whose authority he had relied, but the collapse of the ego-involved institutional structure. Stripped of his military rank and power, Keitel revealed himself as an obsequious, gentle soul who had never really wanted to fight but had always longed to be a country squire. We could hardly resist the temptation of comparing him to Ferdinand the Bull in current American folklore.

Still erect in his stripped gray tunic and boots, his mustache and thin gray hair always well groomed, Keitel was the very model of a well-behaved prisoner. Being deprived of rank, he dutifully bowed to every junior officer who came into the cell. He was suffering physical discomfort and anxiety over the fate of his family, but he made no complaint. There were more important things to worry about.

His main concern was that the International Military Tribunal had set forth in its Charter the principle that obedience to superior orders could not be accepted as exculpation of crime. "I was nothing but the Führer's mouthpiece to carry out his wishes," he protested in one of our first conversations. "As Chief of Staff I had no authority whatever—no command function—nothing. All I could do was to transmit his orders to the Staff and see that they were carried out."

It has sometimes been said that the case of the German generals represented a "special case" that should not have been subjected to ordinary legal conceptions of guilt. They were, the argument goes, only acting in accordance with their military duty, which gave them no alternative but to obey their Commander-in-Chief, Adolf Hitler; they should not have been judged according to the social mores of Western democracies who happened to be the victors. It is not our purpose to retry the case of Field Marshal Keitel from a legalistic or even a moralistic viewpoint; we are interested in the examination of social values, motivation, and character—what it was in the minds of these men that made them support a dictatorship and a disastrous war policy to the bitter end.

In that connection, there are three main questions which present themselves for examination: (a) what the German militarists saw in Hitler; (b) their attitude on the question of war guilt; and (c) their conception of loyalty. Each of these questions has a definite bearing on the issue of how the militaristic mentality may serve the purpose of aggressive dictatorship—at least the manner in which it served Hitler's. To avoid the danger of too moralistic an evaluation of Prussian militarism from the standpoint of our own culture, we shall rely principally on the statements of the German war leaders themselves. We may safely do this, since the war chiefs, outside of Goering and the other revolutionists, were men of some insight and integrity within their own nationalistic and militaristic frame of reference. While Keitel himself was by no means the best example of his breed, his attitudes and values will throw light on these questions when considered in comparison to those of other war leaders.

Attitudes Toward Hitler.—We have already seen that the General Staff were perfectly content to tolerate Hitler as long as he seemed to serve their own purpose of a military resurgence in Germany. General Lahousen, the Austrian who became Assistant Chief of the Abwehr, said (in a statement to the author upon capture) that the generals should have realized that Hitler would get out of hand at least as early as the time of the Roehm purge. "I'll never understand how the Wehrmacht reconciled itself to that. . . . He stood for a complete reversal of their values :—brutality and injustice became virtues of 'hardness'; decency and honor became contemptible weakness." We may therefore justifiably ask just how generals like Keitel could reconcile their rigid code of honor with Hitlerian values, if they were not completely cynical in their loyalty to a militaristic dictator.

Hitler had been well aware of the necessity of selling himself to the Prussian militarists by an appeal to their authoritarian values. Even on the day he assumed the chancellorship, Frank informed us, Hitler had expressed the hope of "winning over" the Junker President, who obviously still had his reservations about the upstart corporal. "The old gent was pleased, though," said Hitler, after the swearing-in ceremony, "when I told him today that I will serve him faithfully as Reich Chancellor just as I did in the old days as a soldier in the army, when he was my hero." (18)   Hitler had left no doubt that his *Führerstaat* was just an application of Junker authoritarianism to civilian government.

But aside from the tradition of obedience to superiors, Keitel was quite aware that there had been a paradox of values presented by Hitler's rebellion against the old order. He could only protest that he had been deceived by Hitler's use of militaristic symbols.

"God knows how honorable and immaculate that Prussian Officers' Corps was!—A code of honor that was the pride of the nation ever since Bismarck, and had a fine tradition going back to Frederick the Great! Why, if an officer didn't pay a debt of twenty-five marks, he was arrested and disgraced.— Why, it never occurred to me that Hitler had any other code. The first thing you saw in his office was a marble statuette of Frederick the Great and paintings of Bismarck and Hindenburg." (Those symbols, at least, were the first things that came into the focus of perception of a Prussian militarist whose motives demanded a reconciliation of his values with those of the dictator who gave him his promotions.) ". . . I can only say that I obeyed him in good faith, and now that I see where it has brought me, I can only say that my loyalty and faith have been betrayed!" He pounded his fist on his knee and repeated the last word with hatred: *"Betrayed!* That is all I can say! . . . And I can tell you that I suffer more agony of conscience and self-reproach in this cell than anybody will ever know. I believed in him too blindly.—If anybody had dared to tell me then any of the things I have found out now, I would have said, 'You are an insane traitor—I'll have you shot!' "

General Jodl made similar charges of deception: "—Especially in the clever way he appealed to the intelligent people. It wasn't just the desperate unemployed and the emotions of women. He appealed to the understanding of intelligent men too. The movement would never have gained impetus if men of repute had not been swept along with it and given the movement some prestige before the German people. That is where propaganda did a terrific job." Jodl described how the pillars of respectability like Von Papen, Schacht, Von Neurath, had given Hitler's chancellorship an aura of solidity that completely camouflaged his contempt of traditional conceptions of law and order. As far as the Roehm purge was concerned, he had shed no tears over the liquidation of the "homosexual swine" who had plotted to liquidate the General Staff, and they had believed. along with the unimpeachable Von Hindenburg, that a threat to national security had been eliminated. Under those circumstances they had little scruple about the methods used.

Thus, at least in the early years of the dictatorship, there were sufficient appeals to the symbols of authoritarian nationalism to overcome the misgivings that many of the protectors of national security may have had about Hitler in the beginning.

But it required more than the clever appeal to symbols to win the respect of hard-headed militarists when the time came to plan and execute acts of aggression, for this was a matter of outright military strategy. Here we can only say there were two schools of thought on Hitler's "military genius." Keitel was one of the few "believers," and almost every other top commander was a "disbeliever."

Even in the midst of his belated resentment over Hitler's deception and recklessness, Keitel could not shake off the conviction that Hitler did have a streak of genius for military strategy in carrying out his reckless gambles:

(*December 25, 1945, Keitel's cell.*) "Please don't tell anybody else until this is over,—but I am convinced that Hitler's decision to attack Russia was a confession of weakness. . . . When we couldn't get across to England—which was impossible because we didn't have enough ships—he just had to do something. What could he do? Take Gibraltar? We wanted to, but Franco was afraid to risk it. Sit tight? Impossible.—That was all England needed to starve us out sooner or later. And all the time the life-blood of our Wehrmacht came from the Rumanian oil fields. Remember that, professor, oil! That was the vital key to the whole situation. Without Rumanian oil we couldn't last a week. And there was Russia; they could cut us off at any time. I think that Hitler must have seen that we were actually in a desperate situation. . . . If we lost the Rumanian oil fields we were finished. Hitler knew that we just couldn't sit and wait. When it comes to strategy, he was smarter than either Goering or Ribbentrop [*sic*!], and of course I don't rate at all. The attack on Russia was actually only an act of desperation, because he saw that our victory was only temporary, and Rommel's little shooting expedition in North Africa was of no consequence. Of course, he talked as if the Russian campaign was a sure thing, and our manifest destiny, and our solemn obligation. But now that I look back, I am sure it was just a desperate gamble."

It was perhaps rather circuitous reasoning by which Keitel upheld his conviction that Hitler was smarter than anybody else when it came to strategy, because he could always see what a hole he had gotten himself into and then take an even more desperate gamble to get himself out of it. But the fact remains that Keitel, who admittedly knew nothing about strategy and had never commanded armies in the field, regarded Hitler as something of a military genius. To evaluate just how much of this was the suggestibility of a passive incompetent, we should consider the judgment of some of the other generals who had commanded armies and tested the hard realities of military strategy.

The most derogatory views of Hitler's skill in strategy were voiced by General von Brauchitsch and General Halder, deposed Commander-in-Chief and Chief of Staff of the army. They considered Hitler's conception of strategy limited to the scraps of tactical information he had picked up at the company and regimental level in World War I. According to them, Hitler had no conception of the broader strategic problems involved in moving whole armies against a well-equipped enemy in modern warfare. Their opposition to Hitler's recklessness and their inability to live up to his fanciful expectations had cost them their military careers. Since their views might have been biased by their ego-shattering loss of command in the midst of a war, we turned to General von Rundstedt, one of Hitler's leading commanders right up to the final collapse, and one of the best-reputed strategists of the German General Staff. The following are some excerpts from an opinion he wrote in answer to our question, "Was Hitler a military genius?"

Like many laymen, Hitler possessed a certain superficial "feel" for operational matters, intuition, determination, and recklessness. However, he lacked: operational training (in spite of his reading of military works); the capacity for the sober consideration of the means at one's disposal, the presumable intentions of the enemy, the *attainable* goals; and the capacity to modify one's overambitious plans in accordance with the reality of the situation and to be satisfied with lesser attainments. . . . Reassured by the early easy victories, strengthened in his autocracy by the adulation of his immediate advisers and by the flattering articles in the press, his autocratic neurosis took on greater proportions in the course of the war. He became more and more intolerant of criticisms, his mistrust of the generals increased, leading inevitably to more and more interference, more fancifully autocratic planning, more perverted appraisal of his own and the enemy's fighting potential and attainable goals, and finally—the collapse!

In the Western Campaign, he already began to interfere in the movements of individual divisions. A big mistake was the halting of two armored divisions just before Dunquerque, which enabled the English to escape over the Channel. *He was already thinking of the second part of the campaign against France.* That is no considered strategy, but the sheer dilettantism of a layman!

The Russian Campaign was the most decisive proof of his strategic ineptness! *No* correct appraisal of his own and the enemy's power, of space, time, climate, or terrain. After the bogging-down of the first advance . . . he commanded the army *himself.* . . . In spite of the ice and snow and the pitiful transport facilities in that winter, he still made *the most grandiose plans,* such as reaching the oil fields of the Caucasus, etc.,—an absolute failure to

recognize the weakening of his own fighting potential in men and
matériel as against that of the enemy. Result: *Stalingrad* (the
turning point of the war!). In 1942-43, failure to recognize the
hopelessness of the situation. No voluntary withdrawal of the
front to a fortifiable line with attempts to negotiate [a peace].
Instead of that—just as in the winter of 1941-42—*stubborn clinging to hopeless positions* on the front with the heaviest losses, *à la*
Stalingrad. So it went until the collapse came. . . . Suggestions
to wage the war differently and if possible to end it by political
negotiation were harshly rejected. . . . He never even saw the
"Atlantic Wall," that great figment of the imagination. . . .

Such expert opinion, even with due allowance for wounded
professional pride, does not support any hypothesis that the
militarists' loyalty to Hitler was based on a common respect
for his military genius. Instead, it helps round out the picture
of an obsessed, neurotic dilettante, thriving on the suppression
of criticism in a dictatorship, giving vent to his obsessive heroic
fantasies by pushing pins across a map of Europe in an era of
mechanized aggression, while fawning courtiers like Keitel and
Ribbentrop help to insulate him from reality.

To summarize what Keitel saw in Hitler: he shared with
most of the members of the General Staff an initial impression
that Hitler would serve their purposes and values and (only
belatedly) the realization that Hitler had deceived them (or
they had deceived themselves). He also had a naïve belief in
Hitler's genius as a military strategist, but this belief was not
shared by most of the other generals. However, it had helped
him keep his exalted status.

War Guilt.—On this question, the generals were in complete
agreement: Hitler was entirely to blame. They had thought
he was bluffing, but he recklessly went ahead with his plans.
Though this obviously had the effect of exonerating them from
any personal blame, according to their own authoritarian conception of responsibility, they would have been glad to insist
that the Allies were to blame, if there had been even the shadow
of a doubt about Germany's guilt in provoking the war. Goering and Ribbentrop did, in fact, make a tongue-in-cheek attempt
to start such a myth, but it rang so falsely in the ears of their

own colleagues that they had to give up the attempt. On the contrary, General Jodl stated his conclusion quite unequivocally:

(*June 5, 1946, Jodl's cell.*) "You can be damn sure that we generals didn't want the war.—God knows we veterans of the first World War had our belly full of it.—When I heard about the English guarantee, I took it for granted that that settled the matter and Hitler would not dare to fight in the face of another world war.—I assure you that the day we heard that war had actually been declared, we were a pretty long-faced bunch of generals in the War Ministry."

"Do you mean to say that Hitler and Hitler alone wanted war, and was able to force it in spite of the general reluctance to fight?"

Jodl stopped in the middle of his supper and answered with conviction and emphasis, "There is absolutely no doubt about it! In this case it was Hitler's will alone that forced the issue! I can only assume that he had his mind dead set on it and all the negotiations were bluff.—I don't know, but it certainly looks that way. Nobody really knows what went on in his mind." Jodl gave the impression that he had been led to believe that the military preparations were bluffed at the time, but he had since come to the conclusion that the political negotiations were the real bluff, and the generals were fooled by him. "I thought he was clever enough to make all the appearances of meaning business in order to get what he wanted, but that he would never really go to war. When England made it clear that they would fight, I took it for granted that he would back down and negotiate.—But instead he just gave the order to march, knowing perfectly well that it meant at least a European war, if not a world war, and once he gave the order there was nothing left for us to do but to obey. Wars are decided by politicians and not soldiers.—Maybe in deciding future wars the General Staffs should be consulted.—But in this war the absolute guilt rests with one man, one man only—Adolf Hitler!"

Even Keitel summarized his analysis of Hitler's military strategy by confiding: "The Russian offensive was madness and the attack on Poland was provided on our side." His only defense for supporting the attack on Poland was that he thought Hitler was still bluffing, seeing how easily he had gotten away with it on previous occasions. It had obviously gone beyond the bluffing stage when Admiral Canaris told him that Himmler wanted Polish uniforms for some secret undertaking. "But I *told* Canaris—'Keep your hands out of that!'—I told him that the Wehrmacht doesn't have to get mixed up in that kind of business. He could just say that he didn't have any Polish uniforms. Believe me, Herr Professor, I had no idea what they were even planning, exactly. And we had absolutely no idea about the attempts of Chamberlain and Roosevelt to prevent war in 1939."

What Keitel did "not know, exactly" or had "no idea about" provides us with another crucial instance of the "normal" self-deception of opportunistic leadership in precipitating war. There are moments in history when the fate of whole nations hangs on the decision of a few men, especially when the initiative is in the hands of a totalitarian government. The days preceding the invasion of Poland undoubtedly constituted such a time. Keitel was certainly one of those whose determined resistance at that crucial moment would have reinforced General von Fritsch's objections and held off the attack—provided that the Foreign Minister had also shown such strength of character. But Hitler had shown uncanny judgment in picking men for his own purposes. It might take more than one man to make a war; but a shrewd dictator could virtually eliminate any operation of social inhibitions or reality-testing by the simple device of placing suggestible sycophants in the positions of greatest responsibility. Like Ribbentrop, Keitel suppressed any full realization of what his collaboration entailed. To have looked further into the question of provocation, to draw the inevitable conclusions and to act on them, as did Von Fritsch, would have required a moral fortitude he simply did not possess. Furthermore, it would have jeopardized any hopes of future status—either as a country squire or as a war lord. At the very least, facing the fact of unprovoked aggression would have confronted him with the dilemma of overtly opposing it or overtly supporting it. Such perceptions were dangerous. It was easier to obviate any full realization of the facts and to divert his attention to other things. The symbols of national tradition in Hitler's waiting room, the images called forth in his appeals to patriotism, and the academic tasks of planning aggressive defenses of national security—these, and not the question about Polish uniforms or the vague reports about diplomatic negotiations were the realities on which an ambitious Chief of Staff could safely focus his attention without provoking a conflict of loyalties.

The obviation and diversion of these dangerous insights was furthermore facilitated by the authoritarian tradition itself. The Commander-in-Chief had, after all, ordered them to stick to their own business. Their duty was merely to obey orders; the responsibility for the launching of the war and the conduct thereof lay entirely with the supreme commander. As for the broader social responsibilities, Jodl argued, if they were to be incorporated in the rules for *future* wars, the generals would be glad to comply.

The Military Code.—Our third and most crucial question in the case of the militarists is their conception of duty. According to their code, if the Commander-in-Chief takes the responsibility for making crucial decisions, and does not delegate any of that responsibility to you, then any value judgments in connection with those decisions are no affair of yours. Keitel said that Hitler made that limitation of responsibility quite explicit and insisted that he "not stick his nose into matters of foreign policy—there were others competent to deal with that." Nothing could have been more convenient for a Chief of Staff who did not have the moral fortitude to face the responsibilities of leadership.

Keitel's first reaction to the indictment was a proper abhorrence of the multiplicity and extent of the atrocities catalogued therein;—but, after all, "For a soldier, orders are orders." If the rigid Prussian code of *correct* (same word in German) behavior had been violated by his Commander-in-Chief, then his loyalty had simply been abused.

We can better analyze the militarists' reaction to war crimes by distinguishing three groups upon whom violence was incorrectly inflicted by Hitler's orders: (*a*) the enemy civilian populations, (*b*) enemy prisoners, and (*c*) the German population. We must restrict ourselves here only to the death and destruction inflicted above and beyond that which would be considered necessary to the conduct of any war, by the rules of the game—rules which were recognized by the Prussian militarists and formulated by the Rules of Land Warfare at Geneva. The consideration of losses in actual combat on both sides, amounting to millions of men, must be omitted from this discussion, for this does not involve any question of criminal guilt by military standards, once the conduct of war is an established fact. That question must be left to the general complex of war guilt as such.

The brutalities inflicted on civilian populations were regarded as inexcusable atrocities inflicted by Himmler's SS and Gestapo, who were not under the jurisdiction of the Wehrmacht. Both Keitel and Jodl were vehement on that score. "I and my colleagues had no deeper insight into the full effect of Himmler's powers," Keitel testified, "and had no idea of the possible effect of these powers. . . . If the entire consequences which arose from granting Himmler's authority in the East had been foreseen, in this case the leading generals would have been the first to voice an unequivocal objection to it." In other words, the Prussian conception of duty did allow for protest against orders that violated the "humane" rules of warfare—provided one had full realization of such violations.

At first Keitel clung to his argument of "deception" and "limited jurisdiction" of the honorable General Staff of the Wehrmacht. At this stage he showed merely embarrassment, as if over a friend's social *faux pas*.

His reaction to the first concentration camp evidence was, "It is terrible. When I see such things, I am ashamed of being a German.—It was those dirty SS swine!—If I had known it I would have told my son, 'I'd rather shoot you than let you join the SS!' But I didn't know.—I'll never be able to look people in the face again."

But it was the mistreatment of prisoners of war that accounted most for any real guilt feelings. These were unquestionably within his jurisdiction and within the framework of his militaristic values. Worst of all, he had transgressed against the most sacred sanction of the Prussian militarist's self-protective code of chivalry: the inviolability of a general's person, friend or foe. Keitel's humiliation over the revelation of his attempt to have Generals Giraud and Weygand caught and assassinated after their escape was more profound than his "shame" over the entire extermination program. "I don't know what to say—that Giraud affair—well, I knew that he was coming up—but what can I say?—I know that an officer and gentleman like you must be wondering.—These are things that attack my very honor as an officer. I don't care if they accuse me of starting the war.—I was only doing my duty and following orders.—But these assassination stories—I don't know how I ever got mixed up in this thing. . . ." It was this revelation, more than anything else that made Keitel lose face among his own military group at the trial. General Jodl quietly "cut" him at lunch thereafter, and the cut left a deep gash in the former Chief of Staff's ego-defenses. The reason was obvious. This was one instance in which the Prussian code of honor would have justified disobedience.

The flexibility of the code of loyalty became more and more apparent as the trial progressed. It was the violation of the *self-protective* and *self-deceptive* functions of that code that accounted for most of Keitel's guilt feelings throughout the testimony that followed. Limited jurisdiction, code of honor, loyalty—all these defenses broke down as the facts came to light. An SS general's detailed report on his brutal razing of the Warsaw ghetto crystallized some long-suppressed insights.

(*December 15, 1946, Keitel's cell.*) "I am dying of shame!—It is disgraceful—horrible! I had at least counted on the honorable record of the Wehrmacht, but now the Wehrmacht too is disgraced. They had too many connections with party organizations.—Like that horrible Warsaw ghetto affair. Imagine Stroop reporting, 'The Wehrmacht engineers, in true comradeship of arms, gave faithful support to the SS in this undertaking, etc.' Why, I could swear the army commander who sent him those engineers didn't have the slightest idea of the dirty business they were intended for. I only wish that I had spent more time in the field. I spent too much time in Hitler's headquarters, and when I went out I consulted the generals. I should have seen what was actually being done at lower echelons. . . . It is clear to me now why [Hitler] always told me to keep hands off police matters. If anything came up, he said, 'That is none of your business.—You are a soldier!' Of course, I did not know that he was planning these horrible things and that Wehrmacht men were getting tied up with it. . . . No, he used three entirely different languages:

one for the Wehrmacht, one for the party leaders, where he discussed his real plans, and one for the Reichstag, which he used as a sounding board for the public.

"There were three main planks to his program, which brought the eventual ruin and disgrace of Germany: the suppression of the church, under the hypocritical motto, 'Every man must find salvation in his own fashion';[1] the ruthless persecution of the Jews; and the limitless power of the Gestapo. These things are clear now. . . ." Keitel made a gesture of a veil being taken away from his eyes, then a helpless shrug, "—but it is too late now."

The veil before Keitel's eyes had, of course, been one of his own making, conveniently reinforced by the authoritarian values of his professional group. There was not one of these belated insights that he could not have achieved much earlier—which he had not, indeed, partially achieved, but suppressed. He had urged commanding generals to "cooperate" with the SS, and let it go at that. He had obeyed Hitler's injunction against prying too much into Himmler's affairs, and had put down his suspicions. He had partially realized the hypocrisy of Hitler's religious "indifference" and his propagandistic appeals to hallowed national symbols but had relegated them all to "politics—out of a soldier's jurisdiction." The realization that no social institution, not even the impeccable Wehrmacht, could remain untainted long in a revolution of values, that no jurisdictional boundaries were respected by social upheaval—this was a catastrophic insight that sent him cowering in shame back to his cell in the Nuremberg jail when it could no longer be suppressed.

Keitel had to admit, upon cross-examination, that the orders he had transmitted were criminal orders and that his own military code had provided for refusing to carry out orders that were against his conscience. All he could say in his final defense (a carefully formulated apologia, which he repeated to us several times) was: "I may be accused of having made mistakes and also of having shown weakness toward the Führer, Adolf Hitler, but never can it be said that I was cowardly, dishonorable or faithless." Thus Keitel could still salvage a little self-respect

---

[1] Motto of Frederick the Great—another one of Hitler's appeals to revered nationalist symbols in democratic guise.

out of his own code of honor, however badly he had mangled it.

But the basic social issue of loyalty, that went even beyond Keitel's power of perception, was raised over the issue of rebelling against the Führer in the last catastrophic phase of the conflict. This was the chief issue of a quiet feud that went on behind the scenes, between the "soldiers" and the "politicians." The generals and admirals, upholding their basic virtue of loyalty, however much they may have sinned in weakness and judgment, roundly denounced the "politicians" (to the writer) for backing Hitler and then expecting the generals to assassinate him when he proved to be a poor choice. They were particularly bitter about a politician like Schacht, who did as much as anybody to bring Hitler to power, then urged the generals to plot against him when he saw that things were not going his way. Jodl conceded that there might have been a moral issue involved in plotting against Hitler, but he felt that a general could not give and withdraw his support like a banker following the stock market.

The politicians, on the other hand, reserved an equal right to having been "deceived" and vehemently denounced the "militaristic mentality" for its blind readiness to obey orders and go to war at the drop of a hat.

Loyalty and Value Judgment.—These varying reactions on the issue of loyalty provided an interesting illustration of how social values determine the nature of perceived meaning. General Lahousen and General von Paulus, who denounced Hitler's "criminal aggression," were denounced in turn by the militarists as "traitors." The politicians considered them the victims of a "human tragedy" for being forced into an intolerable conflict of loyalties by Hitler's reckless leadership of the nation. Lahousen's support of the generals who plotted the assassination of Hitler particularly incensed the generals (who had narrowly escaped assassination by the bomb themselves). Keitel and Jodl were agreed that it was a violation of an officer's honor to remain at his post and plot against the Commander-in-Chief. General Lahousen later noticed these comments in our published *Diary* and wrote the following in rebuttal.

We [of the generals' underground] often confronted ourselves
with those questions [of loyalty] in truly searching conflicts of
conscience. But in these final struggles with one's own inner
promptings, dare one put "officer's honor" ahead of one's own
conscience or ahead of ordinary considerations of humanity? And
did that which Keitel and Jodl did, or helped to do, correspond to
the concept of "officer's honor"?—even according to the sterile and
rigid conception of Prussian military tradition? I grant that the
decision to work against Hitler in the dark was not a heroic one.
(Though one must consider that the circumstances of dictatorship
and the Police State made *open* defiance seem senseless.) But it
was a decision which was better than unconditional and thought-
less obedience. If the dead of the "20th of July" [assassination
plot] achieved nothing more than to show that among this misled
and intoxicated people there were still individuals who, with all
their shortcomings, could resolve to pit themselves against evil,
then they have not died in vain.

The inability of militarists like Keitel to abandon their learned
pattern of group behavior, even in the face of a threat to their
own country's survival, is an all too obvious illustration of the
functional autonomy of derived behavior patterns that have become institutionally fixated to the point of defeating their own
purpose. Clinically, it resembles the maladaptive pattern of
compulsive behavior on a group level.

German national character has, indeed, also been described as
compulsive in nature. But here again we must distinguish between true psychopathology and the cultural epiphenomenon.
It is true that a group of men like the militarists, adapting to the
socially sanctioned values and behavior patterns of their immediate membership group, may carry their ritualistic behavior
to a maladaptive extreme. They may even be aware of this and
feel helpless to do anything about it. But we must not infer
from the apparent maladaptive functioning of the group the
psychopathology of its members. The militarists were not
obsessive-compulsive neurotics, but normal men conducting
themselves in accordance with a broader or more constricted
conception of their indoctrinated values. But it is not always in
the realm of psychopathology that society finds its greatest
threats to survival. The mere difference between broad and

narrow interpretations of group values may be crucial, and this applies even to the military "categorical imperative."

The humanitarian restraints of Western civilization were by no means lost on the Prussian militarists as a group. Their own traditional adherence to certain rules of warfare was a recognition of it, however paradoxical from a pacifist viewpoint. Even Keitel's and Jodl's claim of deception showed that there had been a conflict of values among Hitler's generals. Other spontaneous reactions to evidence, as well as the historical record of actual behavior, showed that there had been an actual threshold-scale in this balancing of values as determining tendencies towards action. Each general "drew the line" at different points in the scale, but few converted their "misgivings" into action. These actions and spontaneous reactions were far more valid than answers to a prepared questionnaire would have been in determining the strength of the military pseudocompulsive obedience. The threshold-scale of resistance to the "categorical imperative" was indicated approximately as follows (in an ascending scale from least to greatest resistance) :

1. Training and planning for armed defense in case of attack (e.g., army maneuvers and border patrol)

2. Increasing armed strength and weapons of offense beyond treaty obligations or needs of defense (long-range bombers, submarines, etc.)

3. Planning attacks on friendly nations as a possible last resort in case of need or provocation ("academic phase" of plans against Czechoslovakia and Poland)

4. Attacking neutral countries for strategic reasons in wartime (invasion of Low Countries)

5. Precipitating war by invading neutral countries without real provocation in peacetime (invasion of Czechoslovakia and Poland)

6. Taking the initiative in violating the Rules of Land Warfare (killing of prisoners, reckless shooting of hostages, blind bombing of enemy territory)

7. Wholesale slaughter of hostile civilian populations (Lidice, Warsaw ghetto)

8. Total destruction of own resources and manpower without strategic justification ("scorched earth" policy after obvious defeat)

9. Systematic large-scale extermination of helpless noncombatants, including women and children, and looting their valuables (extermination of Jews)

We did not actually construct and submit such a threshold-scale of resistance to military obedience, but the reactions of the generals could be cited point for point to support such a scale. Certainly none of the generals expressed any misgivings at levels 1, 2, and 3—nor would the professional militarists of any major power under similar circumstances. Even level 4 presents a possible common threshold of compliance to military duty by the military leaders of the world.[2] But there the operation of "normal" military obedience ends and the influence of aggressive nationalism and ideological dictatorship begins.

The generals expressed increasing condemnation at levels 5 through 9, though they had differed in their willingness to convert value judgments into action. General von Fritsch had drawn the line at level 5. Other generals had been won over to the anti-Hitler underground at various levels from 6 through 9. Keitel had contented himself with "struggles of conscience" to the very limit of pseudocompulsive obedience and had resorted to every possible mechanism to avoid the crisis of conflicting values. As we have already indicated, this involved the obviation and diversion of insights, *but these mechanisms were facilitated by rigid adherence to the group mode of behavior.*

The final crisis in the bitter loyalty controversy between the soldiers and the politicians came over the issue of the "scorched earth" policy. It was War Production Chief Albert Speer who had taken it upon himself to counteract Hitler's order to destroy all production and communication facilities in the face of final defeat. The clear implication of this order had been the total

---

[2] Churchill's memoirs show that violations of neutrality had been reluctantly considered for strategic necessity; but the stigma of aggression may be considered somewhat extenuated by the fact of prepared initial attack on the other side.

destruction of Germany's possibilities for future subsistence, and that was exactly what Hitler had wanted. In desperation, Speer had defied Hitler's orders and had even plotted an aborted attempt against his life. But besides risking his own life, he had had the blind obedience of some of the militarists to contend with. In our conversations Speer complained bitterly about the pig-headedness of the Chief of Staff, who could see no alternative to blind obedience to the Führer, even with disaster staring them in the face for the most primitive basis of survival. The crucial difference in the concept of loyalty, even among the leaders of Nazi Germany, is worth quoting.

> There is one loyalty which everyone must always keep, and that is loyalty toward one's own people. That duty comes before everything. If I am in a leading position, and if I see that the interests of the nation are acted against in such a way, then I must act. That Hitler had broken faith with the nation must have been clear to every intelligent member of his entourage, certainly at the latest in January or February, 1945. Hitler had once been given his mission by the people; he had no right to gamble away the destiny of the people with his own. Therefore I fulfilled my natural duty as a German. (36)

This contrast in conceptions of duty is actually the crux of our case. Speer had also accepted his wartime leadership in 1942 out of a combined sense of duty and ambition. Perhaps, with a deeper sense of responsibility toward Western civilization, or an earlier recognition of it, he would not have gotten into Hitler's good graces to begin with. But he had at least faced the responsibilities of leadership as a German patriot— which was what the Prussian militarists recognized as their solemn obligation. Speer had perceived a tragic violation of a leader's responsibility to the people, even by the paternalistic code of dictatorship. Instead of suppressing his insight under the camouflage of loyalty and limited jurisdiction, for fear of facing an emotional conflict, he had insisted on facing the realities, weighing the conflicting value judgments, drawing the necessary conclusions—and *acting* on them. We are led to believe that such was the action-process of mature leadership that provided the determining tendencies of motivation for men like

General von Fritsch, Admiral Canaris, and the many others, civilian and military, who died in the anti-Hitler underground.

It was on that narrower militaristic conception of duty that Hitler relied for the nullification of humanitarian restraints. It was of such militarists as Keitel that the Tribunal concluded (while not judging the German General Staff an inherently criminal organization) :

> Without their military guidance the aggressive ambitions of Hitler and his fellow Nazis would have been academic and sterile. . . . Many of these men have made a mockery of the soldier's oath of obedience to military orders. . . . The truth is they actively participated in all these crimes, or sat silent and acquiescent, witnessing the commission of crimes on a scale larger and more shocking than the world has ever had the misfortune to know. This must be said.

The fact that some men exercised value judgment in their loyalties, even within the Nazi microcosm, was an affirmation that humanistic conceptions of leadership are not merely artifacts of social mores peculiar to Western democracy. German authoritarian culture and Prussian militarism contained, to be sure, values which could be readily adapted to serve the purposes of aggressive dictatorship. But it was not the best of German culture, nor even the best German military tradition, that supported Hitler to the bitter end.

Chapter 6

THE STATE POLICE

While the military institution has long served the function of defense or aggression against external enemies, police systems have in recent centuries been developed to preserve domestic law and order. Autocratic rulers and oligarchies have made increasing use of police and spy systems to protect their own power and security more than the security of their subjects. The state police system reached the zenith of its development as an instrument of autocratic control in the police state of the modern dictatorships. Hitler's most drastic "contribution" to the development of social institutions was undoubtedly the creation of the SS-police and Gestapo system as the most formidable agency of human destruction in modern times—all within the space of about ten years.

Like an emergent in social evolution, the SS-police state sprang suddenly into being when the Nazi ideology impregnated Prussian militarism to produce a hybrid offspring with which to control the nation. The incubation period came to an end and it emerged full-blown after the Roehm purge, when Himmler was given unlimited police powers and civil liberties were abolished.

The SS-police under Himmler wielded a power that transcended all other agencies of government combined. It was a state within a state. It was subject only to its own laws, which in turn rested entirely on the dictator's personal conception of right and wrong. Through this agency Hitler was able not only to assure his own continuation in power but the execution of his most fantastically paranoid obsessions to eliminate his "enemies." It provided an instrument of brutality to circumvent the inhibiting influences of law, religion, and even the military establishment, in the full realization of his vengeful fantasies.

Organizationally the police state was a multiple-headed monster with tentacles reaching out into every aspect of public and private life. It included the SS (*Schutz-Staffel* or elite guard), a semimilitary organization which manned the concentration camps and special extermination task forces; the Armed SS (*Waffen-SS*), an independent army under Himmler's command, numbering over a half-million men by the end of the war; the paramilitary Security Police under the Reich Security Office (RSHA), with its infamous Gestapo, espionage and intelligence, "research," "resettlement," and other divisions. Through the SS-police network the Nazi dictatorship consolidated its stranglehold on life throughout Germany and throughout occupied Central Europe. Some eight or nine million men, women, and children died in their concentration camps, torture chambers, and slave labor camps.

The values of this new social emergent were cultivated principally through selection and indoctrination of the SS membership. In the cult of those prepared to live and die by violence, the SS were truly the "elite guard," and it was also in this group that militarism reached its apotheosis.

The SS revived the medieval cult of the brotherly "blood-bond" (*Blutkitt*) in its solemn oath to kill or die in the cause without a moment's hesitation. It adopted, in addition to the swastika, the skull and crossbones and ancient mystic runes signifying eternity, death, and racial purity as symbols of its pagan cult. Its conception of all honor was summed up in the motto *Meine Ehre heisst Treue* (My honor is loyalty)—loyalty to one's chief unto death, all other social values notwithstanding. Its formalistic conception of duty outdid that of the most rigid militarism. It was, indeed, precisely because Prussian militarism had been tainted with Christian humanitarian scruples that Hitler and Goering had created the police state. If we may speak of the militarists' "thresholds of resistance to obedience," such a concept would be entirely inapplicable to the cult of the SS. Absolute, unthinking, unconditional obedience under all circumstances was the very basis of life in their microcosm.

Esoteric standards of "good background" were rigidly applied for membership in this elite guard, especially for officers.

Every candidate had to prove his pure Aryan ancestry for at least four generations, and officers had to show an untainted family tree back to the year 1750. A criminal record was not necessarily disqualifying—indeed, political murder (*Fehme-mord*) was a badge of honor, a blood-bond with a long tradition behind it. Those who had missed the chance to prove themselves in this way before admission, soon had the opportunity to do so by service in the concentration camps or "action commandos." Good officer material was selected from the ranks largely on that kind of proof. Certain embarrassing discrepancies occasionally turned up in an otherwise promising SS career, like the discovery of a Jewish ancestor on the paternal side. In such cases, however, the SS officer or candidate could restore his honor by proving that he was an illegitimate child. This rigid selectivity of men of good background broke down somewhat after the expanding needs of the police state led to mass recruitment, and many of the original elite were understandably annoyed that "now anybody can get in."

The leaders of the police state represented a wide variety of personalities and background: ambitious and obedient bureaucrats who reveled in their power of life and death, aggressive imitators and cast-offs of the Prussian military caste, scientists and professional men with strictly academic interests, misled social reformers, and sadistic ruffians of the original Storm Troop variety now parading in the uniforms of the elite. We have encountered the prototypes of these characters before. In the police state the worst elements of revolutionary aggression, political bureaucracy, and militarism were amalgamated into a new role: the human robots engaged in the persecution and extermination of their fellow-humans.

Some of these leaders died by assassination or suicide before they could be examined (e.g., Heydrich and Himmler). However, several of Himmler's chief deputies were captured and examined during the period of our activity in military intelligence and the Nuremberg trial. This included several of the higher SS-police chiefs, the head of the RSHA, the chiefs of administration and espionage (SD), and the chief of the principal extermination camp.

It will be many years before the psychology of leadership in the concentration-camp world will be even dimly perceived. Certainly life in that world cannot be conceived of by those who have never lived in it. The mute evidence of what transpired in those camps was incredible even to those who saw it in the last months of the war. We shall attempt merely to give some suggestion of the interaction of psychopathology and social dynamics which seems to have produced this social emergent. The chief of the main extermination camp will provide the focus of this inquiry.

SS-COLONEL HOESS OF AUSCHWITZ

SS-Colonel Hoess regarded himself as only a minor cog in the wheel of Himmler's organizational machinery. That fact is significant in itself. For this minor cog in the terror machinery of the police state supervised the literal extermination of two and a half million men, women, and children in the gas chambers of Auschwitz extermination camp. We select this case not only for the enormity of the crime but because he was picked by Himmler himself as the very model of an SS officer for such an all-important undertaking. As far as we can judge, Himmler seems intuitively to have selected men who were most like himself to carry out the actual program of extermination. In the lower echelons and in allied agencies there was a greater variety of personalities, but Himmler's extermination deputies were Himmler's alter egos. Just what the nature of this ego-structure may have been is one of the most challenging problems that have ever confronted clinical and social psychology. Since the case so far exceeds the credible, we shall present as much of the data as possible in its original form,[1] making only the most immediate inferences.

Early Background.—Rudolf Franz Hoess was born in 1900 in Baden-Baden, Bavaria. He was the oldest of three children,

---

[1] Consists principally of verbatim records of conversations (recorded in his presence, since there was no danger of inhibiting him) and a detailed autobiography written for the author.

and the only son, in a lower middle-class merchant family. The parents were devout Catholics. The father had not been a serious churchgoer earlier in life, but the contraction of some disease while abroad seemed to have made him suddenly fanatic in his religious observance.

"My father was really a bigot. He was very strict and fanatic. I learned that my father took a religious oath at the time of the birth of my youngest sister, dedicating me to God and the priesthood, and after that leading a Joseph married life [celibacy].—He directed my entire youthful education toward the goal of making me a priest. I had to pray and go to church endlessly; do penance over the slightest misdeed—praying as punishment for any little unkindness to my sister, or something like that."

"Did your father ever beat you?"

"No, I was only punished by prayer—if I teased my sister, or tried to lie, or any little thing like that. The thing that made me so stubborn and probably made me later on cut off from people was his way of making me feel that I had wronged him personally, and that, since I was spiritually a minor, he was responsible to God for my sins, and I could only pray to expiate my sins. My father was a kind of higher being that I could never approach, and so I crawled back into myself—and I could not express myself to others.—I feel that this bigoted upbringing is responsible for my becoming so withdrawn. My mother also lived in the shadow of this fanatic piety."

Young Hoess thus had a role of religious dedication forced on him by a fanatic father who was expiating some guilt feelings —probably over contracting syphilis (nature of disease unknown). This early environment gradually produced a revulsion toward religion and a rather withdrawn and submissive personality generally. Partly in reaction to the suppressive behavior forced on him, he occasionally gave vent to violent outbursts of temper. On one such occasion, at the age of thirteen, he beat up a schoolmate and caused him to fracture his leg. He immediately went to confession. That night his father awakened him and denounced him with the most violent imprecations. Rudolf assumed that the priest had betrayed him to his father. His faith thus broken, he avoided confession thereafter and made up his mind to become a soldier. The family relationship grew more and more distant. The autobiography continues :

> I had no particular ties to my two sisters, and we never grew any closer. Even in later years we had only the loosest ties. My parents were very devoted to me, but I was never completely receptive (*ich schloss mich nie ganz auf*). I fulfilled every wish of my parents, but only out of obedience. My father died in May, 1914. War broke out and from then on my only thought and desire was to become a soldier one way or another. Here I must remark that almost all of my paternal ancestors had been officers and that the career of a soldier attracted me more than that of a Catholic priest. But since my parents' most ardent wish was to make me a priest, I was willing to become a missionary as a last resort. But a soldier above all things. Even at the age of fourteen I tried to smuggle myself into transports going to the front, but I was always caught and sent back home. My mother tried to dissuade me from this plan with all her love and persuasive power, but in vain. My school work was neglected on account of this, but I passed as a good average student, even though I no longer had the necessary interest in studies. At the same time I could often avoid study by being a Red Cross aid. I helped in hospitals and in the unloading of trains of wounded soldiers. My passion to become a soldier grew steadily. I had no friends or comrades of my own. I am not good at making contact (*ich kann mich schlecht anschliessen*), and in my later life I never had any real friendships that went beyond the day-to-day acquaintance. My most pleasant experiences were the holidays which I was allowed to spend with my grandparents on a farm in the Black Forest. There I felt best, and there also grew my love for farming, for nature, and for the animal world. I was regarded as a quiet, sensible youngster, but one dared not irritate me needlessly, because I could get furious.

At the age of sixteen while working as a volunteer in an army hospital, he became acquainted with a cavalry officer who agreed to take him into his regiment. Hoess ran away from home and joined the 21st Regiment of Dragoons, where the above-mentioned cavalry officer was just organizing a detachment for the Asiatic Corps in Turkey. He spent the latter part of the war in Iraq and Palestine. In Palestine he became further alienated from the church by seeing the commercialization of alleged biblical relics. His mother died in 1917 while he was on active duty. However, the military life absorbed his interest completely. "I was wounded twice, had malaria, was cited several times. In 1918 I became a member of the Royal Guards, then scarcely eighteen years old. The life of a soldier pleased me in spite of all the hardships in that theatre of war under the conditions of the time."

In 1917 he had his first sex relations with a nurse while recovering from a wound in a hospital in Damascus. He enjoyed this first experience but became more and more frigid sexually.

After the Armistice in 1918 he made his way slowly homeward through the Balkans.

Soldier of Fortune.—"I visited my sisters and relatives. My guardian wanted to force me to take up the profession chosen for me by my parents even then. But by this time I was inwardly through with the church. . . . I broke all ties to my family. I volunteered for the *Freikorps* in East Prussia and participated in the battles of 1919-1920 in the Baltics; then the battles with the Communists in the Ruhr in 1920; the Polish uprising in Upper Silesia in 1921. After the suppression of this uprising all *Freikorps* were dissolved." In 1922 he officially broke with the church (by formal registration) and joined the Nazi party. The Rossbach "alumni" maintained contact in spite of their dissolution, for purposes of political violence. In 1923 Hoess participated in a *Fehmemord* (political murder) of a traitor to the cause. He was sentenced to ten years' imprisonment for this murder. He served the next five years in solitary confinement in Dachau as a political prisoner. Hoess stated that he felt no guilt for this murder because it was a political murder for the protection of the Fatherland and not just an ordinary criminal murder. His five years of solitary confinement only served to broaden the gulf between society and his "withdrawn nature."

In 1928 he was released from prison and returned to work for some of the landed gentry around Mecklenburg and Silesia, where some of his former *Freikorps* cronies had found refuge. He took to farming and horse-grooming, and joined the farm workers' *Bund*. This was a favorite dodge for the groups of soldiers of fortune who kept together awaiting *den Tag* when German nationalism would once more be on the march.

"I became acquainted with my wife and married in 1929. I was then the leader of the worker's local and had the determined goal of acquiring a farm for my family. These were very difficult years for the two of us, and we had to save every pfennig from our hard work to come nearer to our goal. We lived that way until 1934." During that time a boy and two girls were born to the couple.

At the instigation of the land-owners and the Nazi party, Hoess organized an SS cavalry unit. He had already met Himmler in 1930 at a meeting of some of the "soldiers of fortune" who had turned Nazi. Himmler decided to recruit Hoess for active service in the SS. His record as a political murderer proved that he was good officer material in this elite guard of the party. "Finally he asked me if I would not like to take a job at a concentration camp, where my experience of five years' imprisonment would come in handy after all. I agreed, and so on December 1, 1934, I came to Dachau."

Hoess proved to be an efficient and obedient worker in concentration camps. He accepted the Nazi ideology wholeheartedly and thrived on the military discipline. He rose in rank from sergeant to company-grade officer by 1938. "Things improved materially after I became a lieutenant in 1936." He found nothing particularly distasteful about the work, because the inmates were mostly backsliders who had to be "educated" and the camps were run in a well-disciplined manner.

"When the war broke out in 1939, the number of prisoners increased rapidly and the distribution of prisoner categories changed considerably. If there had been 10 per cent political prisoners before the war, there were over 60 per cent later. Before there had been mostly professional criminals and anti-social elements. Previously the guards were mostly young, voluntary, active men of the *Totenkopf Verbände* (Death's-Head Units), but later they were older men of the *Allgemeine SS* (General SS) who were assigned for this purpose. There was a great deal of work and annoyance connected with this replacement. There are no special incidents to report from this period." (The report mentions nothing further about the influx of new political prisoners at this time.) By 1940 he had been promoted to field-grade officer in the SS. He was now ready for his major undertaking.

Auschwitz.—Himmler detailed Hoess to start construction of a prison camp at Oswiecjim (Auschwitz) in a remote part of occupied Polish territory.

In the spring of 1941 Himmler visited Auschwitz. I was given the order to build up the camp as large as possible, to cultivate about 20,000 *Morgen* of the surrounding land, and to set up model agricultural plants. In the area of Birkenau a PW camp for 100,000 prisoners was to be erected. This was a terrific job, but I went at it enthusiastically. In the summer of 1941 I had to go to Himmler in Berlin, where he imparted to me the following: The Führer had ordered the final solution of the Jewish question. We [the SS] have to execute this. If we do not exterminate the Jews at this time, then they will later exterminate the German people. That is a hard, difficult task. I have picked Auschwitz for this, because it is well situated from a transportation viewpoint, and because the action is to be blocked off for purposes of secrecy. An Obersturmbannführer Eichmann would come from the RSHA to give me further details as to the scope and schedules of the task. I was to keep strictest silence about this order, even toward my immediate superior, Gruppenführer Glucks. I returned to Auschwitz, but at that time still had no conception of what this order really meant. I made camouflaged construction plans without my construction workers having any idea of what it was all about. A short time later Eichmann came to me and described the next steps without giving me any idea of the eventual scope. I then visited a so-called extermination camp in Treblinka near Warsaw and was somewhat shocked by what I saw.

Now as the first transports came from the General-Gouvernement and Upper Silesia, we had just finished the two provisional structures in the two farmhouses and could now begin the action. For the SS men who participated in it, it was a terrible job. I often wondered about it and the men often talked to me about it. But the order of the Reichsführer [Himmler] and his explanation removed any doubts and gave me the strength to remain aloof from all the frightfulness that I had to witness. Of course none of the SS men who participated in this work cared for it, especially since most of them, like myself, were married and had children. But later one became desensitized even in this cruel activity.

Hoess described the actual extermination procedure, to which he and his men had to become desensitized, as follows:

These trains were closed freight cars and generally contained about 2,000 people. After the arrival of the trains on the above-mentioned ramp, the accompanying railway personnel and guards —members of the Security or Order Police—had to leave the place. Only the transport commander remained to complete the numerical transfer to the camp officer of the day. After the un-loading and counting—lists of names were not provided—all the people had to march by two SS medical duty officers, who deter-mined which were fit or unfit for work. On the average 25 per cent were found fit for work. Those fit for work were immedi-ately marched into the camp to change clothes and be taken in. All baggage remained on the ramp, to be stored and sorted after those unfit for work had also been taken away. The men, women, and children of those unfit for work were also separated and marched to the next available extermination chamber. Those who could not walk and women with little children were taken there in trucks. When they arrived, all had to undress completely in rooms which were made to look as if they were set up for delousing purposes.

The steady work detail which worked at these installations— who were also billeted there and did not come in contact with the rest of the camp prisoners—helped in the undressing process and advised the skeptical ones to get ready so that the others would not have so long to wait. They were also told to note where they left their things, so that they could find them immediately after the bath. All this was done to dispel any suspicions that might arise. After the undressing they went into the next room, the gas chamber. This was set up like a bath, i.e., showers, pipes, drains, etc. had been installed. As soon as the entire transport was in the chamber, the door was closed and the gas thrown in through a special opening in the ceiling—it was Cyclone B, crystalline Prussic acid which volatilized immediately, i.e., became effective immediately upon contact with oxygen. The people became stunned with the first breath of it, and the killing took three to fifteen minutes according to the weather and the number of those locked in. After this period there was no more movement. Thirty minutes after the gas had been thrown in, the chambers were opened and the removal of the corpses to the crematoria was begun. In all the years I knew of not a single case where any one came out of the chambers alive.

After being taken out, the hair was cut off the women's heads and any rings or gold teeth were removed by prisoner dentists employed in the detail. In Birkenau there were five installations: two large crematoria with a capacity of 2,000 people per twenty-four hours; i.e., in the gas chamber up to 2,500 people could be killed, inside of twenty-four hours the double ovens (heated with coke) could accommodate 2,000 at most; two larger installations each with four larger double ovens could get rid of approximately 1,500 people. The burning in open pits was virtually unlimited. According to my calculations one could burn up to 8,000 people in twenty-four hours by this method. It was therefore possible to exterminate and get rid of as many as 10,000 people in twenty-four hours by the above-described methods. As I recall, this number was reached only once in 1944, when train delays caused five transports to arrive all on one day. The ashes were pulverized and thrown into the Weichsel River at secluded spots, and were then carried away by the stream.

Among the able-bodied men selected for work in the camp factories, many were starved, tortured, or worked to death before their turn came for extermination. A total of two and a half million men, women, and children were thus exterminated under Hoess's supervision in two and a half years. He himself continued to live what he considered a "normal" family life while this was going on, although he thought that the estrangement between him and his wife increased.

In December, 1943, Hoess became chief inspector of the concentration camps, acting as liaison officer between them and SS-Gestapo headquarters. Epidemics and starvation spread so rapidly among the masses of humanity crowded into these camps from all over occupied Europe that toward the end of the war the living could hardly bury the dead, even after the extermination program was discontinued. A few days before the surrender Himmler called Hoess and his other concentration camp chiefs and told them to hide out, since there was nothing more he could do for them. Hoess obtained a forged naval identification book and was later discharged and assigned to farm work. Ten months later he was arrested and brought to Nuremberg to testify for Gestapo Chief Kaltenbrunner. In 1947 he was tried and hanged by a Polish court.

Observations and Evaluation

Test Results.—This short, soft-spoken, apathetic SS-colonel has the distinction of being probably the greatest criminal ever tested; in point of actual executions, the greatest mass murderer in all of human history.   In view of Hoess's record, the nature of any psychopathology present is of particular interest, though we need have no illusions that this alone could explain the inconceivable magnitude of his crime.

Intelligence Test. The intelligence test showed superior basic intelligence, as with most of the high-ranking *leaders* in the police state. (A small sampling of concentration camp *guards* showed wide representation of the dull and borderline mental defectives.) It would appear that certain cognitive capacities were essential to the mental equipment of the chief murderous robot in the human extermination machine. Thus Hoess showed superior ability in sensorimotor coordination, comprehension, and arithmetic. The relevance of the latter was casually noted when Hoess momentarily blocked on the last multiplication-and-division problem. The examiner urged him on, saying that he had surely had problems like that before in doing his mass-extermination work. Without batting an eye, Hoess replied, "Yes, of course, I had to figure out problems like that all the time—how many days it would take to burn so many corpses, etc." Hoess also blocked in assembling the parts of the human profile and was unable to complete it in the time allowed. These qualitative observations and the poor performance in retention-span were but slight indicators of a mind above average in mechanical efficiency, but far from normal in other respects.

Projective Tests. The projective tests give more substantial evidence of the nature of the degradation of human intelligence as represented by Hoess. Both the Rorschach and the Thematic Apperception Test show a complete absence of human empathy, as confirmed in the inquiry. On the Rorschach he showed sufficient *cognitive* ability to recognize something approaching living human beings on three of the cards, but the humans were as devoid of life as they could be. The only other remotely human figure seen was the gruesome anatomical response on the first card. It is admittedly not a record overflowing with the joy of living when the very first response elicited is "the pelvic girdle of an exhumed corpse—a post-mortem dissection"; the next card produces a kind of *danse macabre* of withered inhuman figures; and the only other two "human" figures are seen as grotesque animated cartoons. Even in testing the limits it is barely possible to elicit an active human figure when suggested. As he states at the end of the inquiry on the TAT, life was essentially a movie film moving before him without touching him—an animated cartoon, we may assume, in which he also sometimes went through some motions without feeling it. Certainly we have here evidence of that detached apathy which was unmistakable in examining the man. The slowness of his responses on the Rorschach also indicates his difficulty in breaking through the block of detachment from real life to use his native intelligence for creative rapport with the environment. It could be seen during the examination that this was not the hesitation and confusion which produces long reaction-time in organic deterioration, but rather the detached wandering of the schizoid.

Accompanying all this are some residual signs of anxiety, which (along with other signs) show that the process of detachment had not proceeded to the level of frank psychosis. When seen in the light of his early development, the schizoid withdrawal would seem to be a defense against the guilt anxiety generated by his bigoted father's religious indoctrination. At any rate, the expected misanthropic reaction is evident in the records of both projective tests.

The compulsion to use whole-figure interpretations went to an extreme in this Rorschach record. It was our observation that both the superficial categorical abstractions of Nazi ideology and the rigid "categorical imperative" of Prussian militarism produced a tendency to pat generalizations in their interpretations. Both of these influences in Nazi-German culture reached their quintessence in the militaristically and ideologically indoctrinated SS. It is therefore not surprising to find here (as in most of the SS leaders tested) a record consisting almost entirely of whole-figure interpretations, with a rejection of the only card on which such an interpretation is almost impossible. His own comment on that card, "I always want to see the whole thing and not the details that don't belong together," shows how actively and consciously this compulsion operated.

The TAT is full of crime and violence, suggesting an easy interpretation in terms of strong psychopathic impulses. However, the inquiry shows the need for caution in such a glib interpretation. Again, because of the essentially schizoid detachment of affect, Hoess was not projecting and identifying in the ordinary sense. He was simply giving free associations with the antisocial milieu of his adult life—the criminals in Dachau at the time of his imprisonment there and the assorted psychopathic rabble he associated with throughout his SS career. Hoess's associations and fantasies as given in the TAT were naturally in terms of the only way of life he had known ever since his revolt against religion. But *no* way of life was very real or identifiable to an ego essentially detached from life and mechanical in its involvements and expressions. This is something different from the basic need and satisfactions of aggression which we find in a true psychopath like Goering.

Hoess's TAT can be better interpreted in the light of these psychodynamic distinctions. The rejection of guilt is a basic motive whenever there is any evidence of projection. On card 7 the father-figure (father-in-law) "is about to beat the young man" but here Hoess blocks, changes the story, and has the young man falsely betrayed to the authorities instead, making him *appear* guilty when he wasn't. This is significant in view of Hoess's feeling that he had been betrayed by his father-confessor to his father, and that he was never punished by beatings (which he would have preferred) but by intolerable guilt feelings and prayerful expiation of sin. Card 14 throws further light on the reactive mechanism. If we substitute his early ascetic religious training for the art motif in the story, we have almost an autobiographical sketch. "Something which he cannot explain is inhibiting him . . . he plunges into a wild life [in Hoess's case, army life and *Freikorps*] . . . becomes more and more detached, shuts himself off. . . ." The final outcome of insanity and suicide was probably very close to Hoess's insight into himself, again revealing the need for adjustment by the schizoid withdrawal further and further from real life.

Schizoid Personalities.—There was nothing about this apathetic little man to suggest that he was the greatest murderer who had ever lived. The only clue to the nature of the personality that had lent itself so readily to such a thing was that apathy, the hallmark of the schizoid personality. Quiet and correct in his military bearing, he stood at attention when approached by an officer, spoke only when spoken to, and then responded to all questions in a mechanical, matter-of-fact way. There was no indication of emotional reaction of any sort as he calmly related how he had received and executed Himmler's orders to exterminate Jewish families by the trainload. Only a certain air of remoteness in his expression, the cold eyes gazing out into space when he looked at you, gave outward evidence of a personality that was not entirely of this world.

To understand what kind of a personality did this thing, we have to understand the kind of a world in which this mind lived. It took time for an observer to project himself a little into this world, even after having learned to understand the values of the other groups we studied. Hoess, who was not lacking in insight, appreciated our difficulty even before we did, realizing it from the naïve nature of some of the questions we asked: How could he have done it? Why didn't he refuse? How could he kill innocent people?—These were questions predicated on the humanistic conceptions of Western civilization. They might have been applicable to ordinary militarism, but not to the new emergent of the SS-police state.

There is a complex interrelationship between social dynamics and psychopathology which must be analyzed before we can begin to understand what produced this phenomenon.

To begin with, there was the basically schizoid personality trend that was well developed before Hoess even heard of any Nazi movement. This was clearly implicit in the case history as he gave it and was confirmed by our observations and tests. Further discussion only strengthened the original impression:

(*April 12, 1946, Hoess's cell.*) "No, I never had any need for friends. I never even had any real intimacy with my parents— my sisters either. It only occurred to me after they were married that they were like strangers to me.—I always played alone as a child. Even my grandmother says I never had any playmates as a child."

Sex never played a great part in his life. He could take it or leave it. Never felt the urge to have or continue a love affair, although he had momentary affairs now and then. In married life he rarely showed any passion. Claims he never even felt the desire to masturbate and never did.

From Hoess's statement that even as a child he had formed no attachments, we might infer that there was probably some innate schizoid tendency in his personality. In our present state of knowledge, that must remain in the realm of speculation. However, the case history does indicate how environmental stresses intensified the withdrawal of affect, while giving him a field of operation that developed from the detached human to the inhuman.

The father's religious fanaticism undoubtedly precipitated withdrawal reaction formation, as Hoess himself stated. "My father was a kind of higher being that I could never approach, so I crawled back into myself—and I could not express myself to others.—I feel that this bigoted upbringing is responsible for my becoming so withdrawn." As often happens, an obsessed neurotic parent had turned a religion of love and human compassion into a compulsive ritual of guilt expiation and unnatural asceticism. Under such an intolerable pressure of guilt anxiety, any possible development of human empathy had been stifled from early childhood. Instead, the detached personality with a low frustration tolerance became increasingly negativistic toward an environment that weighed it down with such a burden of sin and guilt. Any circumstance which seemed to justify an escape from this anxiety-provoking pressure was welcomed and enlarged. Such an occasion was soon provided by the (probably fantasied) "betrayal" by his father-confessor, and later by the exploitation of "religious relics" in Palestine. By the age of twenty-two he had "broken inwardly" with the church sufficiently to complete the severance of the moral umbilical cord and to embrace instead the amoral religious cult of naziism. This satisfied whatever need for group membership remained after his break with the church, but did so without exacting the price of conscience. For him there had been no strong social influence that represented a middle way. A year later he sealed the bond in blood by committing a political murder. The five years of solitary confinement in Dachau virtually completed the withdrawal process. By the time he became "desensitized" to the task of extermination, he was a walking inhuman robot, utterly devoid of human empathy, yet functioning intellectually on a high level of mechanical efficiency with good insight. We learned from an SS inspector who had come to Auschwitz in 1944 to investigate certain "irregularities" that Hoess had said even then, "As for me, I have long since ceased to have any human feelings."

This schizoid pathology seemed to be a selective factor in the executive hierarchy of the concentration camp world. The special task of exterminating human beings, efficiently and systematically, year in and year out, could not be assigned to just anybody. It required men who would not break under the strain. For that purpose, none were better suited than the apathetic little men who had casually sealed their blood-bond in the SS brotherhood and had "long since ceased to have any human feelings."

The fact is that most of Himmler's extermination chiefs whom we examined gave evidence of schizoid tendencies. Heydrich's successor, Kaltenbrunner, was such a personality. This macrocephalic giant with the saber-scarred face appeared docile and harmless in his cell. He had little to say, and it was hard to establish rapport. His sensitivity was so blunted that he shocked the Nazis themselves with his clumsy lying and denials. After being sentenced to death, he appeared too bored by the whole thing to bother with an appeal, but he casually wrote an essay condemning Himmler when we offered him a piece of chocolate for his opinion.

Otto Ohlendorf, a meek little bureaucrat in the SS-police state, had commanded a task force which exterminated a total of 90,000 "inferior elements" in Russian villages. He had a bland philosophical manner and a penchant for transcendental mysticism (like Frank's) but betrayed no vestige of human feeling. These were the men whom Himmler had selected with infallible intuition—because they were like himself.

Hoess gave an illuminating insight into Himmler's personality by describing how he had watched the extermination procedure. "When Himmler came to inspect the procedure, he just watched it all silently and showed no sign of emotion. All he said was, 'It is a hard job, but we've got to do it.'" We asked whether he reacted at all to the sight of people dying in the gas chambers or their bodies burning. "No, you could never see any sign of emotion in his face—never. I always saw him with this iron mask. He was always that way." Others described Himmler's apparent brutality as the camouflage of a very weak nature. He was considered humorlessly pedantic, ascetic, vacillating, but inscrutable. His interests in life, as expressed by the activities of the police state, might best be described as infinitely dilettante. He dabbled in everything from cancer research to human extermination, from animal-breeding to atomic energy, with an uncomprehending indifference. Toward the end of the war he began to barter trainloads of Jews for gold, and he saw nothing inappropriate in his attempt to negotiate a "gentlemen's agreement" with Eisenhower. A schizoid personality to say the least, Himmler may actually have been an ambulatory schizophrenic. He was the man whom Hitler had consciously picked to do the work of "the scourge of God" (Hitler's own words) and who in turn picked deputies who possessed similar qualities. Those who had a flicker of human empathy soon became "desensitized."

But having determined the nature of a personality like that of Hoess and the rationale of selection, we have actually explained very little. Schizoid personalities exist all over the world without getting involved in human extermination. The functional gap between the detached human and the inhuman being can be filled only by complex social interaction. To develop the picture more fully, we must bring into play the dual forces which we have already described as the progenitors of the Nazi police state: (a) militaristic authoritarianism and (b) racial ideology.

The "Categorical Imperative."—Hoess had rebelled against his father's religious fanaticism and discipline; but *he had not rebelled against authoritarianism as such.* That was far too deeply ingrained in the entire culture and was far too convenient a means of escape. On the contrary, he had only sought refuge and security in the more rigid but *amoral* authority of militarism; and he had later found a more secure haven in the still more rigid dogma and behavior rituals of the SS. For the morally maldeveloped, like Hoess, as well as for the overaggressive, overdependent, and sadomasochistic, a superauthoritarian institution in an authoritarian culture provided a common sanctuary against the anxiety of mature social responsibility. Here, at last, was a world in which individual value judgments, responsibility, and guilt feelings simply did not exist, as long as one conformed to the pseudocompulsive pattern of group behavior. One had only to obey orders and not think. To do or die was easy; to reason why, a psychological impossibility. Patiently, Hoess tried to

convey this to us, when we asked whether he had not expressed
any opinion or shown any reluctance to follow Himmler's order:

(*April 9, 1946, Hoess's cell.*) ". . . I had nothing to say; I
could only say *Jawohl!* In fact, it was exceptional that he called
me to give me any explanation. He could have sent me an order
and I would have had to execute it just the same. We could only
execute orders without any further consideration. . . ." I asked
him whether he couldn't refuse to obey the orders. "No, from
our entire training the thought of refusing an order just didn't
enter one's head, regardless of what kind of an order it was. . . .
Guess you cannot understand our world.—I naturally had to obey
orders and I must now stand to take the consequences. . . . At
that time there were no consequences to consider. It didn't even
occur to me at all that I would be held responsible. You see, in
Germany it was understood that if something went wrong, then
the man who gave the orders was responsible. So I didn't think
that I would ever have to answer for it myself."

(*April 12, 1946.*) I asked him if he had ever considered
whether the Jews whom he had murdered were guilty or had in
any way deserved such a fate. Again he tried patiently to explain
that there was something unrealistic about such questions, because
he had been living in an entirely different world. "Don't you see,
we SS men were not supposed to think about these things; it
never even occurred to us.—And besides, it was something already
taken for granted that the Jews were to blame for everything. . . .
But anyway, that really didn't matter. We were all so trained to
obey orders without even thinking, that the thought of disobeying
an order would simply never have occurred to anybody, and somebody else would have done it just as well if I hadn't. . . ."

(*April 27, 1946.*) "It was only about 250 people who knew
about and participated in the exterminations [at Auschwitz].
None of them liked the idea—but don't forget the SS was drilled
to be so hard that one would shoot his own brother if ordered to.—
Orders were everything."

When we see these "desensitized" personalities operating in
such a completely blind authoritarian setting, we begin to get
some conception of the sociopathological interaction that produced this phenomenon. We might interject here a shrewd observation by the philosophical Seyss-Inquart, who had sent many
victims to concentration camps from Holland (but, like Ribbentrop and Keitel, "had not realized, exactly" that they would be
exterminated). He explained the psychology of genocide, as he

figured it out at the trial, thus: "There is a limit to the number of people you can kill out of hatred or lust for slaughter, but there is no limit to the number you can kill in the cool, systematic manner of the military 'categorical imperative.'" At any rate, we can see that the combination of schizoid personality and rigid militarism were important ingredients in the formula for producing murderous robots.

Seyss-Inquart also felt, after hearing Hoess testify, that he represented an interesting German "type"—an amalgamation of two subcultural character trends: the rigid obedience of Prussian militarism and the passionate prejudice of Bavarian provincialism. Speaking from experience, "both had a lot to do with going against one's conscience in moments of decision." Seyss-Inquart's typology need not detain us, but it brings us to the third ingredient in our formula: fanatic racial ideology. Hoess may have felt that this was secondary to the "categorical imperative" of militarism, but he left no doubt about its effectiveness in limiting the frame of reference for those living in his world.

Racial Ideology.—The role of hostile racial propaganda in determining Hoess's conception of his environment was immediately apparent upon investigation:

(*April 16, 1946.*) Tracking down the source of anti-Semitism which made him feel that Himmler's explanation for the extermination of Jews was right, I asked him how he got his anti-Semitic views. He said that he read Goebbels' editorials in *Das Reich* every week for many years, as well as his books and his various speeches; Rosenberg's *Myth of the Twentieth Century,* and some of his speeches; and, of course, Hitler's *Mein Kampf,* as well as hearing and reading most of his speeches. In addition to these authors, there were the ideological pamphlets and other educational material of the SS. He read Streicher's *Stürmer* only occasionally, because it was too superficial. (He noticed that those of his subordinates who had been in the habit of reading the *Stürmer* were usually men of narrow outlook.) Goebbels, Rosenberg, and Hitler gave him more food for thought. All of these writings and speeches constantly preached the idea that Jewry was Germany's enemy.

"For me as an old fanatic National Socialist, I took it all as fact—just as a Catholic believes in his church dogma. It was

truth without question; I had no doubt about that. I was absolutely convinced that the Jews were the opposite pole from the
German people, and sooner or later there would have to be a
showdown between National Socialism and World Jewry. . . .
And if anti-Semitism did not succeed in wiping out this Jewish
influence, the Jews would succeed in bringing about a war to
wipe out Germany.—But *everybody* was convinced of this; that
was all you could hear or read. That was even before the war.
Then, after the war started, Hitler had explained that World
Jewry had started a showdown with National Socialism—that
was in a Reichstag speech at the time of the French campaign—
and the Jews must be exterminated. Of course, nobody at that
time thought it was meant so literally. But Goebbels expressed
himself more and more sharply against the Jews . . . and it was
always stressed that if Germany was to survive, then World
Jewry must be exterminated, and we all accepted it as truth.
    "That was the picture I had in my head, so, when Himmler
called me to him, I just accepted it as the realization of something
I had always accepted—not only I, but everybody. . . . The
problem itself, the extermination of Jewry, was not new—but
only that *I* was to be the one to carry it out frightened me at
first. But after getting the clear direct order and even an explanation with it—there was nothing left but to carry it out. . . .
Yes, when I think back on it all, it is hard to figure out—but at
that time I didn't think of it at all as propaganda, but something
one just had to believe."

In discussing all this, Hoess displayed nothing but the same
detached apathy that characterized most of Himmler's deputies
in the mass-murder machinery of the police state. There was no
question of genuine guilt feelings or genuine emotions of any
kind. Absently, he wondered whether it had not all been "a
mistake."—"Now I wonder if Himmler really believed all that
himself, or just gave me an excuse to justify what he wanted me
to do."

Not that it could have made any difference to Hoess. Guilt
was merely a formal concept in his authoritarian world, attached
only to those who refused to obey orders or shirked their responsibility for giving them. Like all other SS-Gestapo chiefs,
Hoess thought he had been "betrayed"—not because he had
been forced to commit murder on false pretenses, but because
Himmler had committed suicide and left them to take the blame.
According to the code "My honor is loyalty," Hoess had lived

up to his part of the bargain, but Himmler had welched on his.

Similar sentiments were expressed by other SS-Gestapo chiefs. SS-General Pohl, the chief of administration and supply for the police state, who had estimated the "take" in salvaged gold, clothing, valuables, and labor at 1,630,000 Reichsmarks per 1,000 victims, had only this to say in concluding the analysis he wrote for us: "Resistance from Himmler would in my opinion have made this bloody madness impossible. But Himmler was too problematical a character for that. . . . His supporters swore by him up to his death, which no one will forgive him, because every one expected that he would have the courage to defend his cause himself and not leave his people in the lurch."

Even Kaltenbrunner, Himmler's principal deputy, decided the chief of the police state had only "paid lip-service to a fake symbolism and a passé romanticism. . . . He disgraced the SS . . . since according to the motto 'My honor is loyalty' he should at least have died with his Führer."

Hoess ends his autobiography: "Today, when I know that the entire nation has been deceived by false propaganda, it is also clear to me that Himmler's explanation for the order he gave me to exterminate hundreds of thousands, even millions of people, was false. So I face my sentence as a sacrifice [!] of the system in which I believed so fanatically."

All this is a grim commentary on an ideology in whose name a war had been started, millions had been exterminated, tortured, worked, or starved to death. The answer, we think, lies not so much in the individual's capacity for hatred (there is simply not enough venom in the human autonomic and endocrine system to support hatred on that scale) but in the maladjustive, self-defeating, and self-destructive nature of the ideology of hate. This raises a profound question of the meaning and purpose of hostile racial ideology. If we regard it as the instrument used by antisocial psychopathic personalities to serve ulterior purposes, we must recognize at least three different types of personality, for each of whom it has a different meaning and purpose. There is first the paranoid-neurotic obsession of a man like Hitler, who represents the true fanatic. In his case the hostile racial ideology serves a deep psychological need, even more than its material purposes. Then there is the cynical aggressive psychopath, like Goering, for whom the ideology serves a purely utilitarian purpose. For him any ideology or no ideology at all will be acceptable, as long as it enables him to satisfy his predatory and narcissistic drives without restraint. SS-Colonel Hoess, if we consider him a psychopath, was of an entirely different type: the insensitive, unthinking schizoid with the burnt-out superego, accepting the ideology uncritically and mechanically following the course of least resistance in a psychopathic society.

Not all of the servants of the police state were as uncritical and lacking in insight into the material basis of the ideology as was Colonel Hoess. Those whose duty it was to round up victims in the defeated territories to send to Hoess's gas chambers during the German occupation had to be a little more sophisticated in order to get the cooperation of the local authorities. The Gestapo Chief of occupied Belgium and France, SS-Major Dr. Knochen, revealed his hand quite openly in writing to the commanding general of the occupation forces:

> It has been shown that the cultivation of anti-Semitism among the French is hardly possible on an idealistic basis, whereas if business advantages are offered, they are more likely to condone our anti-Jewish campaign. (The imprisonment of around 100,000 foreign Jews living in Paris, for example, would give a large number of Frenchmen the opportunity to raise their [economic] status from lower to middle class.)
>
> I therefore propose an immediate discussion among the participating offices, to bring about the quickest possible solution of this problem as a step toward the final liquidation of the Jewish question, which is the final solution in the sense desired not only by the Führer but by the Reichsmarschall.[2]

But Reichsmarschall Goering, the avaricious entrepreneur in concentration camps, showed a belated partial insight into the utilitarian futility of hostile racial ideology. It took a strange and incredible bit of testimony to bring about this reaction. The testimony was the revelation that in Auschwitz and Treblinka

---

[2] Letter dated January 28, 1941, from Security Police Headquarters to Chief of Military Government for France, Hotel Majestic, Paris; document on file at Centre de Documentation Juive Contemporaine, Paris.

extermination camps, some of the Jews themselves had submitted to participating in the extermination of their fellow-Jews. It was the only time before his death sentence that we saw Goering react in actual panic, and for a long time we were puzzled by this reaction:

> (*August 8, 1946, Goering's cell.*) "Now it is clear to me.—People facing death will do anything. . . . But—*Gott im Himmel!* —surely you must believe that *I*—good God, I never dreamt that people could simply sit down in cold blood and make a business of the extermination of men, women, and children—that they could mechanically submit. . . . *Now* I realize that we could have handled the Jews entirely differently.—We could have liquidated the Communists as Communists and not bothered the Jews as such.—I bet there were plenty who were just as fanatically nationalistic Germans as anybody, and they could have helped the cause.—It was this nonsense of calling Jews Communists and enemies of the State.—God Almighty! . . ."

We can account for this strange outburst (and Goering was really in a panting, sweating panic over it) only by the sudden and belated realization that the racial ideology had been a *catastrophic miscalculation*: that the Jews were *no better and no worse* than anybody else, and could have been used just as well for the purpose of aggressive nationalism; that if Hitler had not been so obsessed by this hostile racial ideology, they might still have won the war or at least escaped self-destruction.

As for Hoess, he had merely been "a sacrifice of the system in which I believed so fanatically." Just how deep this fanaticism ran, it is hard to say. It was hard to find a single Nazi even among the executioners of the police state, who was fanatic enough to insist that the extermination program had really been necessary, once the Nazi microcosm had collapsed. But for Hoess the meaning and purpose that the ideology of the police state had are clear. He had found refuge in a world in which Judeo-Christian conceptions of morality had been abolished, and an ethnocentric pagan ideology, with all its "fake symbolism and passé romanticism," its "false propaganda" and code of loyalty, had served as the supreme criteria of all social values. The dogma had been provided ready-made and all his actions prescribed and sanctioned by higher authority. This had satis-

fied Hoess's personal need to abolish guilt feelings by depersonal-
izing all aggression and submerging the remnants of an
anxiety-provoking superego in the militaristic "categorical
imperative."

It was that combination of absolute authoritarianism and
hostile racial ideology that had crystallized a new set of social
norms in the police state of Nazi Germany and had produced a
new species of schizoid murderous robots, like Colonel Hoess
of Auschwitz.

PART III
PSYCHOLOGICAL IMPLICATIONS

Chapter 7

CLINICAL AND PSYCHODYNAMIC ASPECTS

It has been apparent, all through this study, that the psychology of aggressive dictatorship cannot be explained adequately on either the psychodynamic or the socioeconomic level, but requires an approach that integrates both. The Nazi movement did not come into being simply because of Adolf Hitler's paranoid tendencies, nor was it the inevitable outcome of the Treaty of Versailles. A complex interaction of individual personalities, group interests, critical events, and broader social forces brought about the Nazi dictatorship and World War II. Our examination of the Nazi leaders has provided a convenient focus for this study in social interaction.

If we are to consider the psychodynamic aspects of a social phenomenon like dictatorship, it is clear that we must go beyond the narrower clinical definitions of that concept. Psychodynamics, as currently conceived under the influence of psychoanalysis, is largely predicated on intrafamilial psychosexual tensions. There can be no doubt that much of adult social behavior—even in political leadership, as we have shown—can be traced back to such influences (though even there we cannot overlook the parental role as transmitter of cultural values). These origins of personality development may provide an adequate reference point for ordinary problems of individual diagnosis and psychotherapy. But to apply our clinical insights to the problem of mental health in society, to understand the psychodynamics of ethnic tensions, political demagoguery, social frustration and aggression, a broader conceptual framework is needed. Freud may have been right in suggesting that "all revolutions begin in the cradle," but no one has suggested that the causes of social conflict ended there. On the contrary, we are principally concerned here with the social extensions of clinical psychodynamics—the "connecting links" in the inter-action between personality development and social conflict.

An important requirement of our interactionary framework is to recognize that psychodynamics and social forces represent two different levels of explanation, though there is necessarily interaction between the two. Some of the concepts of psycho-dynamics and psychopathology (like paranoid tendencies) can-not be applied directly to the body politic without making neces-sary distinctions in their phenomenology at the two levels. Other clinical concepts (like frustration and aggression) may come into play on the group level by social facilitation, though they may emerge with additional manifestations.

Furthermore, there appear to be significant processes of ad-justive social behavior which have been largely overlooked by both psychology and psychiatry in their preoccupation with the individual. Thus, in trying to analyze the character and motives of normal political opportunists, as well as the more deviant personalities in this dictatorship, we have found the concepts of adjustive behavior inadequately developed. This is not sur-prising, in view of the discrepancy between the levels of expla-nation required in psychopathology and in social behavior. But the problem is complicated by the sheer enormity and complexity of institutionalized aggression as promoted by the Nazi dictator-ship. Our accustomed concepts do not fit. Even international law has had to formulate new concepts (like genocide) and elaborate on old ones (like conspiracy) to encompass it. To analyze social pathology on that order, clinical psychology will likewise have to develop new concepts and elaborate on old ones. We shall review and elaborate here some of the reconceptualiza-tions suggested by this study in adapting the clinical approach to the study of social conflicts, with particular reference to the challenge of dictatorship.

AUTHORITARIAN REGRESSIVENESS

We recognized at the outset, in examining dictatorship as a cultural phenomenon, that an authoritarian cultural lag predis-posed people to revert to previously learned symbols of authority and security for leadership. Our study of the Nazi leaders has shown in many ways how the reversion to authoritarian behavior provided social mechanisms of defense for leaders as well as masses in a time of social stress. This is a phenomenon which appears to take place on both the individual and social levels and may be called "authoritarian regressiveness."

The concept of "infantile regression" is a familiar one in psychopathology. It means a reversal of the biosocial maturing process in the individual, with a return to a childish or infantile level of functioning, particularly in the emotional sphere, as a result of some strong need to escape the trauma and frustration of adult life. It usually implies an unconscious retreat to child-ish dependency and helplessness, or to a more gratifying earlier level of psychosexual development, for the sake of the secondary gain.

The authoritarian regressiveness we speak of here, however, is the more common and normal variety of immaturity reaction in adult social behavior, of which regression may be considered a pathological extreme. We refer to the common tendency to avoid mature social responsibility in assuming the adult role, to submit to protective leadership and authority, to accept decisions "from above" in order to avoid the anxiety of having to make them, and to submit to paternalistic influences generally. In short, it represents a desire to reap the benefits of youthful irre-sponsibility in adult life. This regressive tendency can take place in the life of any individual in any culture, and it may take place by social facilitation in the life of an entire nation. The psychodynamic processes are the same on both levels (as long as we avoid the concept of regression with its pathological and psychosexual implications). The psychological process at either level is a retreat to earlier patterns of learned social behavior (without actual deterioration) when the maturing process provides too many threats to security. Our particular interest in this process is to elucidate the authoritarian cultural lag which seems to be an underlying condition of the reversion to autocratic rule in societies that have rebelled against it.

In any generation of rapid social change, the pattern of be-havior and system of values learned in childhood is apt to persist—hence the familiar phenomenon of "our conservative elders." Each new generation adjusts to changing values and norms in the natural process of adaptive social behavior. But in times of revolutionary social change, where the whole frame of reference of a cultural pattern is being altered, the vast majority of the entire population may find the rapidity of change beyond the limits of adaptability. This is particularly true if social circumstances accentuate frustration and insecurity, while learned patterns of defense are found no longer applicable. Under such circumstances, the quest for lost meanings and defenses renders the individual and the mass susceptible to propaganda couched in the terms of old palliatives. This may, of course, apply to any previously learned pattern of behavior. But authoritarian regressiveness has such powerful appeal and provides such a persistent social lag, because it has deep roots in the psychodynamics of personality development.

The universal prototype of the paternalistic-authoritarian figure is, of course, the father. In authoritarian cultures he is apt to be more rigidly disciplinarian and autocratic than in democratic cultures. It is through that very fact that the authoritarian pattern is transmitted so pervasively from generation to generation. The submissiveness and lack of initiative or critical value judgments which are thus deeply ingrained in the child provide a permanent basis for submissiveness to authority and lack of independence in adult social behavior. The submission to authority in political life becomes a natural extension of the submission to the father's discipline in the home. The hierarchical social structure provides its own rewards and defense mechanisms in an accustomed frame of reference. It provides the rewards of obedience and parasitism, security of status, outlets for aggression in situations of sibling rivalry and dominance of subordinates. Adjustment to the greatest social crises is the more easily made as long as the social structure remains intact and provides such accustomed defenses. But when that paternalistic-authoritarian frame of reference is destroyed, the threshold of insecurity-tolerance is necessarily lowered. The insecurity of socioeconomic stress, thus accentuated, may even overcome the feeling of liberation that the rebellion against tyranny brings. If not counterbalanced by restructured goals and sources of security, this insecurity may eventuate in a demand for a return to the comfortable protectiveness and familiarity of paternalism—in other words, an "escape from freedom."

In this study we have found that such regressiveness is characteristic of even the highest level of leadership in a dictatorship. Having experienced the insecurity of a destroyed frame of reference for their aspirations, these products of an authoritarian culture forced or welcomed the restructuring of their purposes by a restitution of that frame of reference. The avowed purposes of the movement were to be daringly progressive and revolutionary; but the underlying psychology was retrogressive and counterrevolutionary. Even in borrowing the symbols of racial superiority in a new order in the struggle for survival, rejecting the democratic "myths," the party ideologists expressed their reversion to a primitive and immature level of social behavior. For at the core of this counterrevolution in an age of democratic social change was the rigid adherence to ancient symbols and adolescent fantasies, the inability to adjust to growing social interdependence and responsibility, to control one's own aggressions in the interest of ego-security of a higher order. Even in wielding supreme power, both the dictator and his heir-apparent persistently gave vent to their childish heroic fantasies, their irresponsible egocentricity. In the supporting ranks of the dictatorship, the most common characteristic found was the enjoyment of status without any mature sense of responsibility in their historic roles; the submission to and exercise of authority without any ability to exercise mature value judgments.

This regressiveness was facilitated in various ways among the various identification groups as psychodynamic and social factors came into play. Among the revolutionary fanatics, the close identification with strong leadership was accentuated not only by the prevalent neurotic needs for compensatory power but in some cases by the submissive compulsions of latent or overt homosexuality. Among the diplomats and businessmen who formed the "political bandwagon," it was facilitated by the culturally sanctioned forms of political opportunism : the protection of established institutions in which authoritarianism and class privilege were established norms. Among the militarists and SS the "categorical imperative" of military obedience found its purest expression as an escape from mature social responsibility.

The clear implication of all this is that autocratic government is a primitive and immature mode of social organization which rests on a primitive and immature mode of adaptive social behavior—one that is in fact maladaptive in the present stage of social evolution. We shall return to this hypothesis in discussing the broader social implications of our study.

CULTURAL PSEUDOPATHOLOGY

Pseudoparanoia.—We have stated that insecurity makes people more susceptible to propaganda couched in the terms of old palliatives. Among the palliatives offered by the Nazi propagandists were ethnocentric self-glorification and self-protection of the in-group, with aggression directed to scapegoats of the out-group. These formulas come so close to megalomania and aggressive defenses against delusions of persecution that attempts have been made to explain the behavior of Nazi Germany in terms of an inherently paranoid trend in German culture. (7) Such clinical interpretations create the danger of confusing social pathology with psychopathology. They certainly broke down when the Nazi leaders were actually examined individually. A few, but only a few, of the Nazi leaders showed signs of clinical paranoid tendencies. We are forced to make a clearer distinction between clinical or true paranoia and the cultural "as if" epiphenomenon, or "cultural pseudoparanoia."

The distinction may be defined operationally as follows : In true paranoia or paranoid tendencies, the individual's sense of reality breaks down; he perceives the environment and his relationship to it in terms which do not correspond to the perceptions of other individuals in the same environment. He may develop delusions of persecution or inherent superior power and perceive events as taking place within that subjective frame of reference. But it is also possible that he and most others in that environment have developed, from earliest childhood, attitudes of persecution, superiority, special revelation, or manifest destiny to rule the world as a natural consequence of ethnic identification and indoctrination. Thus a whole culture may behave *as if* it suffered from a paranoid tendency, when viewed from the frame of reference of other cultures. We can describe this as cultural pseudoparanoia, because it is only a cultural epiphenomenon and does not involve the breakdown of the mental reality-testing function. The possibility of reality-testing has simply been artificially limited by the nature of the cultural learning process.

This takes place to some extent in every culture. Prejudices, religious beliefs, national and ethnic myths exist in every society. We do not consider such culturally determined attitudes and beliefs paranoid, or the whole world would have to be considered an asylum of paranoiacs. Such group attitudes might be considered "latent pseudoparanoia," which is universally present. In a totalitarian state, however, the rigid control and distortion of information under the obsessive influence of fanatic ideologists inflames this latent pseudoparanoia and brings about a pattern of national behavior which does *resemble* paranoia. This is particularly true of a state whose leader or dictator suffers from true paranoid tendencies and channels that paranoia into the political ideology of the state. That suffices to create a phenomenon of national behavior which has direct resemblance to behavior prompted by systematized delusions. Thus, in a dictatorship, the paranoid tendencies of a leader become functionally identified with the policies and behavior of the body politic. That is what happened in Nazi Germany: Germany's (i.e., Hitler's) unlimited aggression against her (his) enemies, in "self-defense" against persecution and betrayal from within and without, and to prove "innate superiority" as a defense against inferiority feelings. It must be stressed, however, that most of the members of the culture who shared these attitudes (there were many, of course, who saw through them) were simply responding suggestively to the perceptual frame of reference set up for them. Most of the leaders of the Nazi dictatorship, being more sophisticated and better informed, did not even take Hitler's paranoid obsessions seriously. Men like Von Papen and Schacht laughed off *Mein Kampf* as just another political diatribe for propaganda purposes. Only a few, mostly within the original group of revolutionists, like Hess and Streicher, had likewise channeled their paranoid tendencies into the political ideology. But it was in the nature of an authoritarian system that the entire governmental hierarchy, and all the forces at their command, *behaved as if they did* share these delusions—except for the few who had both clarity of insight and the courage of their convictions. If a sufficient number of leaders had risen above their authoritarian conceptions to apply their reality-testing and agree that "the emperor *has* no clothes!" —that he is in fact a destructive maniac—then the paranoid spell could have been broken. There were such attempts, but too little and too late. Why that should have been the case requires several clinical and social concepts, which we shall consider. One of these might be termed "cultural pseudocompulsiveness."

Pseudocompulsion.—The attempt to explain authoritarian behavior as compulsive also breaks down when individual leaders are examined. This applies to the most rigid of the militarists. There is rigidity and repetitiveness of the behavior pattern, to be sure; but the behavior pattern is not a ritual set up by the individual and adhered to rigidly beyond self-control as a necessary mechanism to deal with anxiety. The militaristic "categorical imperative" *may* be resorted to as a protective device by a compulsive or any other kind of individual, to allay the anxiety of personal responsibility. It was certainly used for that purpose by many Nazis. But this long-institutionalized behavior pattern differed very little from any other cultural or institutionalized behavior pattern. Crossing oneself, saluting, shaking hands, or obeying orders cannot be regarded as compulsive behavior in the clinical sense.

However, we have noted that there is such a thing as a conflict of values even in the militaristic system, and that there is such a thing as a threshold-scale of resistance to the "categorical imperative" of military obedience. Beyond the commonly recognized threshold, the rigid adherence to narrow conceptions of loyalty and duty becomes nonadaptive behavior, even though the individual is carrying out a behavior pattern that corresponds in a narrow sense to the group norm. We can describe this tendency to carry to a nonadaptive extreme the repetition of group behavior rituals as "cultural pseudocompulsiveness." Like cultural pseudoparanoia, it is nonadaptive on a group level but does not imply abnormality in the individual. It may involve a false sense of values, an easy justification for the rewards of conformity, a camouflage for lack of moral courage or independence of judgment, or even a facilitative mechanism for much-needed self-deception in a conflict of motives. That is what happened all too often among the responsible leaders in Nazi Germany, who were not too deceived by the Nazi ideology and did have some misgivings about Hitler's reckless policies but stayed with him to the bitter end. This was particularly true of certain military leaders, like Keitel, and of certain political opportunists, like Von Papen. It was an important ingredient in the terror machinery of the police state.

Hitler was thus able to implement his own paranoid aggressions largely because he was able to count on the normal pseudocompulsion of authoritarian obedience and the latent cultural pseudoparanoia of group prejudices. It is therefore important to make one thing clear: this "pseudo pathology" can be just as maladaptive in group behavior as genuine psychopathology is in individual behavior. The cultural pseudoparanoia of fanatic racial ideology, combined with pseudocompulsive obedience, can drive groups of men to mutual extermination, just as surely as the delusions of the true paranoiac may compel him to commit murder or suicide. The paranoiac has really lost his sense of values in social reality-testing, while the group may merely have failed to test the reality of its social values. But it amounts to the same thing in the end.

This raises the larger issue of the relationships between psychopathology and social pathology; but first we must consider further the adjustive mechanisms in the motivational conflicts of responsible leaders in such a dictatorship.

Defense Mechanisms in Value-Conflict

We have recognized dictatorship as a regressive phenomenon in the conflict between authoritarianism and democratic self-government. This social conflict implies a conflict of values in the generations of men who are living through the social upheaval; more particularly, in the motivations of their leaders. We have seen that for many members of the revolutionary nucleus, the fascist ideology provided outlets for pathological tendencies that had already been deeply rooted in their personality development. In their cases, revolutionary ideological dictatorship provided a means of resolving conflicts, even if it created new ones. In cases like Goering, Hess, Frank, and, we may presume, Hitler himself, their reaction to the collapse of their dictatorship was a reflection of their original motivation in creating it: aggressive reactions to frustration, acting out of heroic fantasies, even hysterical and delusional tendencies.

But in analyzing the motives of the comparatively "normal and respectable" members of Hitler's entourage—the diplomats, businessmen, militarists, Junkers, and such identification groups —the problem was not so simple. There was no escaping the fact that such men, who represented a large part of Hitler's supporters at all levels of leadership, were convinced of their own idealism, their patriotism, their basic humanitarianism. Their drive for prestige and power, even while influenced by the authoritarian cultural lag, was channeled within the framework of cultured polite society, Christian moral values, even democratic conceptions of human rights. The question naturally arises, How could such men have participated in a movement which violated some of their own basic values? How could the same men subscribe to humanitarian values and condone persecution, believe in peace and prepare for war, be pagan and Christian, fascist and democratic, chauvinist and cosmopolitan, all at the same time?

In such cases, we have little evidence for pathological explanations of such inconsistent behavior. Cynical self-interest and authoritarianism did enter into the picture, to be sure, but even these do not provide adequate answers to our questions. These leaders were not immune to the superego restraints of Western civilization. There was definite conflict in their motives and values, and the question to be answered was how they resolved the conflict.

In general, we found that they exhausted the entire gamut of defense mechanisms in adjustive behavior. Conscious rationalization of ulterior motives, especially in terms of patriotism and self-defense; disowning projection of guilt feelings, facilitated by the party propaganda and the authoritarian conception of responsibility; identification with the acceptable symbols and values of their subcultural groups; normal sublimation of aggressive tendencies through cultural pursuits—these were the more or less obvious mechanisms of defense in value-conflict.

But the question still remains, for these leaders as well as for the majority of ordinary Germans: How could they have promoted or condoned war and atrocities, if they knew what was happening, and how could they have helped knowing? We must examine here some little-understood *cognitive* functions in the resolution of conflicting values and motives. We have suggested that it was the "semiconscious suppression of insight," rather than cynical self-interest or pathological defenses that provided the key to the mystery:

> Between knowledge and ignorance there is the limbo of arrested perceptions and inhibited insights. Between calculated hypocrisy and hysteria there is semiconscious self-deception. It is possible to look at things without fully perceiving them,[1] to divert one's attention from the unpleasant to the pleasant, to suspend the process of rational inference in mid-air, and to distort one's insights to avert anxiety. [Cf. discussion of Ribbentrop's case.]

---

[1] This goes back to the Hegelian distinction between apprehension (*Auffassen*) and comprehension (*Begreifen*), a distinction further elaborated by William James and the "functionalist" school of psychology around the turn of the century. Modern experimental social psychology has systematically elaborated the distinction into the basic concept of "social perception" in motivated behavior. (12, 47) We introduce it here as a clinical concept— the basis of a mechanism of suppression. It would likewise apply to the well-known inhibitory and facilitative processes of perceptual anomalies in hysterical, hypnotic, and hallucinatory states.

In other words, in a conflict between hostile-ethnocentric and humanitarian ego-involvements, people may behave inconsistently because they "know not what they do." When the Nazi crowds shouted "God punish England!" and "Throw out the Jews!" and applauded their leaders for taking steps in those directions, many of them simply did not perceive the full meaning of what they were saying. Many of their leaders, in turn, washed their hands (and minds) of any guilt feelings by the same process of arrested insight. It was hard, even for close observers, to believe that the Germans could have been so blind to what was going on around them before and all during the war, but the evidence was there. The extraordinary shock and humiliation of many Germans, when they awakened to the realization that what they had been saying had actually come to pass, was an impressive experience.

This defensive self-deception in value-conflict was by no means peculiar to Nazi Germany. Nor is it merely a defense mechanism of the weak, the immature, the inadequate and ultra-suggestible. To a large extent, it is part of the normal adjustive process of the human quest for security in a world of conflicting values. This adjustive process is so common in social conflict, and yet so largely ignored in clinical analysis, that some elaboration of it would be in order here.

Obviation and Diversion of Insight.—We shall refer to the tendency to obviate or divert insight in value-conflict as "obviation and diversion mechanisms."

We shall define "obviation" as "that mechanism by which anxiety-provoking perceptions are averted by avoiding experiences in which some ego-involved values are likely to be challenged by reality." The avoidance of such threatening experiences and perceptions is not done with full consciousness of purpose; that would involve ordinary conscious evasion or rationalization. There is instead a semiconscious development of negativistic attitudes, habits, and avoidance reactions, which ultimately have the effect of obviating emotional conflicts. Examples of this are: confining one's social contacts to groups and organs of information which only reinforce one's own social values; not "getting around" to reading books, seeing films, or going to places where social issues in conflict with those values are apt to be raised; "following orders and minding your own business," if one is a soldier or a bureaucrat; "keeping too busy to get into mischief"—or to notice one's own negligence of social responsibilities.

We shall define "diversion" as "that mechanism by which anxiety is suppressed by diverting the attention and failing to draw the necessary effective inferences from relevant perceptual data." Here the conflict is "sensed" but suppressed by arrested insight. In contrast to hysterical conversion phenomena, the attendant anxiety is not inhibited by an unconscious process of inactivation or dissociation; nor is it "undone" by some ritualistic behavior, as in the obsessive-compulsive neurosis. The anxiety is present, though suppressed. It may manifest itself to a minimal or maximal degree, at the fringes or at the focus of awareness, but the circumstances that provoke it are not consciously related to the anxiety. Examples of this are: verbalizing one's aggressive impulses without realizing the consequences; dismissing suspicions of criminal intent in the acts of individuals or groups with whom one identifies; noticing signs of approaching physical, financial, or political ruin, but refusing to take them seriously. It may even involve partial insight, as when tyrants shrug off social change with *après moi, le déluge,* refusing to recognize that the deluge is already upon them.

These mechanisms operate in conjunction to form an avoidance-suppression complex that functions on both the individual and social levels. It is the device of the wife who prefers not to know about her husband's infidelities, as well as of the puritanical culture whose sex mores belie its sexual practices. It is true of the invalid who disdains examination by a cancer specialist, as well as of the nation that refuses to face the threat of aggressive dictatorship. It is through such devices that "a man may smile and smile and be a villain," or a privileged in-group indulge in virtuous platitudes while social injustice festers all around. In all of these instances human beings fail to make full use of mature observation and reason for fear of disturbing a comforting belief or set of values. The possible disillusionment over a deeply ego-involved attitude or value may be so catastrophic a threat to the experiencing individuals (or groups) that they resort to semiconscious self-deception.

This, more than anything else, explains the blindness of so many Germans (and others) to inhuman behavior they could not possibly have condoned. In our study, it was particularly noticeable in a man like Ribbentrop, who freely emulated Hitler in verbalized aggression that amounted to collusion in murder, yet broke down when the full realization of actual extermination finally penetrated his consciousness. Similar reactions were found on the part of Von Papen and Schacht, who blamed their lack of insight into Hitler's warlike intentions on the fact that Hitler was "a pathological liar"; while General Keitel claimed that "a veil has suddenly been taken away from my eyes." Economics Minister Walther Funk kept repeating, "We were blinded—not blind, but blinded!" after evidence had been presented that bags of gold teeth and wedding rings had been deposited in his banks. Hans Frank described it best: "Don't let anybody tell you that they had no idea. Everybody sensed that there was something horribly wrong with this system, even if we didn't know all the details. They didn't *want* to know! It was too comfortable to live on the system, to support our families in royal style, and to believe that it was all right."

After the deluge—insight.

Selective Constriction of Affect.—In the realm of affective reactions, there are further adjustive mechanisms that must be taken into account. Self-deception about the existence and extent of atrocities was not always possible. It may be presumed that many who witnessed or unwillingly participated in them had severe emotional reactions out of sheer human empathy. We know that this was true among some of the Nazi leaders and their wives and even some of the hard-boiled SS men. Humanitarian values are not, after all, purely intellectual artifacts, but are rooted in common human emotions that may be considered necessary for survival. The very necessity of self-deception and the emotional breakdowns that accompanied realization proved that human empathy was not dead, but only perverted, in the Nazi microcosm. An unrecognized adjustive mechanism that seems to have been operating here was "selective constriction of affect."

The constriction or dilation of affect has generally been considered as a generalized trait in personality development. It has been customary in clinical practice to test mental patients on that assumption, and to base clinical diagnosis in part on the estimates of general empathy and affectivity. "Flattened or inappropriate affect" in any area of interpersonal relationships is frequently regarded as a major sign of schizophrenic withdrawal.[2] This appears to leave out of account the complexity of social motivation and attitudes. An investigation of group identification, with its attendant loyalties and hostilities, reveals that empathy can actually be a selective function in any given individual or group. We shall therefore define "selective constriction" as "that process by which an individual's group identifications produce selective empathy, indifference, and hostility, with a resultant partial constriction of affect."

This is a natural accompaniment of normal social conditioning. It manifests itself universally in the experience of greater empathy with one's own family than with "the man on the street." However, identification with ethnic groups produces a more complex differentiation of empathy. One may react to injury or persecution of one's own identification group with the same pain or hostility as if the injury had been inflicted on him and yet feel no concern for the same injuries inflicted on members of other groups. Thus sentiment could be aroused among Germans over the "persecution" of their *Volksgenossen* in Czechoslovakia and Austria, with impassioned humanitarian appeals, while many calmly witnessed the beating up of German Jews on the streets of their own cities. In a like manner, some "white, American-born Protestants" can patriotically defend the humane "American way" in defiance of dictatorship, while feel-

---

[2] In our opinion, this accounts for many mistaken diagnoses of schizophrenia, when only exaggerated social attitudes are involved. The same is true of "paranoid tendencies" which (as in Hitler's and Hess's cases) may be part of a neurotic defense system and not symptoms of schizophrenic deterioration.

ing no concern over the mistreatment of racial minorities at their own back door. Many Germans and many Americans, when confronted with these inconsistencies in their professed behavior as decent citizens, recognize the inconsistency intellectually, but still find it difficult to modify their behavior. Insight is not sufficient to overcome the deeply rooted social conditioning of feelings. Perhaps the worst of the Nazi heritage today is the selective constriction of empathy they produced in a whole new generation; for that, more than the relearning of social values, is apt to resist all efforts at re-education.

The *ultimate* effect of this process is often the general constriction of affect so familiar to psychiatry. Our study suggests that the "desensitizing process" of SS brutality facilitated, if it did not create, a schizoid reaction process among its "hard" champions. One cannot go on brutalizing, torturing, killing, or starving the members of enemy out-groups without dehumanizing oneself. Himmler's SS-Gestapo machine consciously cultivated this process to provide a more effective instrument of aggression. The end result of this process has been described in the schizoid personalities who directly supervised the extermination program.

As a general principle, however, the normal social process of group identification and hostility-reaction brings about a *selective* constriction of empathy, which, in addition to the semiconscious suppression of insight, enables normal people to condone or participate in the most sadistic social aggression without feeling it or realizing it.

This is something quite apart from the role that psychopathic personalities may play in social pathology.

Psychopathic Personalities

The suggestion is often made by both clinicians and laymen, when inquiring about the examination of Nazi leaders, that "these men must have been a lot of psychopaths to have done what they did." That statement rests on the popular assumption that since atrocious crimes are abnormal manifestations of social behavior, the people who participate in them must be abnormal. We have already detected a flaw in that assumption. Nevertheless, social phenomena like race riots, lynchings, mass exterminations, wars, and revolutions do not come about simply as part of the everyday activity of well-adjusted individuals participating in the favorite outdoor sports of their culture, even if they are not simply the work of abnormal men. The complexity and confusion in the relationship between psycho-pathology and social pathology lies both at the level of clinical concept and at the broader level of social relationships. We shall examine here the clinical concept and role of psychopathic personalities.

We have already indicated that fairly normal people may become involved in the highly complex manifestations of insti-tutionalized aggression, and we have considered by what devices they become "partners in crime in spite of themselves." It would contribute nothing to our understanding to insist on labeling them psychopathic personalities. The question we must still consider is whether the more deviant personalities who initiated and executed the most extreme acts of aggression (like the Old Fighters and SS-Gestapo-men) were psychopathic personalities.

The concept of psychopathic personality has long been the bugaboo of clinical diagnosis. This, we believe, is due largely to the fact that it is not a clinical entity. It is essentially a so-cially descriptive generic term, grouping all those who display persistently nonconforming or antisocial behavior. For all those who display such behavior, the term "sociopath" is probably a more apt generic designation than are the confusing and ill-conceived designations of constitutional psychopathic personal-ity, psychopathic inferiors with "stigmata of degeneracy," etc. We suggest that the confusion arises out of the traditional rele-gation of all abnormal behavior to the field of psychiatry, with the problems of diagnosis and therapy which are peculiar to the medical orientation.

When a psychiatrist examines a problem child or a criminal, he is ordinarily expected to approach the problem as one of diagnosis and treatment of mental disease. Traditionally, he is confronted with the stumbling blocks of the neat, mutually exclusive categories of Kraepelinian classification and the choice of "indicated treatment" for the diseases in question. Modern psychiatry has, of course, recognized the limitations of the traditional medical concepts in the field of psychopathology and criminology. With respect to psychopathic personality (the "constitutional" part having already been virtually abandoned), the failure to discover any consistent pathology in antisocial behavior has tempted psychiatrists to abandon the term altogether.

Not being bound by medical predilections, the social or clinical psychologist may nevertheless choose to retain such a concept if it has any consistent meaning and serves any useful purpose. In the study of social pathology, the role of personality deviation remains prominent and inescapable. Some means of coming to grips with it would appear desirable, even if we must first disentangle it from its traditional medical connotations. We suggest the retention of the term "psychopathic personality" as an indication of "sociopathic behavior," provided we can clarify what kind of psychopathology is involved.

First, we submit that some psychopathology must be inferred from any persistent failure to adapt to social norms. Adaptability is an essential criterion of normal behavior, and nonadaptability is essential to any definition of abnormal behavior. But that does not mean that the deviations involved in antisocial behavior are clinically specific or that they fit into any particular category of psychiatric diagnosis. Our own experience with criminal and antisocial personalities, on all levels of social relationships, readily leads us to the generalization that such personalities may embrace *any* kind of psychopathology. We would accordingly define the concept of "psychopathic (or sociopathic) personality" as "any kind of deviant personality whose behavior disorder takes the form of persistent violation of strongly sanctioned social mores." Thus the actual mental disorder involved in such behavior may range from mental deficiency through all types of neurosis to psychotic conditions.

In the realm of social pathology, we suggest that three clinical types lend themselves most readily to development into criminal psychopaths under favorable (i.e., socially unfavorable) conditions: (a) the paranoid, (b) the aggressive-narcissistic

personality, and (c) the schizoid personality.[3] This selection
of principal personality deviations in the so-called psychopathic
personality is based on clinical experience before, during, and
after the war, in military as well as civilian life, but the Nazi
leaders provided striking examples of their role in social pathology.

We would challenge at the outset the assumption of some
doctrinaire psychoanalysts that the psychopath is essentially one
who lacks the capacity to develop a superego as a check on his
libidinal drives. If the concept of superego includes, as it must,
introcepted social values and aspirations, then none but the con-
genitally feeble-minded and psychotic lack that capacity. On
the other hand, we would suggest that the basic rationale of
psychopathic behavior is the overruling of the social-conforming
superego function in situations of social conflict, because of the
nature of the pathology involved.

In the case of the paranoid,[4] the distorted conceptualization
adopted to resolve existing anxieties overcomes the strong inhibiting force of social sanctions. Overvalued ideas of persecution, conceptions of innate superiority to compensate for feelings
of inferiority, projections of guilt and aggressive intent, etc.,
may become so powerful as to give rise to violent outbursts of
"defensive" aggression. Libidinal conflicts may well play a
part, as when the aggression is directed against authority associated with the father-figure. All of these factors entered into
Hitler's paranoid aggressiveness, as we have seen. Under the
conditions of social conflict that prevailed at the time, his aggression found outlet first in propaganda, then persecution, and
ultimately in war and genocide. Hitler might therefore be called
a paranoid psychopath, if we are interested in labels. But apart
from the social forces at work, the clinical explanation for his

---

[3] Bromberg (8) likewise recognizes these three types, among others, but
appears to consider them subdivisions of a diagnostic category, in accordance
with psychiatric tradition.

[4] We include here all paranoid conditions, especially the psychiatrically
unrecognized "paranoid neurotic" (usually diagnosed as anxiety neurosis
or obsessional neurosis with paranoid tendencies; sometimes labeled paranoiac
for want of a better category for cases that are not palpably schizophrenic).

behavior is not that he lacked a superego. His extraordinary sensitivity to status and approval by the in-group bespeaks merely a distortion of the superego function. The paranoid aggression took a violently antisocial turn in his case; hence the permissible designation of paranoid psychopath. It need hardly be emphasized that the superego restraints of a well-adjusted individual would not possibly have allowed him to carry aggression to the antisocial extreme that Hitler reached; nor that a healthier social climate would hardly have allowed paranoia to go to such extremes.

The excessively and aggressively narcissistic (ego-inflated) personality may likewise become psychopathic in the social sense under appropriate conditions of social interaction. His excessive aggressiveness (possibly of constitutional origin) and egocentricity likewise bespeak a distortion, rather than an absence, of superego function. He introcepts the social values of his culture only to the extent that they gratify his egotistical needs and provide outlet for his aggressive drive. His drive to dominate and subjugate, even to destroy, is not so much the product of a defensive delusional system as a direct expression of uninhibited infantile impulse. He obtains gratification from manipulating the environment for the feeling of power it affords, to act the aggressive hero for the sheer pleasure of acting. He is too egocentric to love or hate very deeply, though the outward show of such emotions may be part of the role he plays. His violation of the social mores is not a neurotic obsession but an incidental aspect of this aggressive role-playing. In situations of social conflict, he identifies with the group that provides the best outlet of aggression for aggression's sake. Goering was a good example of this type of aggressive psychopath. He joined the Nazi revolution "precisely because it *was* a revolution, not because of the ideological stuff." It was the zest of high and fast living, of heroic play acting, that appealed to him. Craving applause for his showmanship, he would as lief have played the role of aggressive champion of human rights, if the stage had been set for such a role. Like many of his ilk, he presented strange anomalies of sadistic aggression and amiability in his behavior. Here, too, it was the nature of the social interaction that determined his psychopathic role.

Finally, the schizoid personality—the withdrawn, apathetic, rather insensitive individual, who has an emotional valence that is neither sympathetic nor hostile, nor torn between the two, but rather indifferent. He reacts to social conflict by withdrawal, by taking the course of least resistance. He may become a mechanical conformist or a mechanical criminal, as the social pressures dictate. In the latter case, he would qualify as a criminal psychopath. When he violates the social mores, he does so in a more or less passive manner, responding to social pressures or temptations, rather than to aggressive urges or delusions. Though he may at times play the "lone wolf," stealing or killing without compunction to satisfy an immediate material need, he becomes an ideal tool in organized social aggression. This is especially true in an authoritarian environment, when the group prescribes antisocial behavior by demanding the execution of orders without thinking. The psychopathic behavior on his part is not an expression of sadistic urges or desperate defense against danger, nor even aggressive ego-gratification, though he may passively identify with these motives in his leaders. For him it is merely prescribed behavior for the avoidance of the emotional conflict which resistance would entail. This is something different from the suppression of insight that the normally developed superego requires. Nor does it mean that the schizoid psychopath never had the capacity to develop a superego. It simply means that the schizoid has long since learned to resolve his conflicts by emotional detachment and passive withdrawal. It is that very apathy and indifference to social conflict that makes him potentially the most dangerous criminal psychopath of all, in socially organized aggression. While others may encounter conflicts in their ego-gratifications, may initiate aggressive acts and balk at their execution, the schizoid is not likely to do so. In an authoritarian setting, he may go on and on, endlessly committing the most ghastly kind of crime, with the mechanical efficiency of a destructive robot. Colonel Hoess of Auschwitz was that type of psychopath.

It is apparent, even from our brief description of the principal psychopathic types, that it is social interaction that gives the concept of psychopathic personality its meaning and validity. We know of no evidence that there are "born criminal types," who are bound to become antisocial characters and criminals, regardless of the structure and norms of the society in which they develop. The environment provides both the impetus and outlet for such deviant behavior; but society also provides the *definition* of such deviation, which is not clinically specific.

Psychopathic personalities undoubtedly play an important part in major manifestations of social pathology, particularly when they achieve positions of leadership in social groups and movements. It is all too clear that they played a decisive role in the revolutionary nucleus of the Nazi movement, and thus determined the complexion of the government of Nazi Germany. But that does not mean that the crux of our problem is the detection and elimination of such personalities from political life. Even if that were possible, it would be an endless palliative process at best. We have seen that without the support of "normal and respectable" leaders in that society, without a considerable following among the masses of the people, and without the facilitative action of certain cultural trends, it would hardly have been possible for the Nazi leaders to precipitate as great a social catastrophe as they did.

For a fuller understanding of the psychology of aggressive dictatorship and of social aggression generally, we must carry our inquiry to the level of social relationships.

Chapter 8

SOME SOCIAL RELATIONSHIPS

Persistence of Prejudices and Stereotypes

It is well recognized that social group loyalties and hostilities provide the soil in which political conflict and aggression thrive. This is true of all political systems, even though it has particular applicability to aggressive ideological dictatorships.

The racial, religious, and national prejudices which keep international tensions alive from generation to generation often have their origins in historic social conflicts: invasions, religious schisms, persecution and expulsion, slave trade, economic and political subjugation, etc. Many of the unfavorable stereotyped conceptions that various ethnic groups have of each other may be related to such historically precipitated animosities, while others are more obscure in their origins. Whether the prejudices and stereotypes were ever justified by these historic conflicts, even at the time, is beside the point of our discussion. The fact that they *persist* for many generations, even for centuries, is the main problem. Whatever the original motivation or rationale, the significant thing is that they continue to operate long after their origins have become obscured in history. They may even go on to serve entirely different purposes from those they originally served. These attitudes become part of the social conditioning process, transmitted from generation to generation with very little thought to their validity or purpose. Modern man thus labors under an overwhelming burden of such accumulated prejudices.

As we have seen from this study, these social attitudes become grist for the mill of political demagogues and may provide the springboard for unlimited aggression. We have said that certain hostilities, like the German animosity toward the Allies after World War I, were "understandable," i.e., had some rationale in the social conflict experienced by that generation. But the hostility generated among the Germans went far beyond the demand to amend the Treaty of Versailles. The hostility growing immediately out of World War I would probably have been dissipated eventually by amelioration and recovery—but for the exacerbation of ethnic tensions which had festered for centuries. Indeed, but for such tensions there would hardly have been a World War I to begin with, and still less chance for dictatorship and World War II. At any rate, we shall be concerned here only with the psychosocial processes that perpetuate the prejudicial attitudes that play such an important part in the vicious circle of ethnic conflict.

We can distinguish two sets of perpetuating tendencies in stereotypes and prejudices: (a) the gratification of needs and (b) self-perpetuating mechanisms. The former deals with the motivational base that is required for any behavior pattern; the latter is required to explain why these attitudes persist even beyond their motivational rationale.

Need Gratification.—Hitler's case illustrated how ethnic group prejudices provided outlets for aggression born of personal frustration. The stereotypes, slogans, and symbols in which these prejudices were couched provided ready-made formulas for the expression of personal hostility through social animosities that had been generated before he was born. They were merely seized upon and augmented by the political demagogues of his generation, including himself, to provide outlets for current social frustrations. The circumstances under which Hitler first learned the magic appeal of such scapegoat propaganda, and under which he and his cohorts later used it, also made it clear that these frustrations operated on two levels: the psychodynamic (libidinal) and the socioeconomic. For Hitler, the deeper psychodynamic motivation was probably the stronger motivating force. (We have suggested this as a distinction between the ideological fanatic and the political opportunist.) The need to identify with the Aryan Superman stereotype and to vent his aggression on the non-Aryan scapegoat, to rebel against old symbols of authority and to exterminate his fancied enemies, were all deeply rooted in his own libidinal conflicts. For a man like Goering, however, as well as for many of the industrialists and militarists, the socioeconomic needs were probably the determining factors. These leaders did not adhere to these prejudices so fanatically, but used them or condoned them as convenient devices for gratifying their aspirations to fame, fortune, and social status. Goering considered ethnic conflict part of the stage setting of the historic drama, and racial ideology merely entered into his calculations for material gain and power. Even a rather obtuse militarist like General Keitel showed some belated insight into the material motives of ideological "manifest destiny." Banker Schacht made it clear that no sensible man took the ideology seriously; it was just a matter of adjusting economic competition, especially in the professions. The Gestapo chief for occupied France showed how barefaced the socioeconomic motive could be at times, however well camouflaged by "idealistic" propaganda. A good reason for cooperating in the elimination of minority groups, he argued, was to increase the socioeconomic status of the in-group (by taking over the victims' jobs and wealth). The sacks of gold teeth and wedding rings in the vaults of the Reichsbank will forever remain a symbol of the real "idealism" behind race prejudice.

These basic motives in the perpetuation (as well as the origin) of prejudices are fairly well understood. What has not been so well recognized, on the whole, are the devices by which these prejudices perpetuate themselves beyond any motivational rationale. In other words, we have to deal with the hypothesis that part of the reason why prejudice persists is that it already exists and sets psychosocial processes in motion to perpetuate itself. We shall review the *self-perpetuating mechanisms* of ethnic prejudices and stereotypes encountered in this study.

Self-Perpetuating Mechanisms.—*Selective association* is basic to the perceptual bias inherent in biased attitudes. Where any particular group is stigmatized in a particular way, the incidents which seem to confirm the prejudice or stereotype will be noticed, while those that contradict it will simply not be associated with group behavior. Thus, where Jews are regarded as "trouble-makers," any trouble-maker who happens to have a Jewish name will be noticed as such by those aware of the stereotype, while trouble-makers who do not belong to that group will not be associated with their ethnic background. Conversely, the great majority of non-trouble-making Jews will not be thought of in that connection. The same applies to the "dirty-lazy-superstitious Negro" stereotype in America. One notices abundant evidence to confirm the stereotype if one is looking for it, but will not make note of the far greater number of exceptions, nor of the white people to whom these attributes might apply with equal validity. The selective association process becomes even more insistent when the prejudice or stereotype touches on libidinal anxieties. Hence the particularly infectious convictions and concern of bigots over the rape of in-group women by appropriately stigmatized out-groups. (As is well known in psychodynamics, the wish is often father to the anxiety. We have suggested that this was true of some of the Nazi propagandists.) The exceptional case which confirms the prejudice will have sensational repercussions, while the cases in which the reverse is true, or no racial lines are crossed, will pass comparatively unnoticed. Propaganda, of course, facilitates this selective association, and political demagogues make capital out of it. But the same principle applies to the more innocuous stereotypes, though they do not play so important a role in social conflict. One notices the "stingy Scotsman" and the "fighting Irishman," but not the fighting Scot and the stingy Irishman. The stereotypes also obscure the fact that neither Irishmen nor Scotsmen are on the whole stingier or more bellicose than most other people. All in all, people do not form their social attitudes as scientific conclusions based on controlled observation. The mere existence of prejudices and stereotypes provides a basis for selective association, and this in turn gives these biases the appearance of observed reality.

This selective association is facilitated, ironically enough, by the *defensive reactions* of the subject groups themselves. In the case of favorable or innocuous stereotypes, the natural reaction of the group members is to play up the stereotypes as a means of friendly social intercourse and acceptance. Thus there are none who tell more jokes about "stingy Scotsmen" than the Scots themselves; none who play up the fighting qualities of the Irish as much as Irishmen. But the problem is not so simple for those who are subject to adverse prejudices or stereotypes. As in any kind of frustrating experience, both aggressive and avoidant reactions set in. In either case, the defensive reaction tends to perpetuate the prejudice. Those who show resentment of prejudice and compete all the harder in the face of it confirm the "sensitive and aggressive" part of their stereotype. Those who seek acceptance by conforming to majority-group behavior and ignoring the prejudice, give the appearance of being "obsequious and calculating." A few may even go to the extreme of disassociating themselves from the stereotype by confirming it and regarding themselves as "not typical." This *reaction formation* not only helps to perpetuate the stereotype and prejudice but plays into the hands of the political demagogues who capitalize on prejudice.

Reaction formation may also take the form of political appeasement, as it did among the objects of Nazi aggression. Group identification is so complex in modern civilization that even stereotypes allow of a variety of distinctions. Thus Hitler attacked "capitalists," but German capitalists appeased him to turn his aggression toward "foreign Jewish capital." He appealed to German nationalism by attacking "perfidious Albion" and her Allies, but Albion appeased him in the face of the "Communist menace," and "fellow-Socialist" Russia in turn sealed a friendship pact out of their common interest in opposing "Western imperialism." The avoidance-reaction-formation among the objects of Nazi German prejudice only facilitated the ethnic hostilities that formed the basis of the "divide and conquer" policy.

Another process that enables prejudice to perpetuate itself is *social discrimination.* The segregation and discriminatory practices brought about by group prejudices actually bring about subcultural group differences. This in turn provides specious evidence that the stigmatized groups are, in fact, "different." If the discrimination is such as to degrade the group in question, it will create all the appearance of genuine group inferiority. Thus when the ancient Greeks made slaves of the "barbarians," when the Romans in turn used the early Christians as their scapegoats, when Christian emperors later confined Jews to ghettoes and Christian Americans imported Negro slaves, each of these historic events set up a process of segregation and discrimination which became imbedded in the respective cultures for many generations. This could hardly fail to bring about subcultural differences that tended to support any existing prejudices or stereotypes associated with those groups. Since personality development is so largely dependent on environmental influences, it might be said that a kind of social "selective breeding" of personality strains takes place. These are then readily mistaken for inherent group differences.

Let us take the simple attribute of "ignorance" as applied to many groups throughout history. It has always been easy to keep subjugated groups in a state of apparent inferiority by the simple device of denying them educational opportunity. Enslaved groups throughout history, such as the serfs under feudalism, or the Indian and Negro groups in early American history, have been regarded as unfit for self-government because they were "ignorant." Their masters kept them in a state of ignorant subjugation because of that prejudice, and the prejudice was reinforced by that very fact.

Hitler discovered the true secret of perpetuating the master-race myth: Segregate the subject groups, decimate their number, deprive them of education, exclude them from any but menial occupations. This program was already being put into effect against the "inferior Slavic races" in the East. (The Jews were given "special treatment.") The blueprint for this program was drawn up in meticulous detail, by Himmler: Thirty million Slavs were first to be executed as "dangerous partisans" by SS *Einsatzkommandos* (hundreds of thousands actually were), with particular attention to "dangerous intellectuals." A large number of children of "good stock" were to be taken from their mothers for assimilation into the superior Germanic bloodstream. Then none of the remaining inferior elements were to be allowed to rise above the level of labor-foreman, or to receive any education beyond learning to do arithmetic with numbers up to 500. The program might conceivably have succeeded if the Nazis had won the war—until some other group was in a position to apply the same procedure to the Germans.[1]   In the meantime, the stereotypes of "Aryan master race" and "menial Slavic races" would have persisted and been enforced by the actual cultural differences brought about as a result of ethnic prejudice. It has happened before, and an unrestrained aggressive dictator might conceivably do it again.

The exploitation and perpetuation of these ethnic tensions and differences has been a favorite device of political demagogues. This provides us with a challenging reality in any academic discussion of leadership functions in society and in history.

LEADERSHIP AND SOCIAL INTERACTION

American psychologists have in the past drawn up lists of "traits of leadership" sometimes backed up by statistically reliable differences between groups of college students rated on personality trait inventories. The results of such investigations have yielded what amounts to interesting trait-clusters of the American academic ego-ideal. Among the traits frequently listed in such studies are honesty, poise, integrity, tact, tolerance, justice, restraint, etc. These appear somewhat whimsical as yardsticks of leadership, in the light of the present study.

Hitler's worst enemies will not deny that he was a leader; but even his best friends did not accuse him of possessing the qualities so admired in our culture. Goering and the other Nazi leaders made their contempt of "decadent democratic moralistic" values and sentimentality quite plain. "Say what you will about Hitler," Goering told us, "but don't accuse him (or me) of being *moral!*" On another occasion Goering insisted, not without a trace of awe, that "once he made up his mind about something, nothing in the world could budge him." In the Nazi

---

[1] This appears to have been the major concern of the SS General in charge of "partisan-fighting" in the East; cf., testimony of Bach-Zelewski. (36)

microcosm, entirely different qualities were regarded as determinants of leadership: uncompromising hardness and brutality, nationalism with a paranoid tinge, in-group loyalty and out-group hostility. Deceit, treachery, persecution, and murder could be condoned in this militant, ethnocentric frame of reference, and the leader was the one who excelled in these virtues. Clearly, the yardstick of leadership in American collegiate extracurricular activities has not been the yardstick of history. The discrepancy must give us pause.

This discrepancy has its basis, in the first place, in the fact that leadership is not determined by any absolute cluster of traits but by a dynamic interrelationship between the leader and those who accept his leadership. If we would determine what personal qualities brought Hitler to the position of the supreme dictator, out of all the thousands of beer-hall amateur politicians in post-World War I Germany, we must not look for any cluster of admirable traits, but for the psychosocial dynamics that made him a recognized leader *in that social setting*. As Frank pointed out, "one must not say that Hitler violated the German people —he *seduced* them!"

Hitler's Qualifications.—Let us consider the relationships that made *Hitler* the dictator, rather than any of his political rivals. We can do this best by examining the numerous choice-points in his career, at any one of which his leadership might have died aborning or been overthrown. Hitler's functional qualifications (italicized) will be described in their psychosocial setting.

First of all, he achieved his *resonance with the people* (*Einklang im Volk*) because he symbolized more clearly and passionately than even the original founders of the party the *frustration of strivings* common to an increasing number in his culture, particularly in the ego-involvements of socioeconomic status and militant nationalism.[2] Secondly, his own *paranoid tendencies* made him more *outspokenly aggressive in providing objects of aggression* which were consonant with the

---

[2] In this respect our "post-mortem examination" of the Nazi movement confirms the diagnosis made by Cantril (11), Abel (2), and others.

latent pseudoparanoid trends of his culture. This combination of psychosocial relationships was the basis of the early recognition he achieved as "someone the people listen to," so that he quickly became the leader of the nucleus of Old Fighters, the Munich beer-hall dispossessed. In a short time the actual founders of the party were pushed into the background, because they did not capture the fancy of the masses so readily. Thus Hitler was eventually able to tell Frank, "Yes, one must say that very loudly, that Feder founded the party. Who in the world ever hears of him today? . . . We have spoken to the hearts of our people. He who counts on so-called understanding never reaches the masses." Third, Hitler's politically channeled *vengeful heroic fantasies* were consonant with the regressive demand for strong leadership in this confused *authoritarian* culture.

These qualities by themselves would have gotten him no further than his first failure as a rabble-rousing revolutionist in the Munich *Putsch*. To keep on in the years after his imprisonment required a fourth ingredient: *obsessive appeal to national ascendancy*. This went hand in hand with the paranoid tendencies that were pretty well structured by that time, but it was highly suggestive to his more passive followers, like Hess, Rosenberg, etc. It also provided direction and goal for the aggressive needs of leaders like Goering, as well as hope for the normal aspirations of the confused average German.

Nevertheless, it is an anomaly that Hitler actually came to power just when his party was on the downgrade. But for the crucial support of certain other leaders around 1932, Hitler would probably have passed off the stage of German history as just another revolutionary demagogue of the post-war era, and *Mein Kampf* would have remained a minor curio for learned Ph.D. theses on "The Political Cross-Currents of Germany's Great Depression." Certainly his obsession stood him in particularly good stead in that crucial year. Even among the revolutionists, he who faltered or hesitated was lost, as did Hitler's rival, Gregor Strasser, at that crucial moment. But in addition to his obsession of purpose there was still another suggestive quality that was decisive at this time—his *ability to convince other group leaders of their common interests,* even though the various motives could not all be compatible and "honor among gentlemen" was not one of Hitler's obsessions. In other words, the policy of being all things to all men (except for the scapegoats) required *duplicity and insincerity* of the highest order. Intelligent men like Schacht, Von Papen, and Keitel had little cause for moral indignation, perhaps, in denouncing Hitler as a "pathological liar" and for having *"betrayed* us!" since they had allowed the deception for their own ulterior motives, but they were certainly right about these qualities of Hitler's leadership. The shrewdness to divide and conquer by the deceptive suggestion of common purposes in loyalty and aggression was perhaps the decisive secret of Hitler's rise to power. It first helped him achieve decisive support for leadership at home and later proved disastrously successful in dividing the potential opposition against itself while he achieved hegemony in Europe.

But before he was in a position to extend his aggression to the international sphere, there was the choice-point hurdle of consolidating his leadership in 1934. The Roehm purge decided the issue. Here the determinant of leadership was *aggression socially facilitated to the threshold of mass murder.* This was the final psychosocial "qualification" of aggressive dictatorship. Once having crossed that threshold, he was able to consolidate his leadership with a reign of terror camouflaged by a deceptive "benevolent despotism" which crippled while it deluded any potential opposition. The majority of the public showed little concern for the persecution of scapegoats as long as frustration and unemployment had decreased, and they were already conditioned to assume that the leader is always right. The supposedly more sophisticated Junkers, financiers, and militarists failed to deter him because they mistakenly assumed that their interests were being protected by Hitler. When some of these leaders finally awoke to the deception, it was too late. It would have required a major revolution with great risk to depose Hitler's police state by 1938-39. When we asked some of the "not really Nazis" why their plot did not succeed at that time, they pointed out, among other things, that the foreign appeasement of the

Munich Pact cut the ground from under them. Goering regarded it as a matter of course that their success with the Munich Pact rested on the common interest of the West in encouraging Germany's expansion to the East, just as he was able to suggest a "realistic" nonaggression pact with Russia, to enable Germany to settle scores with the West. The final qualification of political leadership in that historical setting must therefore be regarded as the *extension of deceptive common purposes to the level of international appeasement of aggression.* This external appeasement merely facilitated internal appeasement. By the time the appeasers from within and without took action to remove the menace, the damage had already been done.

To add it all up, the chief psychosocial qualifications of leadership for a revolutionary dictator in this social setting proved to be (*a*) the social resolution of frustrations in a manner which had a certain resonance in the needs of the people at the time, and (*b*) aggressive pursuit of goals which had a deceptive identity of purpose with the ulterior motives of other leaders and groups in that culture and abroad.

These are not simple personality traits, nor are they the characteristics of leadership in the American academic ego-ideal. But they are unmistakably the psychosocial relationships that produced a despotic revolutionary leader in a time of social disorganization in an authoritarian culture. The assumed identity of purposes and values is the crucial relationship between any leader and his supporters. The realization of that fact was a very important factor in Hitler's success as a political demagogue.

The irony of it all was, of course, that once having achieved his power by providing direction and leadership for the needs and latent aggressions of his culture, he was able to impose his own aggressions on it to an extent desired by neither the people as a whole nor the leaders who appeased him. It was inherent in the nature of dictatorship that even war and genocide could be brought about by a leader obsessed with such grandiose hostile fantasies. This brings us to the question of the dictator's role in influencing the course of history.

Leadership in History

The principle of psychosocial interaction is already well established in the development of personality and in ordinary group relationships (family, community, etc.). However, there is still a great deal of controversy over the importance of the individual in great historical phenomena like wars and major social movements. One is still asked, "Do leaders make history, or does history make leaders?" Some, like the Freudians and certain philosophers, overemphasize the dynamics of personality in historical leadership. Others, like the Marxists and many social scientists, overemphasize economic determinism. Social psychologists and sociologists tend to stress public opinion and cultural phenomena, as if these existed independent of individuals. The latter viewpoints interpret leadership in history as fundamentally a by-product of social forces. A widely used textbook in social psychology sums up its theme in a recapitulation which states:

> The theme of this book is that the individual plays but a small role on a great and crowded stage and that he plays that role largely in accordance with a socially predetermined script. . . . Should he, furthermore, by force of social circumstances be one of those few who are equipped and expected to provide some measure of individual leadership for others, success will depend mainly on his happening to lead them in the direction in which they happen to be going. With some striking exceptions, the individual counts for little in the social scheme of things. (44)

The escape clause in this sociomechanistic view of leadership is the one pertaining to "striking exceptions." Certainly Hitler was such an exception, and some of the great tyrants of history share the spotlight with him. The highly significant thing that we are apt to overlook in a too socially predetermined view of leadership roles is that such exceptions have become increasingly catastrophic in human history. Indeed, it would take only one more exceptional personality like Hitler to put an end to most of human civilization (given, of course, a similar combination of circumstances). If the direction "in which [we] happen to be going" is ultimate extermination, then we might perhaps just relax until the right man comes along. But assuming that human intelligence can still examine itself and guide its own destiny, we may find an examination of Hitler's role in history rather instructive. We are not prepared to admit that World War II and genocide was the "direction in which they happened to be going" but rather an outburst of latent aggression that could have taken place only in a dictatorship and could easily have been prevented if modern political leadership had been more sophisticated about such things.

Abel has correctly pointed out that the *decision* to wage war is invariably made by the autocrat or group in power far in advance of the actual outbreak of hostilities. It is not a culmination of mass sentiment and war fever "which might be compared to the milling of a crowd getting ready to stampede." From analyzing twenty-five major wars, Abel concludes:

> In every case the decision is based upon a careful weighing of the chances and of anticipating consequences. Many elements enter into the consideration of adequacy preceding the decision, such as relative military strength, available resources, ability to stir up community sentiment, reliability and extent of outside support, and so forth. . . . In no case is the decision precipitated by emotional tensions, sentimentality, crowd behavior, or other irrational motives. The rational, calculating decision is reached far in advance of the actual outbreak of hostilities. (1)

Our study confirms this general thesis, except in one important respect: The irrational behavior of the crowd may not determine the decision, but *the emotional tensions of the leader in an authoritarian system do determine it.*

This may or may not have been true of wars prior to World War II. We doubt that Agamemnon was the last to "launch a thousand ships" in a personal vendetta, though modern wars appear to have a more material basis. We shall never know for certain, because no psychologist has ever been in a position to judge. But our close study of the leaders closest to Hitler, in conjunction with all the evidence presented to them at the time and a study of Hitler's own record, leads inevitably to the conclusion that the final decision to go to war and commit genocide was determined by the irrational obsession of a dictator to "exterminate my enemies."

We have conceded at the outset that Hitler's paranoid tendencies could not, of themselves, have precipitated a world war. Certainly there were historical, socioeconomic, and geopolitical forces at work, and national sentiments that constantly provided a basis for international tensions. But insofar as the subjective element inevitably enters into any decision in the balancing of these forces, the psychodynamics of Hitler's personality played a decisive part. The decisions to risk war over Austria, Czechoslovakia, and Poland, until he finally succeeded, and the further decision to expand it to the East were not entirely the result of cold calculation of relative military strength. They were determined in large part by Hitler's aggressive obsessions, by vengeful heroic fantasies to prove his innate superiority by the victory of arms.

Hitler was, in fact, constantly at odds with the cold calculations of the General Staff, as our study of the militarists has shown; he constantly sought to immunize himself from their "contemptible timidity" and fumed against these "relics of the Ice Age who still do not comprehend my revolutionary ideas." For Hitler's war was a personal vendetta with society, expanded to the proportions of a racial war of extermination. It was for this reason that his Chief of Operations, General Jodl, could tell us with every evidence of sincere conviction, "In this war, the absolute guilt rests with one man, one man only—Adolf Hitler."

Hitler's War Obsession.—Let us briefly review the evidence :

Hitler's actual plan of conquest was crystallized and announced secretly to his war leaders on November 5, 1937, almost two years before the actual outbreak of war. The Commander-in-Chief of the army and the Foreign Minister who showed signs of demurring at his recklessness were forced out of office and more obsequious tools put in their place. All attempts to negotiate a peaceful settlement of outstanding geopolitical problems by the most far-reaching concessions only whetted his appetite. Diplomatic attempts to settle the Polish crisis were deliberately sabotaged by him, and clear warnings from the

Allied nations that further aggression would mean war did not deter him. That this was not based on cold calculation alone is vouchsafed by the fact that his shrewdest advisers, like banker Schacht and several of the High Command, warned him that it was a reckless undertaking, and even the aggressive psychopath Goering was ambivalent about it. It was later revealed that Germany was actually not prepared for a major war. An eleventh-hour attempt to negotiate a settlement through para-diplomatic channels, in which the power and determination of the opposition was pointed out to him, only called forth the heated outburst, ". . . Then I will build U-boats! U-boats! U-boats! . . . I will build airplanes! airplanes! airplanes!— *and I will exterminate my enemies!"* The reactions to the actual outbreak of war (as given to us later, but weighed for their apparent validity) were: a reactive depression on the part of many of the political leaders,[3] "a bunch of depressed generals in the War Ministry," who had "only thought he was clever enough to get what he wanted by bluff," (according to General Jodl); an exuberant readiness to make the most of it, on the part of a few aggressive souls like Goering; and as for Hitler, "he was very calm about it," because "in war, Hitler was in his true element." Hitler, at least, had gotten exactly what he had bargained for. Still, none of this bespeaks cold calculation on the part of the leaders of a nation determined to wage war for material gain.

Even after the war had started, in suicidal disregard of the desperate needs of manpower and full mobilization of resources, his obsessive vendetta went to the extreme of using part of his manpower and resources to exterminate millions of his fancied enemies who might actually have been used to further the war effort if only materialistic considerations had prevailed. It was this maniacal violation of the objective weighing of means and ends in the decisions of war that led the General Staff underground and later the War Production Minister to attempt to assassinate Hitler, in spite of the strong cultural sanctions

---

[3] Ribbentrop and Frank, for example, said they suffered something of a "nervous breakdown" upon the announcement of the invasion. Austrian Chancellor Seyss-Inquart said those were the blackest days of his life.

against treason in war. It also called forth the most violent recriminations from generals interviewed after the defeat and even caused a unique panic reaction in the cynical Goering himself when the stupidity of the miscalculation suddenly dawned on him. Even disregarding morality or sentimentality, Hitler's decisions were irrationally capricious. Over and over again the Nazi leaders clutched their heads and exclaimed, *Wahnsinn! Wahnsinn!* (madness!) as the full record was laid bare in Nuremberg. These were belated insights, to be sure, facilitated by the impending threat of retribution for their complicity, but the spontaneity of these behind-the-scenes reactions was none the less valid. This was true even though some of them had heard Hitler state flatly, well in advance of the attack, that the war to achieve Germany's manifest destiny had to be waged in his lifetime, because no other German leader might have the balance of power *and the determination* to do it. In the social context of autocratic aggressive nationalism, that determination had somehow been perceived differently by them at the time.

The psychodynamics of that obsessive determination have already been discussed, along with the political channeling of his aggressions. We recall how he gave vent to these aggressions in *Mein Kampf* and actually designed a Victory Arch to be erected over his destroyed enemies in an eventual war of vengeance, even while imprisoned in 1923; that he actually stated to his War Production Minister during the war, "How hard Fate has made it for me, that I must wage war to realize my building plans [conceived in Landsberg prison]."

Small wonder that Frank concluded, in reviewing Hitler's career with his clarity of hindsight, "No matter how one twists and turns the facts, there is no escaping the awful conclusion— *Hitler wanted war!*"—Or that Goering admitted, in another unguarded moment, that Germany really had all she could possibly have wanted after the Munich Pact, but "Well, I suppose deep down he really wanted to get revenge for the defeat of 1918."

Our study of Hitler's lieutenants strongly suggested that if any one of them had replaced Hitler before 1939, (even aggressive Hermann Goering, the heir apparent), or if a slight change in circumstances (such as a little less appeasement) had replaced the Nazis with leaders more responsive to the will of the people, then there probably would have been no World War II and there certainly would have been no systematic "extermination of my enemies." As far as we could judge, neither war nor genocide represented the will of the people; nor were they the inevitable outcome of economic needs that could be satisfied in no other way. A dictator was in a position to provide his own social facilitation to reinforce his own convictions on the need and practicality of persecution and armed aggression.

It follows from this analysis that leadership may be crucial in determining the course of historical events. But that does not imply by any means that leaders create history single-handedly. It must be readily conceded that Hitler's warlike obsession would have remained just the vengeful neurotic fantasy of another frustrated political demagogue if it had not been converted into historic decision through the very nature of dictatorship and social interaction. But for the social conditions, cultural lag, and group interests that brought him to power and helped sustain him to the bitter end, Hitler's aggression might have destroyed itself much sooner without involving a historic catastrophe.

Thus the principle of psychosocial interaction holds true of social relationships even on the broad historical level. The psychodynamic factor in leadership may vary in significance in determining historical events, depending on the nature of the social organization and the combination of circumstances under which it operates. But it assumes gigantic proportions when the circumstances and the cultural traditions combine to produce an aggressive ideological dictatorship. Under those circumstances one man's obsession may well influence the course of history. That is particularly true when the dictator in question is obsessed by the prejudices of his culture.

We are thus brought finally to a more comprehensive evaluation of dictatorship as a manifestation of psychosocial interaction in adaptive social behavior.

Chapter 9

DICTATORSHIP AND ADAPTIVE
SOCIAL BEHAVIOR

We stated at the outset that history might be regarded as the developmental record of man's adaptive social behavior in the struggle for survival and security. We must now be more explicit in our conception of "adaptive social behavior." We take it as a basic premise of psychology that the human being, like all forms of animal life, seeks to survive and to live in fulfilment of his basic needs. But the needs of the human being are more highly evolved than those of lower animals. He is a *biosocial* organism. In addition to the physical needs which insure his survival, he has social needs: identification and acceptance among his fellow-men, socially conditioned aesthetic and spiritual needs, a sense of meaning and purpose in his life, and a basic need for emotional security which is related to all of these. The same highly evolved mentality which expresses these needs also provides him with the adaptive capacities for their fulfilment: abstract thought, value judgment, empathy, scientific inventiveness, self-appraisal and social awareness, communication of needs and ideas. All of these capacities manifest themselves on a higher social level as the development of culture, with different modes of social organization and different sets of social values, which often come into conflict in the struggle for survival and security. We have regarded the struggle between democracy and dictatorship as fundamentally a struggle between two modes of social organization and value systems developed in that process of adaptive social behavior. We may now integrate our observations on the clinical and social levels in an appraisal of dictatorship within that broader framework.

Let us examine first the ethnocentric-authoritarian value system of dictatorship and the behavior patterns it fosters.

The Authoritarian Value-System

The cardinal principle in the value-system of aggressive ideological dictatorship is the "categorical imperative" of deference to authority. That which is right is that which is determined by higher authority in a given social hierarchy of power. Correct behavior is primarily obedience and loyalty to such authority; only disobedience and disloyalty are wrong. These attitudes are introcepted from the parents in earliest childhood and continue to provide the basis of social status, approval and disapproval, as the individual assumes the adult role. In any conflict of motives, this "categorical imperative" tends to decide the issue. Any act that might be considered wrong according to legal, religious, or other humanitarian values is devoid of moral stigma if it was ordered or sanctioned by the authority in power. The institutions of law, state, church, and family are either identified with or subordinated to the absolute sovereign. This has been expressed in "the divine right of kings," in the dictum *L'état, c'est moi!* and in the attitude of dictators large and small —"*I* am the law!"

Hitler expressed this philosophy in a thousand ways, and a culture long inured to authoritarian absolutism acquiesced. This cardinal value served as the principal justification for all admitted errors of omission and commission among all the Nazi Germans we studied, from the lowliest *Blockleiter* to the top ranks of leadership. It overruled all other values and nullified the process of critical value judgment and reality-testing of even intelligent leaders.

Attendant upon such an authoritarian ethic is the ego-ideal of heroic mythology: the brave champion of the ethnic in-group, sallying forth to do battle against the group's enemies. The principal hero is surrounded by an entourage of lesser heroes and loyal vassals. The masses are regarded as weak and helpless, unfit to have a voice in their own destiny. They can only be protected and led to victory by heroic champions. The aspiration-level of the masses can only be to be worthy of such leadership, to identify with the leaders' strength by heroic deeds and personal loyalty. The role of the minority groups in the culture is, of course, to serve their masters. The female half of the population likewise enters into the picture only in a subordinate role. Their function is principally to shower admiration on the conquering heroes, to seduce them into marriage, or to be seduced by these virile supermen for the procreation of more little heroes. Females, enemies, and subjugated minorities are all treated with certain condescending protective considerations, according to the rules of chivalry. The rule that supersedes these rules, of course, is that any person or group may be slaughtered if so ordained by the absolute sovereign. He accomplishes this by the simple device of designating them as enemies of the state.

According to the heroic-authoritarian code, only the greatest of heroes has the right to rule. He is either heaven-sent or proves his right by vying successfully with his rivals to seize power by superior guile or force. In modern times, as we have already indicated, the divine right of kings has merely given way to the pseudobiological right of the strong to dominate the weak in the struggle for survival. Because of this natural or divine right to rule, the ruler is sovereign, his authority cannot be questioned. Totalitarian ethnocentricity, with all its suppressive and aggressive devices, is inevitable and natural.

This picture of heroic authoritarianism, which may seem rather overdrawn to the democratically oriented, still captures the fancy of leaders and masses in authoritarian cultures. It provides a rather persistent frame of reference for the structuring of social attitudes in authoritarian regressiveness. This we found to be true in Germany. In a quite literal sense, Teutonic heroic mythology provided the prototypes of the heroic ego-ideal which symbolized the aspiration-level of both leaders and followers in the Nazi movement. When we asked Goering why he thought that Germans would still consider him a hero after he was dead, he answered without hesitation: Every German knew the story of the *Nibelungenlied*—how Hagen had killed Siegfried out of loyalty to King Gunther, so that even Siegfried's kinsmen refused to avenge his death. He refused to renounce his loyalty to Hitler at the trial for fear of losing his heroic status in German history. Even when we found him brooding in his cell, facing death at the completion of his defense, he muttered, "No, my people have been humiliated before. Loyalty and hatred will unite them again.—Who knows but that in this very hour the man is born who will unite my people—born of our flesh and bones, to avenge the humiliation we suffer now!" Goering fancied himself, to the very end, a valiant knight who had sallied forth with his loyal vassals in two world wars, mounting Messerschmitts instead of plumed white chargers, to do battle against the enemies of his sovereign. The fact that millions of his kinsmen as well as their enemies had died while he filled his coffers with loot was beside the point. Heroic loyalty was the thing, and every German, he felt sure, would understand that.

It is only fair to point out that Goering represented an extreme case in the use of the cultural myth to camouflage his own avarice. Among some of the less ego-involved Nazi leaders, the conflict between authoritarian and humanistic values was quite apparent. Von Papen privately denounced Goering for his bombastic oratory when the Reich lay in ruins as a result of his doing. The leader of the Hitler Youth movement, Von Schirach, wavered in his loyalties, but finally denounced Hitler for having betrayed the youth of Germany by the misuse of his authority.[1] The War Production Minister, Albert Speer, acknowledged the "common responsibility" of leaders to the people and accepted his share of the guilt for war crimes. This idea was so repugnant to the authoritarian value-system that Goering denounced Speer behind the scenes and threatened to have him assassinated—for treason to the Fatherland. Every dictator knew that the masses were not fit to decide their fate; that was the exclusive prerogative of their heroic leaders. The idea that the people never want war was cynically dismissed by Goering: "*Of course* the people don't want war. . . . That is understood. But after all, it is the *leaders* of the country who determine the

---

[1] We gained the impression that there was great and genuine disillusionment among German youth at the end of the war. It is a serious question whether we have made wise use of this opportunity to restructure the goals and social values of the coming generation of German leaders or have abandoned them to Goering's heroic fantasies.

policy, and it is always a simple matter to drag the people along, whether it is a democracy or a fascist dictatorship or a Parliament or a Communist dictatorship. . . . That is easy. All you have to do is tell them they are being attacked and denounce the pacifists for lack of patriotism and exposing the country to danger. It works the same in any country."

Propaganda was obviously a convenient tool with which to control the masses in the struggle for survival. The idea of responsibility was ridiculous, because leaders were but the inspired instruments of Nature or Fate.[2] In this struggle for survival, the strongest race with the strongest leaders would naturally dominate inferior races with inferior leaders. If they failed to do so, they simply proved that they did not deserve to survive. It was more than poetic irony, it was almost psychologically inevitable that Hitler should finally commit suicide, decreeing the destruction of the German race because it had failed to prove its superiority over the "Eastern races."[3]

But our evaluation of aggressive dictatorship rests not merely on the fact that the dictator in this case was obsessed by a desire for war, or that he and his henchmen pursued their objectives so recklessly that they were bound to defeat their purposes. It rests on the fact that such leadership exemplifies the maladaptive behavior inherent in such a value-system and mode of social organization—maladaptive, that is, at the present stage of social evolution. This value judgment rests on two considerations: first, the perversion of the adaptive functions of human behavior, and second, the significance of aggression in modern man.

First, by the restriction of any individual sense of responsibility and the relegation thereof to higher authority, the functions of reality-testing and adaptive value judgment are severely impaired. Neither the individual.nor the group as a whole can

---

[2] Although Goering was probably unaware of it, this conception of authoritarian leadership and greatness was clearly expressed by Hegel and other philosophers long before he and Hitler mimicked it for their own purposes. Cf., discussion by Hook. (35)

[3] The "scorched earth" commands were issued by Hitler with the clear intention of wiping out the "inferior remains" of Germany at the same time that he was contemplating suicide. Cf. Speer's testimony. (36)

make full use of intelligence to take account of the environment in a realistic manner, to guide their own behavior for their own best interest. The assumption is, instead, that "higher authority" is the best judge of that. This goes still further. The insistence on obedience in a limited sphere of duty facilitates the suppression of insight in a conflict of values, giving freer rein to unenlightened self interest and ulterior motives. The totalitarian conception of the state exacerbates these defects. The control and suppression of information, the systematic use of propaganda, the regimentation of all social activity, all help to create an artificial social frame of reference which actually limits reality-testing. The dictatorial microcosm is not merely a circumscribed segment of society; it becomes a world unto itself, somewhat removed from reality, so that even a meeting of the minds in diplomatic discussion becomes extremely difficult. Within that microcosm, the function of reality-testing itself may require the normal individual to fall victim to an intensified cultural pseudoparanoia if that suits the purposes of those in control of the media of information. Furthermore, by inculcating fear and hostility toward enemy groups and by encouraging the persecution of scapegoats it helps to constrict human empathy and ultimately "desensitizes" an increasing number of individuals to extreme aggression. This constriction of affect, combined with the militaristic "categorical imperative" and the ideological restriction of reality-testing, produces organized irrational hostility which is not only unlimited in its destructive potential but precipitates a self-destructive reaction.

The outcome need not necessarily be as catastrophic as it proved to be in the Nazi dictatorship, but the tendency of such a system is clear: the crippling of human superego functions and reality-testing, which allow the irrational and psychopathic to become the norm, and the normal individual to become an unthinking member of a society regimented for irrational aggression. The leadership that such a system produces inevitably bears the imprint of the psychosocial relationships it fosters.

Thus it was possible for a man like Hitler to become dictator and to carry out a policy of war and genocide without effective opposition from other leaders; to be supported by a "loyal paladin" who cynically stated that if the leaders want war, the public has nothing to say about it; by a party deputy who was convinced that an international conspiracy was balking his country's manifest destiny and feeding him brain poison; by a Chief of Staff who "didn't know what Hitler was planning, exactly . . . but how can an officer object?"; by a Foreign Minister who verbally implemented aggression incredible to himself, because he was "only in Hitler's shadow"; and by apathetic little deputies of the police state who exterminated human beings wholesale, because "it never entered our heads to disobey orders . . . and besides, it was taken for granted that the Jews were to blame for everything."

It is scarcely conceivable that a free and well-informed democracy, functioning with its free exercise of critical public opinion, its traditional safeguard of minority rights and civil liberties, its checks and balances in government, could have produced leadership of that caliber, or maladaptive social behavior of that order. But the evaluation of dictatorship still cannot rest there. If the philosophy of aggressive competition for survival is entertained, that kind of leadership and social behavior might still be considered adaptive, rather than maladaptive. It is the philosophy of aggression itself that must be evaluated in the light of adaptive social behavior.

Vannevar Bush has recently stated:

> [Dictatorship] has now attained new and frightful power with the advance of science and its applications. This is not only because the application of physical science has brought new weapons and the ability to move far and fast, to speak to multitudes, and to manage complex affairs by reason of gadgeting aids. It is also and more forcibly because distorted reasoning from misinterpretation of physical and biological facts has led to perilous and perverted social theorizing, and because the sciences that deal with man, imperfectly grasped perhaps in their real attainments, have led to very practical applications in propaganda, indoctrination, deceit, and dominance. . . . The law of fang and beak is the only law, in this reasoning. . . . (9)

The significance of dictatorship in the light of aggression as a manifestation of adaptive social behavior deserves our final special consideration.

Dictatorship and the Mechanization of Aggression

We have dwelt on the fact that Hitler (as well as other dictators) regarded racial conflict and warfare as a natural state of existence, derived from an aggressive drive inherent in all animals in the struggle for survival. We need not pause here to argue the thesis of inherent racial antagonism, already disproved by cultural, comparative, and other genetic studies (5, 39, 47). Nor is it necessary to belabor the point that racial ideology has been a convenient pseudoscientific rationalization for the aggression of dictators with abnormal power drives. However, in examining aggressive ideological dictatorship from the perspective of adaptive social behavior, we may well examine the biological usefulness of aggression.

We know how social evolution has modified the basic drives of hunger, sex, and self-preservation (39, 48). Through the evolution of social mores they have acquired different values and modes of expression in different cultures, with derived drives, inhibitions, taboos, and sublimations which modify or even defeat the basic drive. Through the development of institutions like the family and state, religion and law, capital and labor, they have emerged as patterns of behavior which have properties beyond their primitive functions. Aggressive behavior has also undergone social evolution.

If we go back far enough, we can find some conceivable justification for the philosophy of aggression so dear to fascist dictators. But this requires turning the clock back, not merely to medieval history, but to the precultural anthropoid cave-dweller. In this primeval anthropoid, the aggression born of fear, anger, and the frustration of basic drives may well have been necessary for self-preservation. It provided the driving force necessary for escape or combat in the face of danger, for the acquisition of food, shelter, mates, or any other objects necessary to satisfy his basic needs or to overcome any obstacle in the way of their satisfaction. Overt aggression may thus have been an adjustive mechanism of survival and an actual criterion of selection. The apparatus of overt aggression was built into the human being's autonomic, neuromuscular, and glandular systems, along with the primitive feelings of love, fear, rage, hunger, and pain, to insure the preservation of the species. Overt aggression probably continued to serve a biological purpose even at the stage of primitive social behavior, as in community hunting and warfare. Language and group organization served to facilitate community action for defense or attack against commonly perceived threats to group survival.

But like other socialized behavior patterns, aggression became further and further removed from its original biological function as society became more complex. It became institutionalized, traditionalized, and mechanized to an extent that had little direct bearing on its original hypothetical purpose; in fact, it began to defeat that purpose.

In historic times, some cultures have evolved with cooperative social organization, in which aggressive competition is practically unknown. Still others have evolved with hostile national traditions, historic feuds, and mythical "manifest destinies." Aggressive ruling dynasties and military, religious, and industrial movements have at times manifested socialized aggression for motives which seem far removed from self-preservation. At least the extent of the aggression has often been far out of proportion to any actual need or threat involved. In recent generations we have witnessed an ever greater disparity between actual need and the overt aggression inflicted by man upon man.

We must now stop to analyze what has become of human aggression through this evolutionary process, and how aggressive dictatorship fits into the picture. We can do this fairly simply by analyzing the function of aggression at both the individual and social levels according to the classical scheme of analysis of psychological response systems: S-O-R, or stimulus, organic reaction, response. Overt aggressive behavior is the response we are concerned with here.

In our anthropoid cave-dweller, the response system was fairly direct and biologically useful. A perceived external threat or need-object (S [4] produced an emotional reaction in the or-

---

[4] The perceptual process is, of course, a subordinate response system in itself, which becomes a further stimulus to organismic reaction and response. We have condensed it here into the "perceived stimulus" for simplicity.

ganism (O), which gave rise to the necessary overt aggressive response (R) to satisfy the drive. This would hold just as well for hunting for food as for fighting an animal or man who threatened his life. In modern social behavior, however, we have come a long way from that primitive adaptive mechanism.

In the first place, the perception of the threat or need-object (S) is no longer given directly to our individual senses, except in special face-to-face situations. It is mediated through several stages of communication and requires a high order of abstraction and value judgment to reach awareness. The nature of threats and need-objects has become institutionalized in the form of nations, political movements, and economic systems. The very identification of the self, through ego-involvement in complex and conflicting group relationships, further complicates the problem of perceiving who is threatening whom. On the national level, the existence of a hypothetical threat or need is such a complex socioeconomic and geopolitical abstraction that the mass of the people are necessarily dependent on their leaders and the media of communication to interpret it. Propaganda can work wonders in determining the individual's perception of the environment. As we have seen, and as Goering explained with such eloquent cynicism, if the leaders have the power and choose to distort information to evoke the symbols of threatened national security, it is easy to do so quite effectively, even to the extent of plunging a nation into war. But this is particularly true of suppressive totalitarian government. For here the control of information—the sense organs of the nation, as it were— is in the hands of one man and his coterie of loyal supporters. The perception and judgment of whether "a clear and present danger" to national survival exists rests fundamentally with the dictator. A whole nation may be made to perceive its environment in a similarly distorted fashion.

The masses thus alerted do not necessarily react with spontaneous fear or anger (O), but more or less mechanically, or with synthetically produced emotions, to the symbols and the authority that provide the stimulus. For even the emotional driving force of aggression has become socially mechanized. Long-perpetuated latent ethnic hostilities and prejudices may be evoked at any time to provide the anxiety of threatened security. But the hostility thus aroused is for most people but a synthetic, socially facilitated attitude, involving conditioned responses to symbolic stimuli and group identifications, rather than a primitive emotional response to perceived reality. Much of the emotional force behind aggression thus aroused is lost in the process. We are already familiar with the phenomenon of "persuasion without conviction" in public opinion. The prejudices and hostilities of both leaders and followers in Nazi Germany were largely of that order, except for a few fanatics. The hatred of which we heard so much was largely a social epiphenomenon—a response to symbols, whipped up momentarily by social facilitation at mass rallies, and inculcated as a mechanical behavior pattern in ideologically indoctrinated groups like the hard-bitten SS. Most Germans had no active hatred of the Allies, no desire for war, and very little real hatred for the minority groups whose persecution they condoned. Even some of the top Nazi leaders assured the writer that they had always admired the French, or British, or Americans as people, and that some of their best friends were Jews. The irony of it was that it was true. Never in history have more people been killed with less real hatred than during World War II. We are forced to the rather significant conclusion that the emotional component of socialized aggression is something of an entirely different order from "the natural aggressiveness of man in the struggle for survival."

Finally, we come to the overt response component (R). Ever since the invention of gunpowder, it has become abundantly clear that modern technology has removed the implementation of aggressive behavior far out of the realm of adequate adaptive response to biological needs. Today this involves not only the mass production of ever more destructive weapons but also technological advances in communication which immeasurably facilitate their use. It is a far cry from our primeval cave-man, wielding an axe against an enemy, to the modern war machine with its radio communication, rockets and guided missiles, chemicals, airplanes, and atomic bombs, pitting nation against nation in wars of mutual extermination. Add these technological advances in implementation of response to the modifications at the perceptive and emotional levels and we have a new emergent of social aggression, far removed from its original biological function, with a destructive potential that goes beyond anything that could conceivably serve the purpose of selection and survival.

The crucial significance of ideological dictatorship is, therefore, not the validity of its pseudobiological rationale, but its credence in that rationale and its ability to implement it, even though it ultimately defeat its own purpose. The danger implicit in the mechanization of aggression is by no means confined to dictatorships, but totalitarian government and hostile ethnocentricity do accentuate the danger. Our own scientific and political leaders have been quick to recognize the danger of final catastrophe in total war. Some have even espoused the curious logic that the best way to stop it is to start it. But we found, oddly enough, that insight into this danger was not completely lacking even among the erstwhile Nazi war lords. It was recognized by no less an authority than the Nazi War Production Minister himself. This belated insight struck ex-Minister Albert Speer so forcibly in the soul-searching that accompanied his defense at Nuremberg that he cast aside all petty attempts at self-justification in his final plea before the Tribunal, and emphasized instead the crucial danger of dictatorship in this age of mechanized aggression:

> Hitler's dictatorship differed in one principle from all its predecessors in history. His was the first dictatorship of an industrial state in this time of modern technological development. Through the means of developments like the radio and loudspeaker, eighty million people were deprived of the power to think independently. Through these means they were subjected to the will of one man. The telephone, the teletype, and radio made it possible, for example, to transmit orders from the highest authority to the lowest ranking units, where, because of their great authority, they were carried out uncritically. . . . As a result, there emerges a new type of man—the uncritical recipient of orders. We had only reached the beginning of this new development.
>
> The nightmare of many a man, that some day technological developments might dominate entire nations, was all but realized in Hitler's totalitarian system. Today, the danger of being ter-

rorized by technological developments overshadows every country in the world. In the modern dictatorship this seems to me inevitable. The more mechanized the world becomes, the more essential is a counterbalancing influence of individual freedom and responsibility. . . .

This war has ended on a note of radio-controlled rockets, aircraft developing the speed of sound, novel submarines and torpedoes which can find their own target, of atom bombs, and with the prospect of a horrible type of chemical warfare. By necessity the next war will be in the shadow of these new destructive inventions of human minds. . . .

As a former minister of a highly developed armament system, it must be my last duty to say this: A new large-scale war will end with the destruction of human culture and civilization. Nothing will prevent this unleashed technology and science from completing this work of destruction of humanity, which it began in such a dreadful way in this last war. . . . (36)

Ex-Minister Speer's evaluation of dictatorship was not very different from that of our own political and scientific leaders. It is an arresting thought that on both sides of this so-called "struggle for survival," the intelligent leaders responsible for mobilizing men's scientific genius for mutual destruction felt constrained to stop and wonder where the survival value of all this came in and where human evolution was going at this rate. On both sides thoughtful leaders arrived independently at the same conclusion. Restated in terms of adaptive social behavior, it amounts to this : *At the present stage of man's social evolution, aggression no longer serves the purpose of survival but of extinction. At such a stage, dictatorship dedicated to an ideology of ethnic struggle for survival becomes a most potent source of danger to that survival.*

"The new type of man—the uncritical recipient of orders" is not an entirely new phenotype in social evolution, but the reversion to an old one. The same is true of the autocrat and the racial fanatic. However, they now represent something more than psychological anachronisms in an era of democratic social change. They represent the potential mechanization of human intelligence, along with the instruments it creates, into an impersonal machine of mind and matter organized for its own destruction. The specter of a robot war includes not only remote-control weapons but robotized men, responding mechanically to signal and command, in no less automatic and impersonal a fashion than the instruments of aggression they have created. In such a conflict, we are reliably informed, the machines will outlast the creative intellects.

Thus the final implication of the pseudobiological ideology of aggressive dictatorship is that man can be the first to demonstrate how a species may become extinct, not through failure to adapt to its environment but through failure to adapt to its own intelligence. The Nazis' great service or disservice to mankind was in showing how far in that direction such a mode of behavior could go. If the issue was ever in doubt, the thirty million lives sacrificed to Nazi-dominated fascist dictatorship, and the untold misery left in its wake, should resolve that doubt.

Obviously, the technological and scientific progress in man's adaptive behavior cannot and must not be undone, nor can human emotions be extirpated. But the social modifications and implementations of human needs—the philosophies men live by, the forms of government they create for their own security, the leadership and values they cultivate, do lie within the realm of choice.

On the level of international relationships, thinking men are becoming increasingly aware that world government is a necessary corrective to the dangers of aggressive nationalism, that only cooperative international control can safeguard man from his own destructive genius. The larger politico-economic aspects of that need for adaptive social change have been beyond the scope of our inquiry.

On the psychosocial level, our own value judgments confirm, above all, the vital necessity of cultivating the ideal of *mature, liberal leadership* as the goal of democratic education. We rest our case on the conviction that modern man can survive and experience a far fuller life, with greater security than he has ever known, through the constructive use of his intelligence for the common good in a democratic society, with rational adjustment to social change.

This requires leaders who are brought up to think for themselves, to inquire, criticize, evaluate, formulate, and test hypotheses in applying reason to the solution of social problems. It requires leaders who are trained and motivated to recognize their responsibilities, not merely to their narrow identification groups, but to the people as a whole; whose reason is not beclouded by false loyalties and outworn values that require self-deception or provide a camouflage for cowardice and avarice; who have the courage of convictions based on observable realities, including human aspiration as well as material need; whose convictions remain adaptable to changing social conditions and needs, but not to the shifting winds of fashion or personal advantage; who are neither badgered by the ghosts of ancient myths, nor lured by the siren call of ideological panaceas; whose ultimate loyalties are to mankind, and who therefore recognize ethnic hostilities as common threats to survival.

Such leadership must, in the long run, vindicate the democratic way of life in man's struggle for security.

REFERENCES AND BIBLIOGRAPHY

(1) ABEL, T.   The element of decision in the pattern of war.   *Amer. sociol. Rev.*, 1941, **6**:853-59.

(2) ———. *Why Hitler came into power.* New York: Prentice-Hall, Inc., 1938.

(3) ADORNO, T. W., FRENKEL-BRUNSWIK, E., LEVINSON, D. J., and SANFORD, R. N. *The authoritarian personality.* New York: Harper & Bros., 1950.

(4) BARNES, H. E. *Social institutions.* New York: Prentice-Hall, Inc., 1942.

(5) BENEDICT, R. *Race: science and politics.* Rev. ed. New York: The Viking Press, Inc., 1945.

(6) BLOOD-RYAN, H. W. *Franz von Papen.* London: Rich & Cowan, 1939.

(7) BRICKNER, R. *Is Germany curable?* Philadelphia: J. B. Lippincott Co., 1943.

(8) BROMBERG, W. *Crime and the mind.* Philadelphia: J. B. Lippincott Co., 1943.

(9) BUSH, V. *Modern arms and free men.* New York: Simon & Schuster, Inc., 1949.

(10) BYCHOWSKI, G. *Dictators and disciples.* New York: International Universities Press, Inc., 1948.

(11) CANTRIL, H. *The psychology of social movements.* New York: John Wiley & Sons, Inc., 1941.

(12) ———. *The behavior of men.* New York: The Macmillan Co.

(13) COBBAN, A. *Dictatorship, its history and theory.* New York: Chas. Scribner's Sons, 1939.

(14) DUNHAM, B. *Man against myth.* Boston: Little, Brown & Co., 1947.

(15) EBENSTEIN, W. *The Nazi state.* New York: Rinehart & Co., Inc., 1943.

(16) FORD, G. S. (ed.). *Dictatorship in the modern world.* Minneapolis: University of Minnesota Press, 1935.

(17) FRANÇOIS-PONCET, A. *The fateful years.* New York: Harcourt, Brace & Co., Inc., 1949.

(18) FRANK, H. *Adolf Hitler: eine Gestalt-Gestaltung aus Erlebnis und Erkenntnis.* Original MS. in author's collection.

319

(19) FREUD, S. *Totem and taboo.* London: Kegan, Paul, 1913.

(20) FROMM, E. *Escape from freedom.* New York: Rinehart & Co., Inc., 1941.

(21) ———. *Man for himself.* New York: Rinehart & Co., Inc., 1948.

(22) GILBERT, G. M. *Nuremberg diary.* New York: Farrar, Straus & Co., Inc., 1947.

(23) GISEVIUS, H. B. *To the bitter end.* Boston: Houghton Mifflin Co., 1947.

(24) GLOVER, E. *War, sadism, and pacifism.* London: George Allen & Unwin, Ltd., 1933.

(25) GOEBBELS, J. *The Goebbels diaries,* ed. L. P. Lochner. New York: Doubleday & Co., 1948.

(26) GOERING, H. *Germany reborn.* London: Elkin Mathews & Marrot, Ltd., 1945.

(27) GOLDENWEISER, A. *History, psychology, and culture.* New York: Alfred A. Knopf, Inc., 1933.

(28) GREINER, J. *Das Ende des Hitler Mythos.* Leipzig, Zürich: Amalthea Verlag, 1948.

(29) GRITZBACH, E. *Hermann Goering—the man and his work.* London: Hurst, 1939.

(30) HASSELL, ULRICH VON. *The von Hassell diaries.* New York: Doubleday & Co., Inc., 1947.

(31) HEIDEN, K. *Der Führer.* Boston: Houghton Mifflin Co., 1944.

(32) HESS, R. *Reden.* Munich: Eher Verlag, 1938.

(33) HITLER, A. *Mein Kampf.* Munich: Eher Verlag, 1925, 1933. (Amer. ed. Boston: Houghton Mifflin Co., 1933.)

(34) ———. *Hitler's speeches,* ed. N. H. Baynes. London and New York: Oxford University Press, 1943.

(35) HOOK, S. *The hero in history.* New York: John Day Co., Inc., 1943.

(36) INTERNATIONAL MILITARY TRIBUNAL. *Trial of the major war criminals. Proceedings,* vols. 1-24; *Documents,* vols. 25-42 (*Index,* vol. 24). Nürnberg: distr. U.S. Govt. Printing Office, Washington, D.C.: 1947-49.

(37) JACKSON, R. H. *The Nürnberg case.* New York: Alfred A. Knopf, Inc., 1947.

(38) JEFFERSON, THOMAS. *Jefferson, on Democracy,* ed. Saul Padover. New York: Appleton-Century-Crofts, Inc., 1939.

(39) KLINEBERG, O. *Social psychology.* New York: Henry Holt & Co., Inc., 1940. See also *Tensions Affecting International Understanding.* New York: Soc. Sci. Res. Council, 1950.

(40) KOEVES, T. *Satan in top hat.* New York: Alliance Book Corp., 1941.

(41) KOGON, E. *Der SS Staat.* Stockholm: Bermann-Fischer, 1947.

(42) KRAMER, F. A. *Vor den Ruinen Deutschlands.* Koblenz: Historisch-Politischer Verlag, 1946.

(43) KRECH, D., and CRUTCHFIELD, R. S. *Theory and problems of social psychology.* New York: McGraw-Hill Book Co., Inc., 1948.

(44) LA PIERRE, R. T., and FARNSWORTH, P. R. *Social psychology,* 3rd ed. New York: McGraw-Hill Book Co., Inc., 1949.

(45) MARRIOTT, SIR JOHN A. R. *Dictatorship and democracy.* London: Clarendon Press, 1935.

(46) MURPHY, G. (ed.). *Human nature and enduring peace.* Boston: Houghton Mifflin Co., 1945.

(47) MURPHY, G., MURPHY, L. B., and NEWCOMB, T. M. *Experimental social psychology.* New York: Harper & Bros., 1937.

(48) MURPHY, G. *Personality.* New York: Harper & Bros., 1947.

(49) NEWCOMB, T. M., and HARTLEY, E. L. (eds.). *Readings in social psychology.* New York: Henry Holt & Co., Inc., 1947.

(50) NICOLAUS, M. P. *From Nietzsche down to Hitler.* London: William Hodge & Co., Ltd., 1938.

(51) REES, J. R. (ed.). *The case of Rudolf Hess.* New York: W. W. Norton & Co., Inc., 1948.

(52) REICH, W. *The mass psychosis of Fascism.* New York: Orgone Inst. Press, 1946.

(53) ROSENBERG, A. *Der Mythus des 20. Jahrhunderts.* Munich: Hohenreichen Verlag, 1936.

(54) ——. *Die Protokolle der Weisen von Zion.* Munich: Deutscher Volks-Verlag, 1923.

(55) ROUSSET, D. *The other kingdom.* New York: Reynal & Hitchcock, 1947.

(56) RUSSELL, B. *Authority and the individual.* New York: Simon & Schuster, Inc., 1949.

(57) SCHAFFNER, B. *Fatherland: a study of authoritarianism in the German family.* New York: Columbia University Press, 1948.

(58) SCHUMANN, F. L. *Germany since 1918.* New York: Henry Holt & Co., Inc., 1937.

(59) SCHWARTZ, P. *This man Ribbentrop.* New York: Julian Messner, Inc., Publishers, 1943.

(60) STRASSER, O. *Hitler and I.* Boston: Houghton Mifflin Co., 1940.

(61) TREVOR-ROPER, H. R. *The last days of Hitler.* New York: The Macmillan Co., 1947.

(62) VANDAL, C. *L'avennement de Bonaparte.* Paris: Plon-Nourrit, 1903.

(63) WALSH, E. A. *Total power.* Garden City, N. Y.: Garden City Publishing Co., 1948.

(64) WELLES, S. *The time for decision.* New York: Harper & Bros., 1944.

NAME INDEX

Abel, T., 294 f., 299
Adler, A., 84

Bach-Zelewski, SS-Gen., 293 f.
Bismarck, Otto von, 44 f.
Blomberg, Field Marshal von, 72, 76, 100, 210 ff.
Brandt, Dr. Karl, 36
Brauchitsch, Gen. von, 222 ff.
Braun, Eva, 62
Bromberg, W., 283 f.
Brüning, Heinrich, 66, 159 ff.
Bush, Vannevar, 310

Canaris, Adm. 212, 225
Cantril, H., 294 f., 319
Chamberlain, H. S., 48
Chamberlain, Neville, 101, 174
Churchill, W., 125, 126, 173, 234 f.
Cobban, A., 319
Connaught, Duke of, 177

Dahlerus, B., 103
Daladier, Edouard, 101
Doenitz, Adm. 198
Dollfuss, Chancellor, 77
Drexler, Anton, 38

Eden, Anthony, 124 ff.
Eichmann, SS-Col., 245

Farnsworth, P. R., 298, 320
Feder, Gottfried, 38, 295
François-Poncet, André, 101, 187
Frank, Hans, 19, 36, 48, 55, 61, 136-53, 170, 198-99, 278, 302
Frederick the Great, 53, 86, 230 f.
Freud, Sigmund, 265, 320
Frick, Wilhelm, 44
Fritsch, Gen. von, 98, 100 ff., 212
Fritzsche, Hans, 198
Fromm, E., 118 f., 320
Funk, Walther, 278

Gehrlich, 61
Giraud, Gen., 228-29
Glücks, SS-Gen., 245
Goebbels, Josef, 55, 69, 72, 256
Goering, Hermann, 14, 42 ff., 61 ff., 69, 84-119, 133, 151, 168, 198, 259 ff., 284, 289, 293, 302, 306-8
Greiner, Josef, 26-27, 32, 37

Hacha, Pres., 101, 188
Halder, Gen., 222 ff.
Haushofer, K., 55, 121, 123
Hegel, G. W. F., 275 f., 308 f.
Helldorf, Count, 181
Henkell family, 179
Hess, Rudolf, 42, 120-36
Heydrich, SS-Gen., 82, 102
Himmler, Heinrich, 69, 73-75, 82, 215, 228, 237 ff., 244 ff., 253 ff., 292 ff.
Hindenburg, Field Marshal von, 12, 68 ff., 76, 160 ff.
Hitler, Adolf, 12, 16-77, 99 ff., 152 ff., 181 ff., 190 ff., 195 ff., 216-25, 255 ff., 283, 288, 292, 294-97, 300-302
Hitler, Aloysius, Jr., 18, 63
Hoess, SS-Col., 240-61
Horthy, Regent, Nicholas von, 200

James, William, 275 f.
Jefferson, Thomas, 6, 320
Jodl, Gen., 221, 225, 227, 229

Kahr, Minister-Pres. von, 45, 75
Kaltenbrunner, SS-Gen., 253, 258
Kantzow, Karin von, 91
Keitel, Field Marshal, 14, 207-36, 278
Keppler, Wilhelm, 70
Knochen, SS-Maj., 259, 289

Lahousen, Gen., 219 f., 231 ff.
La Piere, R. T., 298, 320

Lenin, Nikolai, 11, 137
Ley, Robert, 42, 73, 82
Ludendorff, Gen. von, 44 ff., 72
Lueger, Karl, 29 ff.

Marx, Karl, 10
Maxwell-Fyfe, Sir David, 171 ff.
Mussolini, Benito, 11, 214

Napoleon Bonaparte, 4-9
Neurath, Baron von, 169, 197 ff.
Nietzsche, Friedrich, 10, 35

Ohlendorf, Otto, 253

Papen, Franz von, 14, 76, 156-75,
  198, 272, 278
Pohl, SS-Gen., 258
Pölzl, Klara, 17
Pötsch, Leopold, 22, 31, 34

Ranke, Leopold von, 48
Raubal, "Geli," 60-62
Ribbentrop, Joachim von, 167 ff., 175-
  204, 278
Roehm, Ernst, 42, 60, 74 ff., 96,
  149 ff.
Roosevelt, Eleanor, 118 f.
Roosevelt, Franklin D., 189
Rosenberg, Alfred, 42, 256

Rundstedt, Field Marshal von, 217,
  223 ff.

Schacht, Hjalmar, 67, 70 ff., 98, 167,
  170, 173, 272, 278, 289
Schickelgruber-Hitler, Aloysius, 16-
  19
Schirach, Baldur von, 62
Schleicher, Gen. von, 70 ff.
Schönerer, Anton, 31
Schopenhauer, Arthur, 62
Schröder, Baron von, 67, 70
Seyss-Inquart, Arthur, 30 f., 255 ff.
Sonnemann, Emmy, 97
Speer, Albert, 47, 234 f., 315 ff.
Spencer, Herbert, 10
Spengler, Oswald, 72, 137, 196
Stalin, Josef, 197
Stempfle, Father, 60
Strasser, Gregor, 55 ff., 69 ff.
Strasser, Otto, 60, 69, 295
Streicher, Julius, 41 ff., 60, 82, 256,
  272
Stroop, SS-Gen., 229

Thyssen, Fritz, 67

Vandal, C., 321

Welles, Sumner, 187 ff., 321
Weygand, Gen., 228 ff.

SUBJECT INDEX

Adaptive social behavior, 3, 268, 304 ff.
Amnesia (Hess's), 126-31
Anschluss (Austria), 31, 44, 100 ff., 163, 188
Anti-Comintern Pact, 184, 198
Anti-Nazi underground, 170, 174, 217, 2 J2, 234 ff.
Anti-Semitism, 29-33, 38, 49-51, 63, 65, 73, 102, 140 ff., 151, 191, 256-60
Appeasement, 117 ff., 174
Ardennes counteroffensive, 217
Assassination attempts (against Hitler), 217, 235
Atrocities, 106, 110, 112-14, 140 ff., 151, 191 ff., 199-203, 216, 228 ff., 244-47, 252-61, 278 ff., 301
Auschwitz, 245-47
Austria, 16, 22, 28-31, 77, 100
Authoritarianism, 3-13, 52, 67 ff., 76, 116 ff., 254-56, 266-70, 305-10, 315 ff.; see also Heroic myth; Militarists and militarism

Blutkitt (blood bond), 238
Büro Ribbentrop, 183

Categorical imperative. 254-56, 305
Catholicism, 31, 44, 77, 159-61, 165, 171 ff.
Christian Socialist Party, 29
Communists, 11, 71 ff.
Concentration camps, 113 ff., 191, 203, 238, 245-47
Concordat, 77, 161
Czechoslovakia, 99-102, 197

Decision in war, 299-302
Defense mechanisms, 202, 226, 274-80, 290 ff.

Democracy, 4-6, 12, 52, 67 ff., 91, 95, 116, 131, 310
Diplomats, 154-204
Divine right of kings, 7, 305
Drug addiction, 94, 105, 114
Dynamic eclecticism, 14 ff.

Enabling Act, 73
England, 99 ff., 116, 123 ff., 184-87, 291
Ethnocentrism and ethnic conflict, 10, 28-31, 37, 52, 89, 99, 115 ff., 132, 140, 256-60, 271, 276, 288-93, 308 ff., 313 ff.
Evolution of aggression, 311-17
Extermination procedure, 245-47

Fascism, 11, 77, 217
Fehmemord (political murder), 239, 243
Four-Year Plan, 98
France, 4-9, 99 ff.
Freemasons, 93
Freikorps, 243

General Staff, 206 ff.
Geopolitics, 55
German Nationalist party, 31
Gestapo, 237 ff.
Gleiwitz incident, 212, 225 ff.
Guilt reactions, 113 ff., 193 ff., 199-203, 227-31, 276 ff.

Heroic myth, 8, 22 ff., 35 ff., 40, 43, 46 ff., 53, 86, 111-14, 119, 132, 305-8
Homosexual tendencies (latent and overt), 59 ff., 69, 98, 149-53
Hoszbach document, 99 ff.

Industrialists, 66-68, 73
I.Q. test, 107 ff., 127 ff., 143, 248

Junkers, 39, 72, 76, 156 ff., 164-69

Karinhall, 97, 105

Landsberg prison, 47 ff.
Leadership, 3-8, 117, 293-303, 305-8, 311, 318; see also Heroic myth
League of Nations, 54, 161
Lebensraum, 36, 99, 102, 189
Legality, 57 ff., 73-76, 138-42, 153
Loyalty, 111 ff., 176, 206, 227, 230-35, 306
Luftwaffe, 90 ff., 104 ff.

Maidanek, 203
Marburg speech (Von Papen's), 162
Mechanization of aggression, 310-17
Mein Kampf, 47-54
Militarists and militarism, 39, 85, 89-91, 97-100, 205 ff.
Munich Pact, 101, 188, 197
Munich Putsch, 43-47, 173 ff., 197

Nacht und Nebel decree, 216
Nazi party, 38-77, 91-96
Nonaggression Pact, 189
Nuremberg Laws, 97
Nuremberg trial, 109-16, 130 ff., 145-51, 169-72, 195-97, 219

Oedipus complex (Hitler's), 20 ff., 25, 64
"Old Fighters," 13, 40-43, 81 ff.

Paranoid tendencies, 51, 64, 124-27, 129, 131-35, 145 ff., 270-72, 283 ff.
Personality and social interaction, 4, 7, 13 ff.; see also Leadership
Plebiscite, 8
"Poison food" (Hess's), 125
Poland, 139-42, 212, 225
Police state, 73, 77, 237 ff.
Political bandwagon, 13, 154 ff.
Prejudice, persistence of, 287-93
Propaganda, 8-11, 27 ff., 31, 37, 40-42, 46, 51-59, 64-68, 72 ff., 133, 151, 221, 256 ff., 268, 308, 313
Protocols of the Wise Men of Zion, 49-51

Pseudocompulsion, cultural, 272 ff.
Pseudoparanoia, cultural, 135, 270-72
Psychocultural viewpoint, 3 ff.
Psychopathology, psychopathic personalities, 82 ff., 115-18, 123, 132-34, 147-50, 203 ff., 266, 280-86; see also Paranoid tendencies; Schizoid tendencies

Racial ideology, 54, 99, 140 ff., 151, 256-61, 269, 292 ff., 308
Reichstag fire, 72 ff.
Reichswehr, 44 ff., 49, 210
Religion, 23 ff., 146, 162, 165, 230, 241, 252
Revolutionary nucleus, 13, 40-43, 81 ff.
Rhineland, remilitarization of the, 184, 210 ff.
Roehm purge, 108 ff., 143-45, 248
Rorschach Test, 108 ff., 128 ff., 143-45, 248
Russia, 17, 116, 189, 190, 214-16, 222-24, 291

Schizoid tendencies, 145, 148, 250-54, 285
Scorched earth policy, 217, 234 f.
Selective association in prejudice, 289 ff.
Selective constriction of affect, 278-80
Self-perpetuating mechanisms in prejudice, 289-93
Slavs, 31, 292 ff.
Social interaction, 3 ff., 7, 13-15, 133-35, 286-303
Social reform, demand for, 10-12, 38, 56, 70 ff., 131
Spain, 11, 100
SS-Police and Gestapo, 237-61
Stereotypes, 287-93
Storm Troops, 42-44, 60, 69, 71, 72, 74-76, 96
Style of life, 84, 178, 181, 185
Sudetenland, 101, 173, 188
Superman symbol, 36
Survival of the fittest, 54, 116, 217, 308, 311-17

Thematic Apperception Test, 128, 249 ff.

United Nations, 116

Value judgment and conflict, 132, 169-72, 200-2, 231-36, 269, 274-78
Versailles Treaty, 37, 49, 92, 209

War guilt, 188 ff., 224-47, 300-3
Warsaw ghetto, 228
Weimar Republic, 5, 12, 53, 57, 69 ff., 73, 95, 159 ff.
World War I, 10-12, 33-37, 47, 90 ff., 158, 178
World War II, 3, 99 ff., 103-7, 123 ff., 188-92, 212-18, 242 ff., 316

AEC 1868

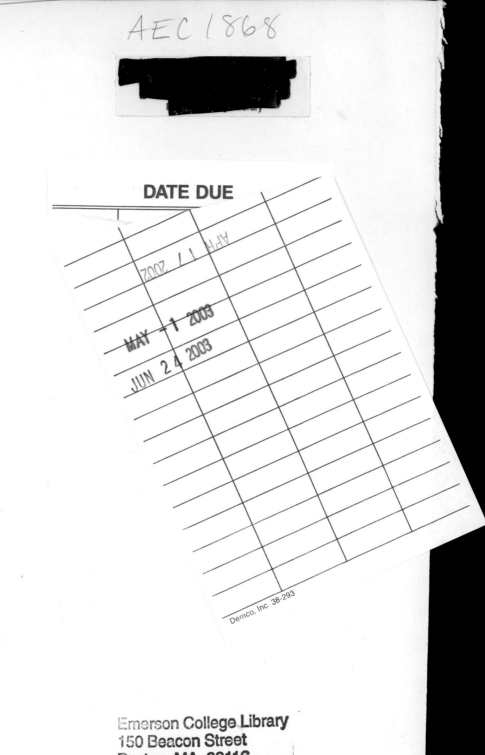